The BOSTON ITALIANS

ALSO BY STEPHEN PULEO

Dark Tide:
The Great Boston Molasses Flood of 1919

Due to Enemy Action:
The True World War II Story of the USS Eagle 56

The BOSTON ITALIANS

*A Story of Pride, Perseverance,
and* Paesani, *from the Years
of the Great Immigration
to the Present Day*

STEPHEN PULEO

BEACON PRESS
BOSTON

Beacon Press
25 Beacon Street
Boston, Massachusetts 02108-2892
www.beacon.org

Beacon Press books
are published under the auspices of
the Unitarian Universalist Association of Congregations.

11 10 09 08   8 7 6 5 4 3 2 1

This book is printed on acid-free paper that meets the uncoated paper
ANSI/NISO specifications for permanence as revised in 1992.

Composition by Wilsted & Taylor Publishing Services

Library of Congress Cataloging-in-Publication Data

Puleo, Stephen.
The Boston Italians : a story of pride, perseverance, and paesani, from
the years of the great immigration to the present day / Stephen Puleo.
p. cm.
Includes bibliographical references.
ISBN-13: 978-0-8070-5037-8 (pbk. : alk. paper)
ISBN-10: 0-8070-5037-7 (pbk. : alk. paper) 1. Italian Americans—Massachusetts—
Boston—History. 2. Italian Americans—Massachusetts—Boston—Social conditions.
3. Italian Americans—Massachusetts—Boston—Biography. 4. Italian Americans—Cultural
assimilation—Massachusetts—Boston—History. 5. Immigrants—Massachusetts—Boston—
History. 6. Boston (Mass.)—Ethnic relations. 7. Boston (Mass.)—Biography. I. Title.

F73.9.I8P855 2007
974.4'6100451—dc22   2006031584

To my mother and father,
Rose and Tony Puleo,

Who blessed me with love, family,
and pride in my heritage

Contents

Even as noon approaches on the clearest of days, shadows still swoop across this cramped street in Boston's North End. The midday sunlight peters out long before it reaches the pavement, giving way to shade halfway down the walls of the century-old brick and wood tenements pinched together and wedged against the tiny lane. Though the tallest of these structures does not exceed four stories, they appear to tower above a street so narrow that an average adult could cross it in three long strides.

Halfway along the east side of this alleyway, a low wooden door, unadorned, marks the entrance to a brick building that houses a small newspaper office. The address of the *Post-Gazette,* at 5 Prince Street, touches historic North Square and is surrounded by layers of American history. It backs up to a second side street on which colonial governor Thomas Hutchinson's eighteenth-century mansion once stood, directly across from another tenement, the birthplace of Rose Fitzgerald in the late nineteenth century. She was the daughter of a colorful and popular Boston Irish politician, John "Honey Fitz" Fitzgerald, and years later, she would become the mother of President John Fitzgerald Kennedy, who, as a Senate and presidential candidate, paid more than one visit to the *Post-Gazette* during his campaigns. The newspaper office is also a one-minute walk from Paul Revere's house, perhaps a brisk five-minute stroll from the famous Old North Church, from whose steeple a sexton hung the two lanterns that sparked Revere's famous midnight ride through the Eastern Massachusetts countryside on the night of April 18, 1775.

But the newspaper that is written and produced on Prince Street spends no time covering the origins of the American Revolution or the Irish rise to power in Boston, though one spawned a new nation and the other a new political force, and both began just moments away from its wooden front door. No, the *Post-Gazette*—as it has done for more than one hundred years under its current name and its previous one, *La Gazzetta del*

Massachusetts—focuses its energy and influence on an entirely different historical and cultural Boston movement, one that began in the late 1800s and continues today. In fact, more relevant to its mission is its proximity to two North End religious landmarks. Nestled halfway between two Italian parishes that opened in the late nineteenth century, St. Leonard of Port Maurice Church and the Sacred Heart Church on North Square, the *Post-Gazette* devotes its coverage to the Italians of Boston.

Like her father and mother before her, and her grandfather before them, Pam Donnaruma believes serving as editor and publisher of the *Post-Gazette* is far more than a job; she has a calling to fulfill, a legacy to protect, and a tradition to continue. Her newspaper carries the tagline "The Italian-American Voice of Massachusetts," and its readers reside as far away as California and the Virgin Islands. Yet, Donnaruma makes it clear that the paper draws its core constituency from Boston Italian Americans, and the strength and vitality of its heartbeat from the neighborhood that has, for nearly a hundred and thirty years, formed the epicenter of Italian life in Boston: the North End.

Donnaruma's small private office, just inside the *Post-Gazette*'s entrance door, is a microcosm of the North End neighborhood. Crowded, friendly, and nostalgia-filled, it's disheveled yet welcoming, rooted in tradition despite the many signs of change. The walls are covered with photos, plaques, awards, certificates, framed letters, and commendations. Dominating one wall is a large portrait of Pam's grandfather, the paper's founder, James V. Donnaruma, the immigrant who began his Italian-language newspaper at the turn of the twentieth century and covered the remarkable progress of his people until his death a half century later. More than anyone, James Donnaruma not only chronicled, but helped shape and define, the Italian experience in Boston. As an editor and a man, his passion and desire to improve the lot of his countrymen drove him into the thick of the action: helping Italian immigrants find jobs, wielding his political influence to battle anti-Italian legislation, raising money to support immigrant health initiatives or expand a home for Italian orphans. Never content to sit on the sidelines, James Donnaruma became and remained a force in the transition of Boston Italian immigrants to Boston Italian Americans. He received help along the way, especially in the early years, from his good friend George Scigliano [pronounced "She-lee-ahno"], but no one else devoted as many years and as much energy to helping Boston Italians as Donnaruma did.

Times have changed, but Pam Donnaruma continues her grandfather's legacy with each issue of the *Post-Gazette*. Her newspaper still celebrates the Italian American experience in Boston, though that experience is vastly different from what it was in decades past.

"My grandfather started this newspaper more than a century ago, written in Italian, to serve as a bridge for Italian immigrants to cross to become integrated into American society," Pam said. "Today, the paper is written in English and the bridge travels in both directions—James Donnaruma's newspaper has become the bridge that lets Italians understand Americans, and Americans understand Italians."

James Donnaruma once used his newspaper's voice to help Italian Americans, many of whom arrived in Boston as immigrants with little more than the clothes on their backs and a flicker of hope in their hearts. Their subsequent settlement, struggle, assimilation, influence, contributions, and enduring legacy remain among America's most important, vibrant, and colorful ethnic sagas.

This book tells their story.

Between 1880 and 1921, more than 4.2 million Italians entered the United States, as many as 95 percent of them through Ellis Island in New York. Historian Roger Daniels observed that no other ethnic group in American history sent so many immigrants in such a short time. Nearly 80 percent of them were from villages and hill towns of Southern Italy and Sicily, where they had tilled the land, fished the sea, or worked with their hands, and fled their homeland due to impoverishment; more than half were illiterate, or barely literate, in their own language. When they arrived in America, some settled in small mining towns or on farms, but the overwhelming majority flocked to America's large cities and quickly established tight-knit, insular enclaves, Little Italies, which acted as buffer zones of comfort and familiarity in the midst of a strange and hostile urban landscape that was strewn with pitfalls and prejudice.

It was within the cocoon of these enclaves that most Italians settled, purchased property, worshipped, shopped, socialized, and, in some cases, worked. It was from these enclaves that Italians ventured out, albeit slowly, to expand their job opportunities, learn English, and finally, assimilate into American culture. This story repeated itself in most American cities, including New York, Chicago, Philadelphia, Buffalo, New Orleans, San Francisco, and Boston.

Thus, this book looks at the Boston Italians within the broader context of the overall Italian experience in America, and that includes why so many left Italy seeking a new life in the first place. More than those of any other major ethnic group, Italians' life experiences in the Old Country directly affected their patterns of settlement, manner of living, reliance on family, process of assimilation, and relationship with other Americans.

But many elements of the Boston experience *were* unique. Italian immigrant leaders like Donnaruma and Scigliano had a greater proportional impact than their counterparts in other large cities thanks to the relatively small geographic footprint of Boston in general, and the Italian neighborhoods of East Boston and the North End in particular.

Then there is the North End itself. With due acknowledgment to the descendants of Boston Italian immigrants who settled in East Boston, Roxbury, Hyde Park, Roslindale, Dorchester, and the West End, this book's main focus is on the North End, the neighborhood that has been the heartbeat of Italian life in Boston for more than a century. The other Boston Italian neighborhoods are important and are dealt with here, but when the Boston Italian experience is examined and dissected, all roads lead to the North End, the city's oldest and most enduring Italian neighborhood.

There are many reasons for this, almost all of them due to the North End's size and geographic proximity, which helped stabilize the neighborhood more quickly than other Italian enclaves and, eventually, accelerated the rate of assimilation among its residents. The North End's nearness both to the downtown business section and an ever-thriving port and dock area contributed to these factors. Italian immigrant colonies in most cities were close to one or the other, but the North End abutted both, a postage-stamp neighborhood wedged between dual engines of commerce. Such a location meant access, within walking distance, to a multitude of jobs for people with limited skills: laborers, fruit vendors, barbers, waiters, and porters downtown; fishermen, warehousemen, longshoremen, stevedores, shippers, merchants, and packers along the docks and the waterfront.

And the North End's closeness to downtown provided something else. It afforded Italian immigrants a convenient opportunity to observe and eventually join the American mainstream. While most Italian immigrants spent the vast majority of their free time with family and friends in the neighborhood, thousands left the neighborhood daily to work. In this way, they learned a little more about the United States and its people each day, and carried that knowledge back to the North End with them. The geographic location of the North End placed Italians literally on the edge of the American mainstream, serving as a window, rather than a closed door, to the larger American society. Italians could get a taste of the bigger American picture during the day and retreat to the relative safety and familiarity of the enclave at night.

The final geographic consideration that made (and makes) the North End so vital in defining the Boston Italian experience is its small size—less than a mile square and consisting of only a half square mile of inhabitable space once the waterfront section is excluded (one historian pointed out that the livable portion of the neighborhood is smaller than the parking lot at Disney World). The downsides to this were the North End's population density, congestion, and dreary tenement housing and the proliferation of disease, especially in the early years of immigration. Conversely, the neighborhood's cozy size served, after a fashion, as a unifying factor, helping Italians move beyond identifying themselves only as members of regional enclaves—Sicilians, Avellinesi, Calabrians—and strengthening their ethnic identity as Italians in the United States. Like virtually all Italian immigrants, Boston Italians first settled in America with family and friends from the same village, or *paese,* in Italy. But because of the compactness of the North End, residents from different regions of Italy were all but forced to interact with each other. They could, therefore, eventually submerge their regional differences to deal with more common problems of survival and assimilation, such as finding jobs and overcoming discrimination. This did not occur immediately; the North End, as much as any Italian neighborhood, initially was composed of strong, well-defined regional enclaves-within-an-enclave, a major component of settlement whose remnants exist even today. Yet, the neighborhood's size accelerated the eventual identification of the North End as a vibrant *Italian* neighborhood more rapidly than in other Little Italies. It is worth noting that the North End's George Scigliano and James Donnaruma, the most important Italian immigrant leaders in Boston and major figures in this book, consistently championed the causes of Italian immigrants as a group and almost never focused on regional differences.

Even if Boston-area Italian Americans have forgotten all the reasons why, the fact that they continue to make periodic pilgrimages to the North End to understand the essence of their heritage is a testament to the neighborhood's predominant and rightful place in the history of Boston Italians.

Readers will note that more than half of this book covers what I refer to as the Great Immigration and Settlement Years, stretching from the beginning of the Italians' arrival in Boston (around 1875) up to the onset of the Great Depression. These were the most crucial years of the Italian experience in America, and they define to this day how Italian Americans view their own heritage and how other Americans assess us. The people who defined these first fifty-plus years were the immigrants themselves, who struggled to get to America, overcame enormous odds once they arrived, contributed their sweat to help build a country, carved a place for themselves and their children in the American mainstream, and forged an ethnic identity that still evokes pride a hundred years later.

To many second- and third-generation Italian Americans, including me, these immigrants were members of their own "Greatest Generation," years before the phrase was applied to their children who fought in, and supported the home front during, World War II. As the years go by, and history provides distance and the opportunity for fresh assessment, their sacrifices and accomplishments appear all the more remarkable.

Finally, the story of the Boston Italians is my story, too. Three of my four grandparents were immigrants, members of that first "Greatest Generation." My two grandfathers and paternal grandmother arrived virtually penniless, with few skills, and unable to speak English. My paternal grandfather was barely literate in his own language. Both my grandfathers eventually became citizens and entrepreneurs; my grandmother never obtained her citizenship and was even classified as an "enemy alien" at the outset of World War II, despite the fact that three of her sons would eventually fight overseas while serving in the United States Army. My paternal grandparents settled in the North End and stayed for years; my maternal grandfather spent a few years there before moving to the nearby city of Everett. Theirs were the quintessential experiences of Italian immigrants.

My parents and aunts and uncles also shared the experiences of thousands of other children of Italian immigrants. Several of my aunts worked in the garment industry, which was flooded with Italian American women in Boston. As a young girl, my mother worked in my grandfather's cobbler shop, lighting the small stove to provide heat in the wintertime and waiting on customers after school, contributing to the family business as thousands of other Italian American schoolchildren did. My father and two of his brothers served in World War II, which was a defining period for Italian Americans, one in which they were forced to prove their loyalty to America as the United States battled not just Germany and Japan, but Mussolini's Italy.

Thus, I have woven the Puleo story through the course of this book as illustrative of the overall fabric of the Boston Italian experience, a rich and colorful tapestry of enduring strength and value, one held together for a hundred and thirty years by the legacies of struggle, perseverance, hard work, and the bond of family.

PART I

GEORGE SCIGLIANO, JAMES DONNARUMA, *and the* BATTLE *for* NORTH SQUARE

CHAPTER I

A cool breeze blew through Boston's North End on the morning of June 20, 1906, carrying the last trace of dampness from the previous day's rain and a tang of salt from the harbor. Wind skittered along the brick and wood tenements, rustled through the alleys, and tousled the hair of thousands of men, who, heads bared and bowed, lined the narrow streets of the city's largest Italian neighborhood to mourn its favorite son. Some men, the merchants and shopkeepers who had closed their businesses this Wednesday morning to pay their respects, wore expensive clothing, carried gold pocket watches, and held soft wool fedoras between their fingers. The vast majority, though, stood in awkward silence, clutching rumpled hats and looking uncomfortable in their starched white collars, ill-fitting suits, and worn shoes. These were the shoemakers and the stonecutters, the fruit peddlers and the fishermen, the bricklayers and the butchers, the carpenters and the common laborers, men with calloused hands and weathered faces, mostly immigrants who hailed from places like Sicily, Calabria, Avellino, and Abruzzi, many of whom had risked their livelihoods by skipping work this morning to honor a comrade.

Boston newspapers would later report that the funeral procession that wound its way along Hanover, Cross, North, Richmond, Parmenter, Salem, and Prince streets was the largest in the North End's history. More than fifteen hundred mourners from dozens of Italian neighborhood societies marched in silence, followed by seven horse-drawn carriages filled with flowers, and finally the hearse itself, in which rested the bier that supported a plush, open casket lined with white silk and trimmed with gold handles. The body inside was hidden from view by an enormous flower arrangement sent by a score of Boston's most prominent businessmen. As the hearse passed, men stepped off the sidewalk and fell in behind the official procession. They were joined along the route by women and children, one account noted, "many of whom had known him from childhood, or had met with kindly assistance from him," swelling the ranks to several thousand who would accompany the coffin to the funeral mass at St. Leonard of Port Maurice Church on Prince Street, established thirty years earlier as the first Italian parish in New England.

Despite the sheer number of mourners, the procession traveled in eerie silence. The normal cacophony of voices and sounds that filled the North End on a weekday morning was stilled, replaced only by the soft breeze, the rhythmic clip-clop of horseshoes on pavement and cobblestones, and the occasional rasp of a mourner clearing his throat. "Never was any higher honor shown to the memory of any civilian in the North End," the *Boston Globe* pointed out later.

It is likely that most of the mourners had known the deceased, George A. Scigliano, if not on a first-name basis, then certainly to exchange cordial greetings with when they encountered him on the street. "He knew personally, probably more North End Italians than any other resident," the *Globe* noted. But had they only known *of* him, these mourners still would have flocked to his funeral to honor him for his contributions.

A prominent lawyer, businessman, politician, and champion of Italian immigrant causes, Scigliano had died three days earlier, just two months shy of his thirty-second birthday, at his in-laws' home in Millbury, Massachusetts, near Worcester, about sixty miles west of Boston. The reported cause of death varied, depending upon the source of the information; speculation included acute kidney failure, "organic" disease, Bright's disease, and hemorrhaging of the bowels. The first Italian American elected to public office in Boston and only the second to the Massachusetts legislature, Scigliano had been in failing health for the past two years. In February, he had collapsed in his office and had to be carried from the State House. He recovered briefly, but by early June was forced to abandon his representative's duties due to illness. His wife and family hoped a quiet convalescence away from Boston could help him regain his strength and health. Instead, he became violently ill on Friday, June 15, and died around 9 A.M. Sunday morning. "The large amount of work [he] conducted proved too much for him, his friends say, and he overtaxed his strength," the *Boston Post* reported on the morning of his funeral.

Scigliano's body had arrived in Boston Sunday night, where it was prepared for viewing at his home at 232 Hanover Street. For two days North End Italians filed through the Scigliano house, paying their respects to his wife, Florence, who was now left alone to raise three children: Florence, age five; Jessica, four; and an infant son, George, Jr., two months. For Boston Italians, the tragedy of Scigliano's death was compounded by the age of the children he left behind. All night long Tuesday, mourners streamed through his living room to view his body and gaze upon his face—the dark wide-set eyes, patrician nose, sharp-cut jaw—and filed out in tears. They hugged his wife and held his children, murmured their condolences, and knelt in prayer. More than a thousand mourners entered from Hanover Street, walked through the Scigliano home, and exited back onto the pavement again, their numbers as strong in the early morning hours of Wednesday as they had been Tuesday evening. "So great was the desire of the people of his own race to see his face before the grave enclosed it that since the body arrived [in Boston] . . . there has been a steady stream of people about his bier," the *Boston Globe* reported. To the twenty thousand Italians who lived in the North End, Scigliano was a hero and an idol, and to pray before his body and catch one last glimpse of his face was to accord him the honor he deserved. The funeral mass was scheduled for 9:00 A.M., but it was 9:45 A.M. before the throng outside the Scigliano home cleared and the hearses finally began moving through the streets of the North End.

At St. Leonard's Church, the procession was met by Scigliano's friend Pastor Ubaldus Panfilio, who offered brief prayers before the six pallbearers—a state senator, a state representative, a city councilman, and three close friends—gently lifted Scigliano's coffin from the hearse and carried it into the church. Scigliano's wife, Florence, who had collapsed with grief late Tuesday night as mourners visited their home, was assisted into the church by friends as she carried her infant son in one arm and guided her two young daughters with the other.

Inside, three priests assisted Father Panfilio with the funeral mass, including Father Valerianus Piangiani, who delivered the eulogy. He spoke of Scigliano's long connection with the church; the deceased had "grown up" along with St. Leonard's, and both the man and the parish had become beloved by North End Italians. Father Piangiani paid Scigliano a handsome tribute for his "moral and upright life, his kindness to the poor and afflicted, his interest in the welfare of the Italian people at large and of the poorer classes in particular."

In reality, Scigliano's intelligence, passion, and ability to identify so closely and personally with his countrymen made him more than a legislator to Italian immigrants in Boston, and more than a neighborhood leader who would risk his political standing for poor day laborers. Many Italians, certainly those who listened to Father Piangiani's remarks in church, regarded Scigliano as a larger-than-life figure who fought tirelessly on their behalf against any number of people who sought to do them harm.

Here was a man with education, financial wherewithal, and political influence who provided leadership to people who had none of these things.

Here was a hero whose valiant efforts made the New World seem less strange and hostile to Italian immigrants in Boston, and offered hope and encouragement that there was room for them in America.

George Scigliano was born in the North End to immigrant parents on August 26, 1874; he and his family were among the earliest Italian residents of Boston. His father, Gennaro, hailed from the ancient town of Scigliano in Italy's southern Calabria region. George was born shortly after fearful smallpox epidemics had racked the North End in 1872 and 1873, killing more than a thousand people. There were no suitable hospitals in Boston for contagious diseases; city officials charged three dollars for fumigating one room and five dollars for a tenement. "As a result, the most needy houses were neglected," according to one report. "The deaths made clear that the sanitary administration of the city was inadequate."

On February 26, 1876, George Scigliano turned eighteen months old and the Boston Archdiocese dedicated St. Leonard of Port Maurice Church, built on the corner of Prince and Hanover streets, as the first Italian parish in New England. It stood on land the archdiocese had purchased for nine thousand dollars. Father Joachim Guerrini became the first priest specifically assigned to care for the Italian community of the entire archdiocese—about eight hundred in the North End, eleven hundred in Boston, and perhaps two thousand more scattered toward the North and South Shores and throughout the Merrimack Valley. "As if the task of administering to such a scattered group were not taxing enough, [Guerrini's] work was made even more difficult by his religious superiors" when he was ordered to hear confessions in English, according to historian William De-Marco. "It appears that the archbishop hoped to encourage the Italian congregation gradually to make a transition to the English language by this introduction of bilingualism at Saint Leonard's Church."

By the time George Scigliano turned six years old and began school in 1880, the North End neighborhood stood at the edge of astonishing ethnic change, poised to experience its second major demographic metamorphosis in fifty years. Boston's first neighborhood had once been the city's most prestigious residential area, home to colonial governor Thomas Hutchinson, silversmith and renowned midnight rider Paul Revere, and wealthy shipping magnates and business merchants. But by the mid-1800s, the economic condition of the North End had deteriorated with the arrival of thousands of German and Irish poor, while Boston's well-to-do fled the neighborhood and moved to Beacon Hill and, later, the newly developed Back Bay. The Irish famine of the mid-1840s, especially, drove the poorest of immigrants across the Atlantic to the North End, and by 1850 the once fashionable address had become Boston's first slum neighborhood. By 1880, about twenty-six thousand people lived in the neighborhood, most of them still Irish, another three thousand Jewish and Portuguese immigrants had settled there, and the North End Italian population had crept up to a thousand (of Boston's total twelve hundred Italians), most of them immigrants.

However, during the next twenty years, the ethnic face of the North End, and Boston in general, was to undergo yet another remarkable transformation, its most dramatic population shift since the arrival of the Irish and Germans in the 1830s and 1840s. New immigrants, desperate to escape punishing economic conditions in Italy and pogroms against Jews in Russia, drastically altered the city's ethnic mix. In 1900, the year George Scigliano was admitted to the bar following his graduation from Boston University Law School, there were still twenty-four thousand people in the North End, but the Italian population had swelled to nearly fifteen thousand. The Jewish population hovered around five thousand, but only a few thousand Irish remained; like their Brahmin counterparts seventy-five years earlier, most Irish had achieved enough upward mobility to leave

The Paul Revere house on
North Square was a tenement
building in this 1895 photo,
and ten years later, as depicted
in this postcard, it housed
an Italian immigrant bank.
The structure was restored
as a historic house in 1909.
*(Courtesy of the Boston Public
Library, Print Department)*

the city's poorest, tenement-ridden, disease-stricken neighborhood, this time choosing to move to areas such as South Boston, Charlestown, and Dorchester.

Five years later, a year prior to Scigliano's death, the North End population had grown to twenty-seven thousand, of which twenty-two thousand were Italians, and the neighborhood's character was unmistakably Italian. Virtually no English was spoken in the neighborhood. On newsstands, most newspapers and magazines were printed in Italian. More than thirty Italian mutual benefit societies and organizations had emerged, each representing immigrants who hailed from a different village, or *paese,* in Italy. Italians owned more than $2 million worth of real estate and Italian businesses had begun to flourish. Pietro Pastene, who opened his first food shop at 229 Hanover Street (right next to the Sciglianos) in 1874 (the year George was born), had expanded his business dramatically and now filled the space between 69 and 75 Fulton Street. His company would one day become the New York–based Pastene Corporation, one of the largest Italian food importers. One of the earliest Italian immigrants to the North End, Alessandro Badaracco, who had settled there prior to the Civil War, ran the largest fruit business in Boston by 1900. The Boston Macaroni Company, headed by John Ponte, began operations in 1890, and slightly later, the Prince Macaroni Company launched the operation that would one day become a highly successful pasta company and a Boston institution. Other businesses were not nearly as large, but they were important signs that the North End had transformed itself into a vital and vibrant Italian neighborhood: Italians established fruit, produce, and meat shops, grocery stores, bakeries, and barber shops.

By the beginning of the twentieth century, the North End was home to more than 85 percent of the city's total Italian population. Despite small and cohesive Italian enclaves that had begun to spring up in East Boston, the West End, Hyde Park, Roslindale, Dorchester, and Roxbury, it was the North End that epitomized and represented both the positive and negative aspects of Italian immigrant life in Boston. Congestion and overcrowding, substandard housing conditions, and poverty beset the neighborhood, but strength of family, industriousness, and generosity were also hallmarks of the Italian immigrant experience in the North End. Italians who moved to other neighborhoods in the city returned to the North End for religious functions, socializing, or weekly shopping. "They would even be provided bed and/or board in their parents' and relatives' apartments whenever needed," William DeMarco noted.

Thus, when George Scigliano emerged onto the public stage as a new century dawned and became a leader of North End Italians, his labors and success, by definition, benefited all Italians in Boston. Scigliano, who turned twenty-six years old in 1900, had grown up in and with the North End, and thus grew up immersed in the totality of Boston's Italian immigrant experience.

With pride, vigor, tenacity, and eloquence, he dedicated himself to helping his countrymen adjust and succeed once they crossed the ocean and encountered the chasm between the Old Country and the New World.

CHAPTER 2

Like so many great leaders, George Scigliano rose to prominence as he
helped his people in their struggle to overcome hardship. For even as Italians were establishing a foothold and an identity in Boston, they—like
other immigrant groups before them—were fighting poverty, disease, and
discrimination. A high level of illiteracy in their own language, the inability of most Italians to speak English, and religious and cultural differences
with other immigrant groups made it painful for Italian immigrants to
assimilate into American culture or find work that lifted them above
poverty levels.

Illiteracy proved the most severe handicap for Italians to overcome. "If
I could read," one peasant said in explanation of his difficulties, "I should
have four eyes, but now I see naught." Illiteracy, coupled with the language
barrier, meant Italians were frustrated in their attempts to compete in
America's growing industrial society. Thus, Italians came to the United
States primarily as unskilled laborers and were among the nation's lowest-
paid immigrant groups. In 1905, households headed by Southern Italians,
who accounted for about 80 percent of all Italian immigrants by that time,
earned an average of $360 annually, far below German, Swedish, and Irish
immigrants, and slightly below Russian Jews, all of whom had far higher
literacy rates. In Boston's North End, the figure was even lower, about $338
annually.

And beyond their economic plight—indeed, perhaps because of it—
Boston Italians endured two other major problems as they established
themselves as Americans: unhealthy living conditions and intense discrimination.

The North End in particular was beset by nearly intolerable living conditions. Southern Italian immigrants, who hailed from farming and fishing
communities in Italy, were crowded into a neighborhood of dilapidated

tenements as they struggled to make ends meet. The inhabitable portion of the neighborhood is only about eighty acres, and by the first decade of the twentieth century, the North End rivaled Calcutta, India, in population density. City investigators found the tenements adjoined so closely that sufficient air and light could not enter outside rooms; and except for those on the top floors, inside rooms were dark and musty. The Boston City Council reported in 1896 that "in the North End the tenement houses are today a serious menace to public health." One author who reported on slums in Boston in 1898 described tenements along Fleet Street: "In none of the houses is there any thorough ventilation; air shafts were not thought of when these houses were built. Though the sun shines into some rooms on the top floors, all the lower rooms are very dark."

These conditions took their toll in the North End. Italians quickly became susceptible to tuberculosis, even though they were among the least likely to contract the disease in Europe. "And how could it be otherwise?" asked Dr. Antonio Stella, a physician and member of the Italian Committee on the Prevention of Tuberculosis. Dr. Stella cited the infectious nature of the disease and the overcrowded conditions of tenements inhabited by people "made up chiefly of agriculturalists, fresh from the sunny hills of Tuscany and Sicily, abruptly thrown into unnatural and dark sweatshops, a population overworked, underfed, poorly clad, curbed with all the worries and anxieties of the morrow." Stella even argued that many cases went unreported, often because sick Italians were likely to return to their native villages, preferring to die there. The number of Italian men and women who contracted tuberculosis in Boston and other cities was so high that the Sicilian town of Sciacca, which sent thousands of fishermen and farmers to America (including my paternal grandparents), built a small sanitarium on its outskirts to receive the stricken who came home to die. "Six months of life in the tenements are sufficient to turn a sturdy youth of Calabria, the brawny fishermen of Sicily, the robust women from Abruzzo and Basilicata, into the pale, flabby, undersized creatures we see dragging along the streets," Stella observed. Addressing a Tuberculosis Congress in Washington, D.C., one investigator said: "If we had invented machines to create tuberculosis, we could not have succeeded better in increasing it."

Apart from unsanitary housing conditions, which were considered mainly responsible for the spread of tuberculosis, Stella's committee found that certain occupations popular among Italians in Boston and other big cities were particularly hazardous to the lungs—including bootblacks, plasterers, marble and stone cutters, and cigar makers.

Other diseases and miseries also plagued Boston Italians. In 1898 and 1899, the North End had the largest number of deaths in the city from pneumonia, meningitis, typhoid fever, and diphtheria, and the second-largest number of deaths from infant cholera and bronchitis. Not only did the North End lead the city of Boston in births in 1898 and 1899, it also led in number of deaths of children under one year of age and between the ages of one and five. Referring to the death rate among North End Italians, writer Robert Woods noted in *Charities* magazine in 1904: "This is no doubt largely the effect of extremely close tenement quarters upon people who belong out of doors in a sunny land."

Italian immigrant laborers sweep up a North End street in 1909 as a young boy looks on. *(Courtesy of the Boston Public Library, Print Department)*

———

In addition to their physically demoralizing situation, Boston Italians battled psychological hardship as they sought a foothold in America. Like their countrymen across the United States, Italians in Boston faced intense discrimination during this period—though not as violent as Italians faced elsewhere—particularly at the hands of the Irish, who had themselves suffered persecution fifty years earlier.

Beyond a general tendency for the more established ethnic groups to be suspicious of newcomers, a number of other factors intensified Italian-Irish tensions. First, the two groups competed with each other for jobs. Second, Italians' illiteracy and inability to speak English made them objects of Irish scorn. Then there was the belief by the Irish, largely accurate in the early days of Italian immigration, that Italians were "birds of passage" who traveled back and forth between Italy and the United States for seasonal work and had no interest in settling in America permanently. Many Italians were apathetic about obtaining citizenship, which also stoked Irish fears that Italians had no desire to make a commitment to the community. As late as 1909, less than a quarter of North End Italians had become American citizens and their political apathy stirred contempt among the Irish, who had made strong inroads into the Boston power structure by this time. Writing three decades later of the Italian-Irish clash in Boston, sociologist William Foote Whyte explained:

> The Italians feel that they were badly handled by the Irish and some bitterness remains even now. This, however, need not be taken as an indictment of the Irish. It may be that any new racial group always suffers at the hand of the older, more established race. Certainly, the Irish have for years complained of Yankee discrimination against them. The Irish resented the intrusion of Italians, whom they considered an inferior people. As a matter of fact, the new immigrants had few educational opportunities and most of those from Southern Italy could not read or write . . . The Italian laborers were competition for the Irish working class; both for jobs and places to live. It was between these groups that the sharpest struggle took place, and many fiercely contested battles were fought on North End street corners.

Whyte noted that battles took place away from the street corners too—most symbolically, in the boxing ring. In the early years of Italian settlement of the North End, and even into the early twenties, boxing was controlled by Irish promoters and largely patronized by Irish fight fans. Organizers believed it was necessary to have an Irish or at least a non-Italian name to achieve success in the ring, and thus Italians were forced to change their names to fight at all. "Al Delmont, Mickey Landis, Eddie Waters, Little Jack Dempsey, and Sammy Fuller, were a few of the many Italian fighters . . . who had to change their names," Whyte pointed out. "Yet this did not eliminate the race rivalry from the contests. Sammy Fuller and a real Irishman, Andy Callahan, fought six times, and each time large crowds of Italians and Irish turned out to cheer their favorites."

Finally, and perhaps most visibly, there was the strange and unusual form of Catholicism practiced by Italians who arrived in a Boston Archdiocese governed almost exclusively by the Irish. While both nationalities were predominantly Roman Catholic, Italian Catholicism, which included street processions and festivals to honor saints, differed greatly from the more traditional and moralistic Irish Catholicism. "While the Italians professed the same religion, their language, customs, and dress were incomprehensible to the Irish," Whyte noted. The Irish hierarchy in Boston had a strong concern about what was known across the chancery leadership as "the Italian problem." Historian Susan Walton wrote years later, "The Italian form [of Catholicism] combined Catholicism with the older folk religions and customs that many Irish Catholics saw as pagan and idolatrous." In addition, the Irish "resented the anti-clericalism among Italian men and charged they did not see to their children's religious education."

In the view of Irish church leaders, this perceived lack of loyalty to the faith made Italians particularly vulnerable to attempts by Protestant and other religious leaders in Boston to convert newly arriving immigrants. Methodist and Episcopalian ministers were active in the North End in the early twentieth century, and even Unitarians were hopeful of converting Italian Catholics. "Is it possible to imagine a Unitarian Italian?" wondered the *Pilot,* the Boston Archdiocese newspaper. "The Italian can be nothing else but a Catholic." One priest who met immigrant ships at the South Boston docks was alarmed when he saw "Protestant ministers passing among the newcomers, conveying the message . . . that to be true Ameri-

The North End is decorated for All Saints' Day in 1929. *(Photo by Leslie Jones. Courtesy of the Boston Public Library, Print Department)*

cans, they had to relinquish the faith of their fathers and join the Protestant mainstream of the United States," noted religious historian James M. O'Toole. After William Henry O'Connell became Boston Archbishop in 1907, he designated the Boston Catholic Charitable Bureau (CCB) as the agency responsible for, among other tasks, protecting Italian immigrant parents and their children "from the insidious efforts of proselytizing forces that infested the North End."

Irish Catholics were also dismayed by Italians' seeming apathy about parochial education for their children. One article in the *Pilot* highlighted the founding of St. John's School for Italian children in the North End, while expressing concern for neighborhood children who were "almost entirely unversed in their faith." Finally, historian Robert Lord pointed out that Irish Catholics in Boston reviled the majority of Italian immigrants for never receiving any sacraments except baptism, and that "this hostility was often manifested in inequity toward the Italians."

Summing up Irish-Italian religious differences, scholar Amy Johnson wrote: "Italians believed in family before nation and celebration of ethnicity over ritualistic liturgy, and this resulted in the Italians clashing with the Irish authorities . . . aspects of Italian life from language to politics, from education to worship style clashed with those already established by the Irish at the turn of the twentieth century in Boston."

As they fought against the burdens of poverty, congestion, disease, and discrimination, Boston Italians drew strength from families and friends, but it was George Scigliano who stepped into the breach to offer them hope amidst their desperation. His bold leadership instilled confidence in thousands of Italian immigrants and sent a message that someone in a position of power was concerned about their welfare.

CHAPTER 3

In August of 1904, George Scigliano, already a beloved figure in the North End and among Italians across Boston, attained near legendary status when he publicly announced that he would ignore death threats from the mysterious Italian *La Camora* criminal organization and defy its demands that he resign as chairman of a local vigilance committee. Prominent North End Italians had formed the committee "to aid the police in hunting down a gang of Italian and Sicilian thugs who infest the lower portion of the city." *La Camora* publicly marked seven Boston men for death, including three police officers and Scigliano. LA CAMORA, SICILIAN SOCIETY, TO STOP POLICE INTERFERENCE WITH ITS WORK, STARTS BLOODY CAMPAIGN OF EXTERMINATION, the *Boston American* headline shouted in a Sunday edition. The paper also printed *La Camora*'s warning to its intended targets:

> Your death is at hand; your life shall be destroyed in a manner which will freeze the blood of those like yourself who are spies and friends of the police. You have betrayed your countrymen and you have tried to have them sent to prison. Now, this is your last notice you will receive, and unless you at once leave Boston, never to return, you will be killed.

"It doesn't seem possible that this can be true in Boston," the paper's lead article stated. "If law and order are to be supreme anywhere it seems that it must be here, in the shadow of the gilt dome that has covered the lawmakers of the most lawful State in the Union." In the anti-Italian language commonplace for the period, the *American* added: "But down in the North End, where dark doorways and dismal alleys shelter swarthy people whose deeds keep them in constant war with the police, strange things are said and done."

After *La Camora*'s threat became public in the third week in August, several of Scigliano's relatives "flocked to his house" to provide protection. "Mr. Scigliano may walk about the streets of the North End, seemingly indifferent to what goes on about him," one newspaper reported. "But not far away, with the young attorney never lost to their sight, may be seen two or more of his faithful relatives, not one of whom but is ready to jump into any danger to save him."

In the face of *La Camora*'s public threats of violence, Scigliano remained undeterred and publicly defiant. "We are going to purge the city of Italian criminals," he said. "The committee does this to protect the public and also in the interest of the respectable, hardworking Italians here. There are a small percentage of Italians in Boston that would be far better behind prison bars than at large and these we have determined to get their just desserts. They can threaten, cajole, or plead, but justice will be meted out to them."

That Scigliano was tough enough to ignore death threats and stand up for what he believed bolstered his standing among, and endeared him to, law-abiding Boston Italians. More important, though, were his public utterances—and from all accounts, his private beliefs—that his work would benefit hardworking North End residents who were simply trying to earn a living and improve their standing in America. Scigliano was well aware that other Americans often viewed Italians as a criminal class. "From some of the lurid accounts given by sensational newspapers, it might be thought that *all* Italians went around looking for plunder and blood," he said in an interview with the *Boston Traveler*. "Of course there is a criminal class that comes from our land as well as any other European country. I think, though, that the percentage of evil-doers from Italy is far less than from other countries. Be that as it may, we are determined to arrest Italian criminals in Boston and have them put in jail or expelled from the city as their degree of crime allows."

By fighting against criminal elements like *La Camora,* while at the same time reminding the public that those criminals did not represent the thousands of honest Italians in Boston, Scigliano became not only a leader but a folk hero among Italians.

His reputation and accomplishments leading up to the 1904 *La Camora* threats had built an impressive foundation. In 1900, at the age of twenty-six, Scigliano was elected to the Boston Common Council, where he served three one-year terms. In November of 1903, he was elected to the Massachusetts legislature, where he would serve for two and a half years before his premature death. His continued election during these years was evidence of his widespread support in the North End from all ethnic groups. The Italian population was too small—and included too low a proportion of citizens—to provide him with sufficient votes to win. Scigliano needed a substantial number of votes from Irish and Jewish residents to win elections.

Once in office, though, Scigliano poured the bulk of his energy into assisting Italian immigrants, using the legislative process, his personal relationships with Boston's business and political leaders, and the bully pulpit accorded him by a Boston press eager for an articulate voice in the growing Italian community.

Scigliano recognized that improving Italian immigrants' economic fortunes would cure many other ills his people faced. Thus, his two major legislative thrusts were designed to protect Italian immigrants from unscrupulous people and business practices. Within a matter of months after taking his seat in the Massachusetts legislature, he became the leading force behind the state's decision to abolish so-called immigrant banks and to do away with the often corrupt *padrone* labor system.

Scigliano scorned the immigrant "banks," which often were little more than unregulated grocery stores whose proprietors collected money from immigrants and sold steamship tickets at the same time. Bankers demanded cash from depositors, paid no interest on funds, and maintained shoddy records. When filing his first anti-bank bill, Scigliano submitted to the legislature a list of North End Italians whom immigrant bankers had swindled out of $150,000. "The pending peril by absconding the earnings of Italians and other laborers was one of the great evils which came to my attention," Scigliano told his fellow legislators. "There is no statutory requirement as to the opening of such banks, and the experience gained along this line by disaster, from the absconding of funds, and the readiness with which the small grocers ... open up a banking department, presents an evil hardly without parallel in this State."

Public and press response to Scigliano's initiative was overwhelmingly supportive. Boston newspapers had long opposed the immigrant banks, perhaps based as much on their support of the downtown banking establishment as their concern for immigrants' financial welfare. When Scigliano filed his bill, newspapers hailed his courage, calling him the "father of the anti–immigrant bank bill," and published numerous stories decrying the business practices of the immigrant banks. "There is absolutely no law at present that applies especially to the operation of these immigrant banks," asserted the *Boston Herald* in 1904. "The thousands of dollars that represent accumulations from months or years of hard toil are absolutely at the mercy of the men who hold them in their hands." The *Herald* described a possible example of abuse: "One of these men, for instance, not only cares for deposits, but carries on a bakery and a printing establishment. He could with impunity appropriate every dollar that has been placed in his keeping, and then claim it had been lost in some one of his business enterprises, and there would be absolutely no legal redress . . . To regulate the practice of these bankers, and protect their ignorant depositors, is the purpose of [this] bill." Other Boston papers echoed the *Herald*'s editorial slant.

Scigliano's bill called for any bank to file a bond of at least $25,000 with the Board of Commissioners of Savings Banks "for the purpose of indemnifying such depositors against loss by any default or wrongdoing on the part of said bank." Despite strong support on Beacon Hill, the bill did meet some resistance. Bank commissioners objected to their potential increased workload from monitoring immigrant banks, and, as one newspaper described it, "while everyone has admitted the misfortunes of the system, it has been a task to draft a law which would not hit the big private bankers on State Street."

Scigliano would not live to see his anti–immigrant banking bill pass, "but while he has met with many rebuffs, he has kept at it until victory is in sight," one newspaper said in January of 1906, shortly before Scigliano suspended his legislative duties for health reasons. "For his success in something which is devoid of red fire, of tremendous moments of excitement, of the enthusiasm which brings renewed and redoubled voting strength, all praise to Scigliano."

———

Scigliano's passion and tenacity were also single-handedly responsible for the decline and eventual end of the *padrone* (or boss) labor system in Massachusetts, which he described as "perhaps the greatest evil which has beset the Italian immigrant in this country." Employed by businesses as "labor agents," opportunistic *padroni* greeted Italian immigrants as they arrived and promised that they could find jobs and housing for the newcomers, in return for a fee of one or two dollars per man. Often, this meant herding immigrants who had arrived in major Northeastern cities onto trains and transporting them to rural areas in the South and West to toil in mines or on farms, or lay track for railroads. Once the immigrants were employed, *padroni* charged them a weekly fee to keep their jobs, collected the immigrants' wages from the company or business owner, kept a percentage of that as an additional fee, and were supposed to pay the remainder to the immigrant laborer.

But dishonest *padroni* extorted exorbitant fees from the unsuspecting immigrants, held back full wages for weeks or months, and collaborated in rural areas with owners of company stores, forcing Italians to purchase goods at inflated prices. "These men, bound by contract to the *padrone,* must buy the necessaries of life from the contractor's store, live in the miserable shanties which he puts up, and often submit to the withholding of the greater part of their pay until the end of the season," a *Boston Post* editorial explained. "When that time comes, the *padrone* contractor may 'skip' and leave them swindled." When he submitted legislation to abolish the *padrone* system in Massachusetts in early 1904, Scigliano told his fellow legislators: "In almost all cases, where payment is held back, the money is not paid to laborers, and so, at the end of the season, late in the fall, after the first frost sets in, the laborer returns to the city, and is to house himself for the winter without funds."

In the cities, too, *padroni* held sway over newly arriving Italian immigrants who were confused by the language and the urban setting. "Southern Italian peasants [were] grist for the urban mill," one historian noted. "[They] served their time with pick and shovel, brick and mortar, manning the battalions that built skyscrapers and dug pipe lines, sewers, and subways. For the average immigrant, the initial years were the hardest... he greatly depended upon intermediaries" to find work and survive.

Sometimes, *padroni* participated in blatantly fraudulent schemes to prey on unsuspecting Italian immigrants. Scigliano himself thwarted the potential swindle of hundreds of victims in the North End in May of 1904, just a few months after he filed his anti-*padrone* bill. One brazen *padrone* had stood in the middle of North Square and announced that he was seeking a thousand Italians to work on a major construction project in Providence, Rhode Island, about sixty miles south of Boston. He said the work would last for nine years, that laborers would work "but nine hours a day," and that wages would range from $1.50 to $2 per day. Potential workers would simply have to pay a $1 "registration fee" for the privilege of being hired and another $1.05 for car fare to Providence. "The glad news spread through the North End like wildfire," according to one report, "and in less than 24 hours, half the little colony was flocking to the meeting place... where successful applicants were supposed to deposit their registration fee ... Several hundred names and several hundred dollars were secured in this manner."

Scigliano, in his role as president of the Italian Protective League as well as state representative from the North End, received word of the "gilded promises held out by this unknown contractor" and immediately requested that friends in Providence investigate the claims. "The answer came back quickly that the contract was a fictitious one," the *Boston Post* reported. Scigliano contacted police and accompanied them to a building on Washington Street in downtown Boston, where they arrested the *padrone* while he was "allegedly counting the cash that the Italians had already paid over." Scigliano then oversaw the effort to return the money to the swindler's victims, further burnishing his stellar reputation in the North End.

Boston newspapers applauded Scigliano for educating the city on the "evils of the *padrone* system," and supported his bill enthusiastically and without exception. "It may not be possible to eradicate altogether the so-called *padrone* system, but it is entirely practical to abolish the abuses which have made the title of *padrone* a name of infamy," the *Post* declared. A *Traveler* editorial more forcefully condemned the practice, albeit while invoking other social prejudices of the era: "It is clear that Massachusetts sentiment does not approve of these Shylock methods being applied to the workingmen in this state, even though they are helpless foreigners...we believe that if Representative Scigliano's bill provides an adequate remedy for the evils for the *padrone* system, it should be passed."

Ironically, on the day of Scigliano's funeral, one blatant case of *padroni* mistreatment of Italian immigrant laborers reached the highest levels of the United States government. Italian consul C. G. Montagna wrote to U.S. secretary of state Elihu Root, demanding that the government investigate *padroni* abuses of Italians employed by the Spruce Pine Carolina Company, a North Carolina construction company. A few months earlier, in March of 1906, the company had hired *padroni* to recruit labor from among immigrants arriving in New York and Boston, ostensibly to build railroad track beds. Yet, upon their arrival in North Carolina, the "Italians were deprived of their liberty and reduced to a state of peonage," according to one affidavit Montagna sent to Root, who added:

> The condition in which they appeared was most pitiful, their bodies being broken down by the hardship of the long journey made in great part on foot and by lack of food, and they being stripped of their goods and demoralized...the treatment all these Italians received was practically that of slaves. They were guarded day and night by armed guards and not allowed to leave the premises. They were compelled to do underground work when they had contracted to work above ground...When they refused to do this work...they were whipped and suffered other abuses.

Root intervened with the governor of North Carolina, who exerted enough political pressure on Spruce Pine for the company to agree to pay indemnities to injured Italians "and never again to employ those agents... [who] have been shown to be guilty of ill treatment and abuse of laborers."

Scigliano never knew of the Spruce Pine case, but his bill was passed by his colleagues shortly before his death, establishing such stringent regulation of *padroni* that it virtually outlawed the *padrone* system in Massachusetts. Other states followed suit and the practice was all but eradicated in the United States by about 1910.

More than likely, Scigliano's unflagging and successful efforts to abolish the *padrone* system in Massachusetts benefited scores of Italian men who mourned him on that cool June morning in 1906.

CHAPTER 4

Scigliano's political battles against shady *padroni* and immigrant bankers topped his legislative agenda and sated his desire to improve his countrymen's economic fortunes, but he endeared himself most ardently to Boston Italians with his unwavering public demands that their culture and, more important, their reputation, be treated with dignity and respect. Again and again, he represented the Italian immigrants' point of view to the Boston political, business, and press establishments; he embodied the Italians' spirit, pride, and hope.

Even as illness took its toll, Scigliano remained a clear and indefatigable voice for Italian interests. He founded the Italian Protective League in Boston to assist immigrants, helped form the first Italian workers' union in the North End, worked to kill a bill that would have required laborers to be naturalized, pushed for legislation to establish the first Italian cemetery in the Forest Hills section of Boston, and convinced the state legislature to designate October 12 as Columbus Day in Massachusetts. Of the latter action, one news account reassured its readers: "He is a business man as well as a lawyer, and does not ask that a new legal *holiday* be added to the list. He does ask that this little courtesy be paid to the discoverer of the new world: He wants it provided that the governor shall each year issue a proclamation naming that date as Columbus Day and giving it standing."

Scigliano even traveled outside Massachusetts to help Boston Italians. He visited western states several times seeking outdoor employment for Italian immigrants, on farms or in fruit groves, work that many of them were accustomed to in their home country, accompanied by living conditions that suited them better than the crowded urban tenements of the North End, East Boston, and other sections of the city.

Scigliano also wrote and spoke extensively against those who discriminated against Italians or criticized the North End neighborhood, emotional appeals that further elevated his standing among Italian immigrant workers. In 1901, the United States senator from Massachusetts, George F. Hoar, spoke forcefully against a law excluding Chinese laborers from citizenship, disparaging Italian and Portuguese immigrants in the process. "The Chinese, who is absolutely fit for citizenship, is excluded, while the Portuguese or Italian, who is absolutely unfit, is admitted," Hoar said. Scigliano, then a Boston city councilman, responded the next day in most Boston newspapers: "Why, in espousing the cause of one people, should Senator Hoar take occasion to condemn another? The Italian emigrant, as well as the Portuguese...are courteous, gracious, and just, when treated courteously, graciously, and justly...[They are] frugal and thrifty, eager to educate their children, who...stand shoulder to shoulder and rank every bit as high as pupils of other nationalities. I cannot believe that a man of his [Hoar's] exalted standing could be guilty of such an unwarranted and discriminating censure upon a people." When a Boston Baptist minister charged that the influx of Italians had increased "crime and immorality" in the North End, Scigliano wrote: "On the whole, anyone who lives in this quarter knows that it compares favorably with any other—socially, morally, and educationally. Our troubles are not inherent in our neighborhood...my people have done and are doing their best to lead lives that will benefit themselves and the country which offers them asylum."

Even Scigliano's ceremonial responsibilities and accomplishments helped him achieve revered status among Boston Italians. In the summer of 1905, he joined a distinguished Massachusetts delegation whose members visited Portland, Oregon, for the Lewis and Clark Centennial Exposition. "Massachusetts is well represented, we feel sure," said one Boston newspaper account. "This is about as able a collection of men as could be called upon to uphold the name of the Bay State, and even if codfish and baked beans will be scarce, these Bostonians will be enough to give the Portland pilgrims the proper Boston flavor." That same year, Boston Italians cheered when they heard that the king of Italy had bestowed knighthood upon Scigliano for his efforts and service on behalf of Italians in America, an honor also celebrated by non-Italians in Boston. "President Charles V. Eliot of Harvard college [*sic*], who was given the same title for his work in Italian literature, is the only other man in America who has been knighted by the King of Italy," the *Worcester Telegram* boasted.

In short, Scigliano's influence as a legislative leader had immediate economic impact for Boston Italians; but his influence as an inspirational leader produced long-term psychological benefits. Scigliano's position at the State House was a source of pride among Boston Italians, who viewed his political accomplishments as a sign that Italians could sit confidently at the table with other power brokers in the city. Yet, staking his hard-earned reputation on their behalf, making public utterances in their defense, helping them believe in themselves—these were Scigliano's lasting gifts to Boston's Italian immigrants. They saw in him a man who possessed everything they did not, but one whose life they might one day emulate: a favorite son of financial means who was educated, articulate, tough, urbane, and, perhaps most of all, respected.

In 1903, Scigliano wrote of Italian immigrants: "People who leave their own for another country do so usually because they are dissatisfied with their lot in their native land, and hope to secure a greater measure of happiness under the flag of some other nation."

George Scigliano died years before Boston Italians secured real happiness in America, but his life exemplified the promise of their new country, and his legacy instilled optimism among Italians that, one day, the promise would be fulfilled.

When Scigliano's funeral mass ended in the late morning of June 20, 1906, the procession reformed outside of St. Leonard's Church and slowly made its way to Commercial Street and then Atlantic Avenue, on its way to Boston's South Station. There, Florence Scigliano and her children, other relatives, and friends boarded the 1:00 P.M. train to Worcester. The casket bearing George's body was placed on a rear car, in preparation for a second funeral mass that would be celebrated the next day at St. John's in Worcester, the same church in which Florence and George had exchanged wedding vows exactly six years to the day earlier. Monsignor Thomas Griffin, who married the Sciglianos, would deliver George's eulogy at St. John's. "Monsignor Griffin laid particular stress on the fact that six years ago today he united in marriage the deceased man and his wife," one account reported. "The strange coincidence made the services especially sad to the immediate family...there was hardly a dry eye in the church when [Rev.

Griffin] recalled to the minds of his hearers the uncertainty of life and the magnificent example of good citizenship set for them by the young man whose life was plucked out last Sunday while he was yet in his very prime." For many Italians, "the peculiarly sad coincidence" of Scigliano's Worcester funeral occurring on his sixth wedding anniversary surrounded his death with the aura of a tragic opera or a celestial event.

That Scigliano was being eulogized in Worcester at all came as a disappointment to Boston Italians. North End clergy and residents and Scigliano's brothers and sisters repeatedly implored Scigliano's widow to bury her late husband in the Italian cemetery that he helped establish in Boston's Forest Hills. Florence Scigliano refused each time, choosing to inter George at her family's plot at St. John's Cemetery in Worcester. A group of Boston Italian businessmen approached her a second time, promising to erect a $15,000 monument in Scigliano's memory, and provide perpetual care for a Forest Hills gravesite. But Florence held firm, explaining to one reporter that "if her husband's body was interred in Boston, she would have to go to that city frequently, and that her grief would be more hard to bear in meeting the friends that she and her husband had known in his every day life."

With Florence Scigliano's decision final, another prominent North End Italian believed he had a more creative idea about how best to honor George's memory in Boston for decades to come. James Donnaruma, a peer and close friend of Scigliano's who served as an usher at the funeral, was also the publisher and editor of the North End Italian-language newspaper, *La Gazzetta del Massachusetts*. Donnaruma would need help from politicians and city officials to transform his plan into reality, but that didn't faze him. He had a bold vision and friends in high places; he knew he would succeed.

What he did not know in June of 1906 was that eighteen months later, his plan would embroil the Scigliano name and memory in a political and cultural maelstrom that would touch the city's historical core, test the influence that Italian immigrants exercised in their own neighborhood, and threaten Boston's very power structure in the early twentieth century.

This controversy, this clash of wills, has no official name in Boston's historical record. It is probably most accurately labeled "The Battle for North Square."

CHAPTER 5

James V. Donnaruma and George Scigliano shared a friendship and a mission, their energy and dedication to the latter no doubt strengthening the personal bond they had enjoyed since their youth. Donnaruma was born in 1874, the same year as Scigliano, in San Valentino-Torio, a section of Salerno, Italy, and emigrated to Boston with his parents in 1886 at the age of twelve. His adolescence and young adulthood, like Scigliano's, coincided with a decade of struggle by Italian immigrants, and like his friend, Donnaruma committed himself at a young age to helping his countrymen assimilate into urban American society. He became fluent in English and established himself as a proficient writer.

In 1896, at age twenty-two, ten years after he arrived on America's shore and settled in the North End, Donnaruma founded his first Italian-language newspaper in Boston, *La Stampa,* dedicated to providing information that would ease Italians' transition to the United States. In 1903 (now married to his wife, also named Florence, and the father of a son, Caesar), he bought his second weekly, *La Gazzetta del Massachusetts,* and merged *La Stampa* into the new publication, a four-page broadsheet, printed entirely in Italian, that sold for one cent a copy and carried the masthead tagline "The Italian Weekly Newspaper in the State of Massachusetts."

In the three years between his purchase and Scigliano's death, *La Gazzetta* had become an important voice in the Boston Italian community. Their illiteracy rates notwithstanding, enough Italians could read their own language to share news with friends and relatives. On street corners and in grocery stores, in taverns and private clubs, groups of Italians gathered around one reader to hear, and then discuss, the weekly news. Donnaruma filled his pages with information about Boston, surrounding towns, the United States, and regions in Italy from which most of his readers hailed. He wrote "letters from the publisher" that explained American laws and customs. A family biographer noted that *La Gazzetta*'s classified ads listed steamer passage prices and the times ships sailed to and from Italy, as well as retail stores where immigrants could find food and consumer goods imported from the Old Country. *La Gazzetta,* one of more than five hundred Italian-language newspapers already in the United States by 1906, certainly fulfilled the mission of ethnic newspapers to serve "as a bridge between life in the European village and that in the American city," in the words of one historian. "The Italian-language press addressed itself to people who had seldom—if ever—read newspapers or anything else, for that matter, in the homeland...and eased the first critical years of immigration adjustment to the United States." Years later, Donnaruma's daughter-in-law would describe *La Gazzetta*'s role in those early years as the Italians' "passport to belonging."

As *La Gazzetta* became more influential in Boston, Donnaruma's prominence grew, to the point where it was perhaps second only to Scigliano's both within the Italian community and beyond, in the city's and state's political hierarchy. Donnaruma was friendly with Mayor John F. "Honey Fitz" Fitzgerald, with city councilors, and other men who wielded power in the corridors of city hall and the State House.

Shortly after the death of George Scigliano, James Donnaruma began circulating through those corridors advancing a plan to properly honor his friend's memory.

Donnaruma's idea was simple enough. He believed the appropriate and permanent way to honor Scigliano was to rename North Square, one of Boston's most historic and famous squares, "Scigliano Square" and erect a monument on the square in Scigliano's honor. Shortly after Scigliano's funeral, Donnaruma began sharing his plan with North End businessmen and residents, the vast majority of whom agreed with him; for a year, Donnaruma continued building momentum at a grassroots level, before approaching Boston city councilman James T. Purcell, a close friend of Scigliano's. In the fall of 1907, Purcell agreed to introduce an order in the Common Council to rename North Square Scigliano Square.

Donnaruma handled one other thorny political issue to improve the chances of the name-change bill. George Scigliano's brother, Alfred, a

North End resident who had achieved some popularity since George's death, was threatening to support Republican mayoral candidate George Hibbard over Mayor Fitzgerald in the November 1907 election, due to his dissatisfaction with many of Fitzgerald's policies. Yet, Fitzgerald's support was necessary for the name-change order to pass: first, he had supporters on the Common Council who were likely to vote according to his wishes; and second, Fitzgerald himself would have to sign any order passed by the Council. Donnaruma convinced Alfred Scigliano to withdraw his support for Hibbard and publicly express his backing of Fitzgerald, in exchange for Fitzgerald's endorsement of the name change. For his part, Fitzgerald knew his race against Hibbard would be tight and sought as many ethnic votes as possible in his reelection quest. Despite the relatively small number of Boston Italians who were naturalized at the time, every vote would count. "Names of streets and squares can be used as political assets by desperate politicians looking for votes when votes are hard to find," the *Boston Journal* asserted.

Ironically, despite Alfred Scigliano's eleventh-hour reversal and endorsement, Fitzgerald lost the November election; Hibbard would become mayor in January of 1908. Given Alfred Scigliano's last-minute reversal and declaration of support for Fitzgerald, a furious Hibbard would not support the North Square name change after he took office.

If Donnaruma and Purcell were ever to stroll through Scigliano Square in Boston's North End, the new name would have to be in place before the end of 1907.

With a lame-duck Mayor Fitzgerald voicing his support, Purcell filed his order for the North Square name change at the Common Council meeting on Thursday evening, December 12, 1907. The measure passed on a voice vote with no debate. All that remained for the change to become official was the expected final approval on December 23 from the Boston Board of Aldermen—the upper body in the city's then two-tiered legislative form of government—and Mayor Fitzgerald's signature, considered a foregone conclusion.

If Donnaruma, Purcell, or the Common Council thought that the Christmas season would provide enough cover and distraction to divert attention from the "Scigliano Square" vote, they badly miscalculated the depth of opposition from Boston's powerful elite and traditionalists. For the next ten days, what began as Purcell's quiet legislative maneuver to honor an old friend and a neighborhood leader erupted into a citywide political donnybrook, involving city and state officials, business leaders, blueblood patriotic societies such as the Daughters of the American Revolution (DAR), the entire Boston press establishment, and residents from most of Boston's neighborhoods.

On one side were the majority of North End and Boston Italians, most of them immigrants, led by Donnaruma, who supported the Common Council's decision to rename North Square and believed it was a fitting way to honor a man who had given so much to the neighborhood in which the square was located. On the other side were patriotic organizations, many Boston political officials, and most of the press corps, who believed, in the words of the DAR, that changing the name of North Square was "a sacrilege...as well might they...change the name of the glorious frigate *Constitution.*" North Square, after all, was the site of Paul Revere's house and just a few blocks from Old North Church. In the eyes of the guardians of Boston's Puritanical and Revolutionary legacy, renaming the square to honor an Italian immigrant leader was tantamount to desecrating the venerable site.

The *Boston Globe* cringed the morning after the Common Council vote, expressing a subdued anti-Italian bias about the impact the new name would have on North Square's proud historical lineage: "It is safe to say that the new name for the square, Scigliano, will not drop lightly from the tongue of all visitors to that region. The name North Square is one of the richest names of Boston in its historic associations, and the change will certainly create a necessity for many textual changes in local histories before the rising generation can become habituated to describing Paul Revere, Increase and Cotton Mather, Governor Thomas Hutchinson, Sir Harry Frankland, and Sir William Phipps as connected with Scigliano Square."

The *Boston Post* and *Boston Journal* quickly joined the *Globe* to vigorously oppose the name change, although they devoted a substantial number of column inches to present the views of Scigliano Square supporters. The *Journal* published an editorial cartoon entitled BALLOON VIEW OF

BOSTON RE-TAGGED that showed famous Boston landmarks renamed; Copp's Hill was labeled "Cosmopolitan Terrace" and Faneuil Hall was named "Cabbage Arcade." The *Post* quoted Dr. Francis Brown of the Sons of the American Revolution when he learned of the Common Council vote: "Give up that old name, so identified with history and life of Boston? Why it is an outrage! There shall be a protest against such an action."

Brown's words proved prophetic. As Bostonians prepared for Christmas, as shoppers visited downtown stores to purchase gifts, as North End Italians anticipated the fish, vegetable, and meatless pasta dishes that would crowd their tables during their Christmas Eve feast, Boston newspapers covered the North Square controversy on their front pages and inside virtually every edition. The Common Council vote had opened a floodgate of passion and conviction on each side of the issue. Historical societies, politicians, businessmen, Italian and non-Italian Boston residents—all of them weighed in on whether an Italian's name would adorn a square in the oldest section of Boston, the city's first neighborhood.

"I don't believe in such changes," said Levi L. Willcut, a director of the Bostonian Society. "Mr. Scigliano was known throughout the district, but the name of North Square is known the world over. The home of Paul Revere and the center of such historic happenings, it should be considered an almost sacred spot." A letter writer to the *Post* protested, "Scigliano Square? Very euphonious, but having nothing to connect it with the time that tried men's souls. In the name of the true American sentiment, which saved the old frigate *Constitution,* the Old State House, the sacred Old South Church, and many other monuments of American history, I protest most vigorously against any destruction of the ancient landmarks." Charles Francis Adams, president of the Massachusetts Historical Society, said that to rename North Square would be "the worst kind of vandalism . . . there should be decided protest and it could not be made too strong!"

The North End was not excluded from such protest. Two dozen North End merchants, all non-Italians, signed a petition protesting the North Square name change. One banker commented: "We have over a million envelopes marked '3 North Square.' We don't want a change, we'll fight a change, and if there is a change, we won't pay attention to it."

Not even all North End Italians supported changing the name of

North Square. A reporter visited the neighborhood and "was surprised that some of the very men who most had reason to rejoice at a change in name shook their heads and spoke against having the place known to coming generations as Scigliano Square." One Italian attorney and friend of Scigliano's, Domenic Romano, spoke strongly: "I am opposed to the change, absolutely opposed to it. Mr. Scigliano was a dear friend of mine and I have in my possession the last letter he ever wrote. I am glad to see that they want to honor him, but I cannot see why they want to change a name so widely known for its historic associations. If they absolutely must change the name, name it Paul Revere Square and preserve American history."

Despite these pockets of protest in the North End, the overwhelming sentiment in the Italian enclave was to rename North Square to honor Scigliano, particularly among the average working Italian immigrants he touched so deeply. Italian immigrants did not understand the historic significance of North Square, and there was little about the area to remind them. The building that had been Paul Revere's house had become the *Banca Italiana* (Italian bank) and the F. A. Goduti cigar shop; only earlier in 1907 had interested citizens formed the Paul Revere Memorial Association to preserve the home of the patriot and silversmith (it was restored in 1909). Virtually all other structures on North Square bore the flavor of the Italian neighborhood. Sacred Heart Church, a second Italian Catholic parish established in 1888, anchored the southeast end of the square; the Hotel Rome apartment building dominated the center; and an Italian notary public, an Italian café, and an Italian grocery store dotted North Square's perimeter. As much as the North End was the center of Italian life in Boston for most Italian immigrants, so too was North Square the center of Italian activity and vitality within the North End. Renaming the square in honor of Scigliano seemed natural and appropriate to most Italians.

In a December 22, 1907, *Post* article headlined ITALIANS INSIST THAT THE NAME OF NORTH SQUARE BE CHANGED TO SCIGLIANO, North End Italians poured out their sentiments. Achille Forte of 5 North Square noted: "George Scigliano was not a politician. He looked out for the poor and the lowly, letting his own interests go to benefit others . . . He did more to promote the interests of his race than any other Italian in Boston. The naming of this square would not be too great an honor to this man among men."

St. Leonard's pastor, Ubaldus Panfilio, who the previous year had presided over Scigliano's funeral, strongly favored the name change. "It is a deserved tribute to a man who performed great works for his race and whose memories will ever be cherished." Another St. Leonard's priest added: "A most beautiful character had Mr. Scigliano and all that he did was for the interests of his own people. He deserves the honor of having the square named after him."

Italian organizations enthusiastically supported the name change. Columbus Associates argued that renaming the site to Scigliano Square was the least the city could do to honor the most prestigious Italian in Boston's history. Members of the organization accused newspapers who quoted Italians in opposition to the name change of "misrepresenting" the views of Boston Italians, "and from now on every effort will be made by this organization to have the upper branch of the city government endorse the action of the lower body." Michael Cellica, president of St. Michaele's Society, said: "By all means, let the square be named after the man."

Prominent Italian businessmen, including doctors, bankers, and shopkeepers, also wholeheartedly endorsed the name change. Druggist Felix Laurello said: "I believe that the square should bear the new name. It would be a just tribute to his [Scigliano's] worth." A physician, Dr. John Cecconi, probably best summed up the feelings of the North End when he said: "I believe in calling it Scigliano Square. If a vote of the residents of this section were taken, it would be practically unanimous."

Nonetheless, in the days between the Common Council vote and the Board of Aldermen meeting, momentum built swiftly against the name change outside the Italian community. The influential Charles Read, secretary of the Bostonian Society, argued that North Square had borne its name since the Revolution and was "known from one end of the country to the other . . . it would be a shame to make the change proposed." Charles Darling, president of the Massachusetts Sons of the American Revolution, chose a softer approach: "I want to respect the memory of Mr. Scigliano, but I think that if he were alive today, he would not sanction any such change . . . we can be considerate of the Italian population without taking such a step as that." The press continued its opposition, publishing several stories in which reporters allegedly "summarized" the general feelings of those they purportedly interviewed. "They condemned generally the policy of making changes in the names of old streets and localities," one piece in the *Globe* said. "They thought it strange that an outgoing city government should at the last moment consider such a radical and unreasonable change in the square's name, and said that if the order passed the Board of Aldermen and the mayor didn't have the backbone to veto it, then the new mayor, upon assuming the duties of office, would find it put up to him to rescind the order." The paper never acknowledged whether the "they" who expressed these views were ordinary Boston residents or its own top editors, though it is worth noting that the *Globe* printed identical sentiments on its opinion pages.

For his part, Councilman Purcell, who proposed the name change, did not back down in the face of the protest and said he would continue his support at the Board of Aldermen meeting. "I am somewhat surprised at the agitation," he said. "I think the Italians of Boston and vicinity should have some recognition . . . to their former leader, George Scigliano, and for it there is no more appropriate location than North Square . . . the Italians of Boston and vicinity practically look upon this square as their own."

Yet, as the Board of Aldermen meeting approached, it was clear that Purcell's proposal, the Common Council vote, and James Donnaruma's carefully crafted plan to honor his friend were in jeopardy. The death knell for Scigliano Square likely occurred when Mayor Fitzgerald publicly backpedaled in the midst of the controversy, and finally said he was opposed to the name change. In fact, in the most disingenuous assertion of the debate, Fitzgerald claimed that he first learned of the plan to change the name of North Square when "the matter first appeared in the newspapers stating that the Common Council had passed such an order." Supporters of Scigliano Square knew that, even as a lame duck, Mayor Fitzgerald wielded significant power among the Board of Aldermen. Fitzgerald may have suffered a defeat in his November reelection bid, but he had strong future political aspirations (he would one day again serve as mayor of Boston and later as a congressman from the city); the fervor with which Boston's old-guard establishment and his Irish supporters opposed the North Square name change almost certainly caused Fitzgerald to reconsider a legacy in which he would be identified as the man who penned his signature to the official document that would create "Scigliano Square."

Donnaruma was disgusted at the tone of the debate. "Instead of North Square or Scigliano Square, it ought to be Blackmail Square," he said. "The bankers have opposed the project because Scigliano got the banking bill passed, regulating their business and making them keep their books in good shape. His *padrone* bill also proved to be of immense benefit to the poor laborers who had been swindled out of their pay."

In the end, of course, Donnaruma and other allies of the late George A. Scigliano were thwarted. At its December 23 meeting, the Boston Board of Aldermen declined to concur with the Common Council vote, opting instead to "indefinitely postpone" the proposed North Square name change. The vote was unanimous, with aldermen citing the intense pressure from historical societies and businesses against the change. NORTH SQUARE STANDS the *Globe* headline crowed in its Christmas Eve edition.

One week later, at their December 30, 1907, meeting, in what amounted to a consolation prize, the aldermen voted "without debate" to change the name of the North End Park near Copp's Hill to Scigliano Park. Mayor John Fitzgerald, in one of his last official acts before leaving office, approved the change.

Despite the outcome, the Battle for North Square represented a watershed event in the history of Boston Italians: It was the first major political battle they had waged with any kind of consensus or unity. While it would be many years before Italians wielded any real power in Boston, the North Square controversy helped them develop a sense of political savvy that had eluded them to this point. It was as if George Scigliano's advocacy and activism had rubbed off on them, and galvanized them to fight for something in which they fervently believed.

Moreover, the fight helped Italians make the transition from being strangers in a strange land to finding a new place they called home. The experience of taking on Boston's most powerful people and institutions unified Boston Italians and strengthened their sense of belonging. From then on, despite a long wait before they would achieve political power, their status changed from itinerant newcomers to one of Boston's largest and most *socially* influential ethnic groups. Whereas before the Battle for North Square, the North End had merely been the place where they lived, afterward they viewed the neighborhood as their own and quickly developed a sense of community pride. This cohesiveness would become ingrained in the North End character for decades to come, becoming the central reason the neighborhood thrived and its voice represented all Boston Italians.

Finally, the Battle for North Square was a defining moment for James Donnaruma. With Scigliano's death, Donnaruma became the strongest voice for Italians in the North End and Boston. As Scigliano's memory faded, Donnaruma's stature and influence grew. From behind the editor's desk of *La Gazzetta del Massachusetts,* Donnaruma became the new champion of Boston Italians, a title and distinction he would hold for the next fifty years.

PART 2

WHY THEY CAME

CHAPTER 6

In the period between George Scigliano's death in June of 1906 and the Battle for North Square eighteen months later, my paternal grandparents left the ancient fishing village of Sciacca in Sicily and emigrated to America. Their story epitomized the experience of millions of Italians in the late nineteenth and early twentieth centuries, a period of mass exodus from Italy to other parts of Europe, South America, and the United States, one of the great voluntary migrations in the history of mankind.

My grandfather, Calogero ("Charles") Puleo, came first, traveling by train to Palermo and boarding the SS *Italia* bound for Ellis Island. He arrived in New York on August 30, 1906, two weeks after his twenty-fourth birthday, with twelve dollars in his pocket, a pregnant wife back home, and an unquenchable desire to begin laying the foundation of a life for his family in America. That meant earning enough money to send for my grandmother, who was expecting their first baby five months later, and his newborn, as soon as the child was old enough to survive the difficult two- to three-week voyage in steerage. My grandfather had traveled to the United States once before, four years earlier, to work temporarily, a classic Italian "bird of passage," who earned a few dollars in the spring and then returned to his economically depressed homeland a little better off. This time, though, he arrived in America, speaking virtually no English and without skills, with plans to stay permanently. He found work as a ditch digger and laborer and began saving money.

Nine months later, my grandmother, Angela, and her six-month-old daughter of the same name made the grim and grueling trip across the Atlantic Ocean aboard the same SS *Italia*. The passage took more than three weeks in conditions that were crowded, filthy, uncomfortable, and often dangerous, especially for an infant.

Aboard the *Italia* and all immigrant ships, lice, scurvy, and seasickness all contributed to the misery of steerage passengers. Italians, including my grandmother, brought along knapsacks full of cheeses and salami to supplement the wretched soup doled out to passengers by the steamship company. Passengers were "crammed into overcrowded berths, stacked to the ceiling below decks, breathed foul air, suffered from seasickness, contracted diseases, and continually feared the ship would sink," in the words of one writer. Italians later remembered the Atlantic passage as the *via dolorosa,* the "sorrowful way." Immigrant Angelo Pellegrini, who was nine years old when he boarded the *Toramina* in Genoa, bound for New York, recalled as an adult: "Peasants who did not understand why some objects float . . . had to accept on faith the phenomenon of a floating ship. Their faith, of course, was severely taxed. Every time the ship rolled, or dropped groaning into the trough of a wave, accompanied by the clatter of falling tin dishes with which each steerage passenger had been provided, she was presumed to go down." Pellegrini saw an elderly woman, miserable with seasickness, complain to a crew member who assured her that she would not die. "She shot back at him, with unintended humor, that he had taken from her her last hope." One emigrant saw the voyage as an extension of the hardships he had faced in Italy: "The passage across the ocean seemed to have been so calculated as to inflict upon us the last, full measure of suffering and indignity," he wrote. The voyage seemed designed "to impress upon us for the last time that we were the 'wretched refuse of the earth' and to extract from us a final price for the privilege we hoped to enjoy in America."

The brutal voyages eventually did end and passengers jammed the decks of the immigrant ships as the Statue of Liberty and the New York skyline came into view; 95 percent of Italian immigrants entered the United States through Ellis Island, while other ships docked in Boston, Providence, Philadelphia, and elsewhere. On June 15, 1907, the *Italia,* with my grandmother and aunt aboard, arrived in New York, where my grandfather met them in a joyful reunion. After my grandmother and her infant cleared the Ellis Island inspection, the little family traveled by train back to Boston, where they would live briefly with my grandmother's brother at 1 North Square before establishing their own household.

Over the next eighteen years, my grandparents would have nine more children—one every two years—until their tenth and final child, my father, Anthony, was born in 1925. Like millions of Italian immigrants, they carved out a life in America under the most difficult of circumstances.

My grandfather worked as an unskilled laborer until a few years after my father was born, then earned his citizenship in 1931 and supported his family as a peddler selling his fruit and produce from a pushcart. The Puleo family lived first on Garden Court Street and then North Street in small tenement walk-up apartments, surrounded by *paesani* from Sicily who spoke their dialect and shared their customs. My grandparents shopped, socialized, and worshipped in the North End; indeed, my family's growth coincided with the North End's transformation into a nearly exclusive Italian neighborhood.

By 1910, after a decade of unprecedented immigration, the North End's population approached thirty thousand people, of whom more than twenty-eight thousand were Italians. The vast majority of the Irish population and virtually the entire Jewish population had left the North End and "moved up" to Roxbury, Dorchester, and Hyde Park. By 1920, forty thousand people crowded into the North End; Italians represented 97 percent of the neighborhood's population, and more than 50 percent of the overall Italian population in Boston. Of the North End, one Yankee journalist lamented: "No where in Boston has father time wrought such ruthless changes as in the once highly respectable quarter, now swarming with Italians in every dirty nook and corner." The influx of Italians made the neighborhood unrecognizable, he noted. "In truth, it is hard to believe the evidence of our senses, though the fumes of garlic are sufficiently convincing... those among us, who recall something of its vanished prestige, [do not] feel at all at home in a place where our own mother-tongue no longer serves us."

Why did these Italians decide to come to America when most of them had never before traveled outside of their own village or town? Why did my grandfather risk leaving his pregnant wife and traveling thousands of miles alone, virtually penniless and illiterate, to a land where both the language and the way of life were foreign and hostile? From where would my grandmother, a young twenty-two-year-old mother at the time of her departure from Italy, find the inner reservoir of strength to bundle up her six-month-old daughter and embark on a wretched and harrowing four-thousand-mile journey in the bowels of a dirty steamship, likely fearing for her daughter's safety and health every moment for three weeks?

To fully understand why Italians flocked in droves from the Old Country to America and Boston, why they were willing to endure the hardships of settlement and assimilation in crowded urban neighborhoods so different from the villages and small towns of Italy, and indeed, why they ultimately persevered and thrived in the United States, it is important to understand why they left Italy in the first place.

More than anything, Italians sought a new life in America in a desperate attempt to end years of suffering in Italy. My grandparents and millions of others had little choice but to emigrate to survive.

CHAPTER 7

Early in the first decade of the twentieth century, Italian prime minister Giuseppe Zanardelli made a trip through one of the southern provinces. The mayor and chief men of one town, Moliterno, met the minister at the train and escorted him to the central square, where an enthusiastic crowd greeted the important visitor. The mayor mounted a platform, looked down upon the crowd, and delivered his opening remarks to the esteemed prime minister: "I welcome you in the name of the five thousand inhabitants of this town—three thousand of whom are in America and the other two thousand preparing to go."

Exaggerated, even flippant, perhaps, but the mayor's remarks to Prime Minister Zanardelli carried enough truth to accurately portray the magnitude of emigration from Italy at the end of the nineteenth and beginning of the twentieth centuries. The records are incomplete, especially in Southern Italy, but government estimates and scholarly research indicate that between fourteen and fifteen million people left Italy between 1880 and 1920. More than four million of this number came to the United States, about 80 percent of those from Southern Italy and Sicily. From 1900 to 1910 alone, more than two million Italians, including my grandparents, flowed through American ports, as the Italian inundation reached a crest higher than that from any other nation; nearly three times as many arrived in the first decade of the twentieth century as had in the preceding ten years.

In 1900, Italians composed less than 4 percent of the foreign-born population in the United States and about 2 percent in Boston. By 1920, nearly 16 percent of the populations of both Boston and the United States were either Italian immigrants or their children.

"Necessity is not only the mother of invention," immigration scholar Francis E. Clark wrote early in the twentieth century, "but of a good many other children, including emigration." And necessity was the driving force prompting Italians to leave the farms, fishing villages, and citrus groves of the Old Country to settle in crowded urban American neighborhoods in New York, Boston, Chicago, Philadelphia, New Orleans, Buffalo, San Francisco, and elsewhere. In Southern Italy and Sicily, particularly, from where the vast majority of immigrants hailed, the exodus was born of desperation caused by the harshest of economic realities, natural disasters, disease, and cultural issues between Northern and Southern Italians in a country that had become unified only a few decades earlier.

Southern Italy, the nation's *mezzogiorno* region (the word means "midday" in Italian and is a reference to the strength of the midday sun in Southern Italy), became known instead to the peasants who lived there as the land of *la miseria*.

Like weather fronts colliding, a stunning forty-year combination of natural disasters and poor political and economic decisions converged upon Southern Italy. In the 1870s, just a few years after Italy was unified in 1860, the Italian government in Rome forced southern peasants to pay exorbitant taxes on diseased vineyards. In 1910, the eruption of Mount Etna in Sicily killed ten thousand people. Sandwiched between these two events, Southern Italians endured an apocalyptic litany of misery that they recalled again and again as they rode the trains bound for embarkation ports and boarded steamships for America, and once again in the grocery stores and coffee shops of Boston:

- To raise revenue in the late 1870s, the Italian government heavily taxed wheat, which had already fallen to a record low price, and salt, which Southern Italians used as a preservative, creating overwhelming hardships for peasant farmers.

- In Avellino in 1880, virtually all of the region's agricultural crops suffered from disease, and its peasant population was forced to absorb the loss by absentee landlords who lived in the North.

- Bread riots broke out when more than 60 percent of the Naples-Avellino population could not find work in 1881. A cholera epidemic ravaged Naples in 1882, further devastating the region.

• The citrus crop, the pride of parts of Campania and Sicily, suffered several poor harvests in a row due to drought and diseased trees, enabling the American citrus industry to gain a toehold in the world market in the late 1890s.

• Similar conditions destroyed vineyards and enabled the French wine industry to encroach on that of Italy, which until the turn of the twentieth century had been dominant in Europe. The loss of market share further bludgeoned the Southern Italian economy.

• In addition to the Mount Etna eruption, other natural disasters added to the belief of thousands of Southern Italians that their homeland was cursed and that flight was their only option. In 1905, a series of earthquakes rocked the provinces of Calabria and Basicalata, killing thirty thousand people. The following year, Mount Vesuvius erupted, burying entire towns near Naples. And in 1908, just a year after my grandmother and aunt left Sciacca, one of the worst disasters in Italian history occurred when an earthquake devastated Messina in Sicily. More than one hundred thousand people were killed in the city itself, and another twenty thousand died across the Straits of Messina in Regina di Calabria.

• Disease, especially malaria, ravaged Southern Italy during this period. "It stands forth as one of the prime forces that have made for emigration," wrote immigration historian Robert Foerster, explaining that malaria needs stagnant water to flourish and spread. With six months of heavy rain and six months of almost no rain, Southern Italy proved the perfect breeding ground for the disease to thrive. In 1887, for example, more than twenty-one thousand people died of malaria in Southern Italy.

All of these factors—poverty, natural disasters, and disease—had a crushing impact on the Southern Italian economy, but perhaps a more debilitating effect on the psyche of the region's residents. "Of all the consequences," Foerster wrote, "the most serious is probably psychological, the creation of a mood of helplessness, or even worse, of apathy restraining at once the impulse to progress and the energies needed for accomplishment."

Italian officials and writers echoed the mood of helplessness that permeated Southern Italy. In a widely publicized essay in the 1880s, one writer described the harsh conditions in the South:

> Our peasants there are in worse conditions than the serfs of the Middle Ages. The landlords treat them like slaves. Peasants live like beasts. Their sense of dignity seems to have died centuries ago. They have two equally hard choices before them—submission and work until an untimely death, or rebellion and violent death—unless they are willing to escape to somewhere else.

In 1900, Giustino Fortunato, who represented one of the poorest districts of the South in the Chamber of Deputies, described to his colleagues "the sadness of the physical and social landscape of the provinces of Calabria and Basicalata and the tragic reality of regions where peasants live for months and years without ever seeing a happy face...It is unlikely that these people will learn to smile as long as they stay in the deep South."

The prolonged agricultural depression pounded Southern Italy so fiercely that one official reported: "The cost of oil and other items is so high that people are forced to leave for overseas to avoid starvation." In the spring of 1894 he added: "People are leaving in large numbers; they think they have no alternative, and they are unwilling to face another winter here. Poverty seems to have broken their will to fight. Their departure is like the flight of people who have nothing to lose by going." Financial capital to develop industry and commerce was virtually nonexistent, as peasants could not afford interest rates on loans that hovered close to 100 percent. Even the once proud Southern Italian fishing industry was devastated by the depression. The mayor of Santa Flavia declared in 1895: "The fishermen of this town are forced to leave. The basic reason is that they cannot sell their catch. There is simply no cash in the region, and commerce has come to a standstill."

While the stagnant economy made jobs scarce, even those who *did* work earned virtually unlivable wages for their efforts. Carpenters in

Southern Italy received as little as a pitiful thirty cents per day, or $1.80 for a six-day week. Their counterparts in the United States earned about $18 for a fifty-hour week. General day laborers in the United States earned three times more than those in Italy, and in some of the poorest regions of Southern Italy, laborers earned no more than twelve to twenty cents per day.

Perhaps most destructive of all to the Southern Italian economy were the burdensome taxes levied upon its citizens, most already desperately poor, by virtually all levels of government. By the end of the nineteenth century, taxes in Italy were the highest in Europe and weighed especially heavily on those least able to pay, the *contadini* (peasants) and the *giornalieri* (day laborers) of the South. Rome imposed excise taxes on salt, sugar, tobacco, wine, flour, bread, and macaroni, all items integral to Southern Italian households and the region's economy. Not only did the central government levy taxes equal to more than 30 percent of income, but provinces and communes taxed day laborers to excess also. "In Italy, the taxes fall heaviest on the poor," Francis Clark wrote. "It is progressive taxation topsy-turvy; the less a man has, the more he pays." When considering the emigrant, "two words may describe the forces which drive him from his native land, and these two words are poverty and taxes. Perhaps the formula may be reduced to one word—poverty—for his poverty is in no small measure the result of the direct and indirect taxes he has to bear."

This tax burden not only contributed to the near bankruptcy of Southern Italy but also bred resentment among Southern Italians against the central government and the Northern Italians, who held the most powerful positions in Rome. This exacerbated a feeling that had existed in the South since Italy's reunification in 1860—that northerners viewed their southern countrymen as inferiors, a sentiment that continued in Boston and America. Usurious taxes imposed by Rome also heightened the Southern Italians' general distrust of authorities and government, suspicions that also carried over to the New World and would affect Italians' attitudes for years to come. "[When] Rome provided for graduated taxes on the grinding of [wheat], Southern Italians considered this grist tax discriminatory, since wheat was the major grain in their diet," historians Luciano Iorizzo and Salvatore Mondello suggested in a 1980 study. "They believed that Northern Italians, who relied predominately on corn, were favored."

Through all of this, while Southern Italy and Sicily struggled with disease, economic blight, and a skewed tax system, the birth rate continued to rise, placing an enormous strain on families mired in poverty and a region with virtually no semblance of a working economy. Between 1881 and 1901, Italy's population increased nearly 20 percent—despite the emigration of millions of Italians to other countries. As if conditions were not terrible enough, overpopulation became another factor Italians weighed in their decision to emigrate.

Amid this bleak backdrop, it is no surprise that Southern Italians looked outside Italy to escape the land of *la miseria* and overcome the poverty and desperation that filled their lives. "Purely economic causes were responsible for practically all emigration from Italy," wrote historian Humbert Nelli. "The emigrants were driven by a desire to escape abject poverty and a vicious system of taxation, the burden of which fell almost exclusively on poor peasants."

By the late nineteenth century, traveling to America had captured the imagination of Italians, especially the poorest residents of Southern Italy. Farmers, fishermen, tradesmen, and laborers not only sought to escape their desperate plights, they were further encouraged by family members and friends who had traveled to the United States and returned with money, or sent funds back to Italy while continuing to work in America. In 1896, the *prefetto* (prefect or magistrate) of Palermo reported: "America seems to have an irresistible attraction for these people. Sicilians have traditionally been unwilling to leave the island, even to go to Italy. But America seems to be different. Or is it that they have no alternative, and anything is an improvement over their present condition in Sicily?" An American visitor to Southern Italy wrote:

> There was constant talk of America on the trains, on the road, and in towns. In a small southern town, I saw a great throng of people. Upon inquiring, I was told that they had been to the station to say goodbye to 120 of their townsmen who had just left for America. Even in the most isolated communities, emigration to America was the topic of discussion. There were many people who could name the president of the United States but not the King of Italy.

When word began trickling back about opportunity in America, and money began flowing from Italians in the United States to families in Italy, Southern Italians saw hope for the first time and viewed emigration as their final chance to escape *la miseria* in Italy. "America has become a disease, but of necessity," wrote the president of an Italian agricultural society.

Or, as a Southern Italian peasant who had traveled several times between the United States and Italy answered when he was asked the difference between the two countries: "The main difference was bread. There was always bread in America."

Still, even after Southern Italians left their homeland to improve their desperate economic conditions in America, they found it difficult to stay away. Despite the perilous conditions in Southern Italy and Sicily, the love of family and village called many back to the Old Country, a siren's song whose mesmerizing strains were strengthened by the chaos, confusion, discrimination, and homesickness Southern Italians experienced in American cities. "There is a strife between the desire to earn [in the United States] and that to return to Italy... there arises a contest between the old home and the new, the one calling, the other seducing," historian Robert Foerster wrote in 1919.

The entire phenomenon of return migration from the United States was a unique and vital aspect of the Italian immigration experience, one that made Italians different from other immigrants and evoked a mixture of wariness and suspicion among Americans about the motives of Italians who entered the country. As they traveled back and forth across the Atlantic, driven by economic, meteorological, or psychological considerations, Italians were disparagingly labeled "birds of passage" by Americans who questioned their character and their commitment to the United States. As they arrived in America in springtime to take advantage of outdoor seasonable employment and returned to Italy when the weather turned colder, Southern Italians were scorned by other ethnic groups whose laborers, born in America or naturalized citizens for years, fought for the same jobs. And as they sent millions of dollars back to family members in Italy, money they had earned from those same jobs, Italians triggered resentment among Americans that often hardened into hatred and violence.

The birds of passage influenced the entire character of Italian immigration, and thus the American response to it; even those Italians who crossed the Atlantic only once and stayed in the United States permanently were tainted, in the eyes of Americans, by their migratory countrymen. It is impossible to understand the immigration of Italians to the United States, and their assimilation into American society, without recognizing the significance of the birds of passage and return migration.

Records from the very early years of immigration are incomplete, but the numbers that exist are stunning. Return-migration scholars estimate that of the approximately 4.2 million Italians who arrived in the United States between 1880 and 1920, as many as 1.7 million were birds of passage who migrated back and forth between the two countries, and well over 1 million returned to Southern Italy permanently despite the depression that gripped the region.

Repatriates most often were unable to make the cultural and sociological adjustment from the largely pastoral setting in Southern Italy to a frenetic urban pace in America. Others simply missed family and loved ones at home. "Without question," historian Betty Boyd Caroli wrote in a 1973 study, "the repatriates I interviewed listed economic reasons for going back to the United States and emotional attachments drawing them back to Italy." Edward Corsi, who later became President Franklin D. Roosevelt's commissioner of immigration, pointed out that his mother was despondent from her arrival in America until her departure. She hated the "dingy tenement house" in Harlem in which she and her family lived. It stood in such contrast to the open fields outside her Italian village. Corsi recalled of his mother:

> She loved quiet and hated noise and confusion. Here [in the U.S.] she never left the house unless she had to. She spent her days, and the waking hours of the nights, sitting at one outside window staring up at the little patch of sky above the tenements. She was never happy here and, though she tried, could not adjust herself to the poverty and despair in which she had to live.

The Italian love of family and *paese* was a powerful force to many immigrants, strong enough to overcome the horrendous conditions in Southern Italy. An Italian physician who resided briefly in the United States asked a group of his countrymen, all seasonal laborers, why they insisted on sending money back to their families in Italy when they seemed to barely subsist on minimal necessities in America. One man in the group replied: "Doctor, we brought to America only our brains and our arms. Our hearts stayed there in the little houses in the beautiful fields of our Italy."

As they wrestled with the emotions of leaving their homeland, Italian birds of passage to the United States were also assisted by their government.

In the late nineteenth and early twentieth centuries, the Italian government strongly encouraged *temporary* emigration and regulated its flow, viewing it as a necessary safety valve offsetting population increases that would have made economic conditions worse. Italian minister of foreign affairs Tommaso Titoni said in a 1904 speech: "Emigration is a necessity for our country. It would be terrible if this safety valve did not exist, this possibility of finding work elsewhere." One Italian journalist added: "It is quite evident that emigration must continue; otherwise the country will not be able to support its inhabitants."

In 1901, Italy established the *Commissariato dell'Emigrazione,* under the minister of foreign affairs, to manage and oversee temporary emigration— and encourage repatriation to Italy—as a matter of national policy. The agency disseminated prices and times of voyages to America, guidelines for what emigrants should bring on their trips, and conditions in U.S. cities. The Italian government in Rome hoped its southern citizens would make seasonal trips to America to earn money and alleviate pressure on the anemic Italian economy, and then return to infuse cash into a resource-starved Southern Italian region.

The *Commissariato dell'Emigrazione* published a bulletin, the *Bollettino dell'Emigrazione,* which provided information to potential emigrants on a wide range of topics—from mining conditions in Pennsylvania to land prices in the southern United States, from sleeping arrangements available to emigrants in ports of departure to the types of food they would find aboard ships.

Italian officials simply believed, at least in the early years, that the benefits their country could derive from temporary emigration, particularly the remittances from America, far outweighed any problems. Deputy

Paolo Falletti, speaking in the lower house of Parliament, voiced his body's predominant opinion: "Repatriation is certainly an advantage for us, because it represents what permanent emigration is not...because of this, I maintain that we must preserve ever stronger the ties of the mother country with our emigrants in order to facilitate their return." Falletti even recommended that his government appropriate money for schools in the United States to "teach nationals better Italian" and strengthen their attachment to Italy, a plan that never came to fruition.

The Italian government did appropriate funds to Italian immigrant aid societies in the United States (money derived from a tax on emigrants' steamship tickets), and further encouraged emigration by reducing train fares for both emigrants and repatriates between their homes in Italy and port cities. "The great current of returning emigrants represents an economic force of the first order for us," asserted Italian senator Edoardo Pantano in a speech before Parliament. "It will be an enormous benefit for us if we can increase this flow of force in and out of our country...if we can increase temporary emigration." And the Italian foreign minister reminded emigrants that when they returned to Italy after working in the United States, "the mother country will never refuse to recognize them as her sons."

Initially, the Italian government's emphasis on encouraging temporary emigration literally paid enormous dividends for the country's economy, especially in the *mezzogiorno* region. One writer estimated that by the First World War, Italian immigrants in America had sent nearly $750 million to their relatives in the mother country (this practice continued even after most Italians began to settle permanently in the United States). The Italian National Bureau of Economic Research concluded, remarkably, that between 1902 and 1920 "the transfer of savings to Italy by Italian laborers in foreign countries constitutes one of the principal credit items in Italy's balance of international payments." One Italian immigrant study, summarized by historians Iorizzo and Mondello, concluded: "This infusion of fresh capital helped bolster the Italian economy and encouraged the development of agricultural and industrial improvements, which created jobs for many peasants and laborers... *some areas of Italy owed almost their entire economic development to remittances* [my emphasis], and the Italian mer-

Dominico Iovino (left) stands in the doorway of Siculo Express on North Square around 1906 or 1907. The establishment housed a steamship agent who provided Italian passports to immigrants traveling back to the Old Country. *(Courtesy of Paul Yovino)*

chant marine was virtually built upon them. Without a doubt, money from abroad had become a potent factor in the economic and social life of Italy."

Most interesting about these remittances is that the money flowing from America entered regions and sections of Italy in amounts that corresponded proportionally to the number of emigrants those regions sent to the United States; as additional *Avellinesi* poured into America, a corresponding increase of money traveled back to Avellino. Not surprisingly, after the turn of the twentieth century, the vast majority of remittances flowed back to Southern Italy and Sicily.

As one Italian writer observed: "The enormous amount they [immigrants] send back to their relatives in Italy in the form of postal remittances are staggering when one recalls what they were earning—many of them one dollar per day."

———

Temporary emigration benefited the Italian government and economy but harmed Italian immigrants' entry and assimilation into American society. Many Americans, likely a majority, deeply resented what they considered a double insult: not only did this group of foreigners, most of them illiterate and desperately poor, compete for jobs with natives, but then they sent the money they earned back outside the United States. One citizen shared a popular sentiment when he said: "The American race will eventually be wiped out by these alien hordes. Even now every city has its Little Italy... in which the people do not learn the English language, do little business except among themselves, and send all the surplus earnings back whence they came." Another American writer concurred: "Taking into consideration the innumerable 'birds of passage,' without family or future in this country, it would be safe to say that half, perhaps two-thirds of our Italian immigrants are *under* America, not *of* it."

The birds of passage, temporary emigration, and Italian repatriation are woven into the fabric of the Italian immigrant experience in Boston and in the United States generally. They help to explain Italians' actions and attitudes: the continuing strength of their attachment to their home villages, their commitment to assist financially those family members left behind in the Old Country, their slow economic progress within American society, and their early reluctance to become citizens. The temporary nature of much of Italian immigration also profoundly influenced the reaction of Americans toward Italians, especially Southern Italians; most notably, the birds of passage offered many people an excuse to fan the flames of discrimination as they questioned the commitment of these immigrants to the United States.

It was not until halfway through the first decade of the twentieth century, around the time of George Scigliano's death and my paternal grandparents' arrival in the United States, that this level of commitment began to change for hundreds of thousands of Italians.

An attitudinal shift among Italian immigrants that had begun almost imperceptibly around 1900 became seismic in nature several years later: more and more of them decided to settle permanently in America.

"Why and how did these Italians who remained in the United States change their minds?" historian Dino Cinel asked. "We can speculate that the returnees failed by and large to achieve their goal of a good life in Italy, and that this failure discouraged others from going back to Italy. Perhaps too, life in the New World changed the immigrants' goals . . . Immigrants were realistic enough to compare the opportunities in the New World with the deprivations of the old."

The Italian government, which had provided its poverty-stricken citizens with a taste of better things in America, recognized that its plan to encourage temporary emigration had backfired and attempted too late to shift gears. By 1905, the government was forced to take the opposite side of the emigration issue, desperately urging Italian citizens not to leave for the good of the mother country. Adolfo Rossi, a regional inspector for the *Commissariato dell'Emigrazione,* lamented in a magazine interview that "the character of emigration has changed in recent years . . . this excessive emigration is working a harm to the nation at large in that it takes from us the flower of our laboring class."

Emigration thinned out the population, but it often emptied whole villages of able-bodied men. "The young men have all gone to America," one village leader said in 1908. "We are rearing good strong men to spend their strength in America." The departure of these men changed the very character of scores of small communities in Southern Italy. The town of Amalfi, a thriving town of ten thousand people before emigration, was a tiny village of fewer than three thousand people by 1907. "America has all the rest," one journalist wrote. "This explains why the factories cannot run and why the vineyards are going to decay." In the same article, he summarized the perilous shift that had occurred in the nature of emigration. "When emigration had not assumed such enormous proportions as the present time, the Italian government looked upon it with favor, for it served as a kind of balance wheel to the economic equilibrium of the country . . . but the great bulk of emigration today is a very different sort. It is the *permanent* tendency in the tide of emigration which is occupying the attention of those most keenly interested in the welfare of the country as a whole."

The birds of passage certainly did not disappear during this time; indeed, during periods of economic depression in America right up until World War I, they traveled back and forth between Italy and the United States. But after 1905, the character of Italian emigration underwent a transformation—from generally temporary to most often permanent. Too many Italians, many of them Italy's "good strong men," had either traveled to America at least once or had received word from loved ones that the United States, though in many ways so foreign and so hostile, was still an improvement over the deplorable conditions in Italy.

Midway through the first decade of the twentieth century, the perma-nent exodus from Italy had become a floodtide "with no parallel in history," in the words of one historian. "The land literally hemorrhaged peasants." One Italian writer described how one day the peasants of a Sicilian village gathered around the feudal lord who owned the land on which they toiled. They threw down their shovels and posted a notice: "Sir, do your farming yourself—we are going to America." Years after his ancestors boarded ships en route to America, Yale University president (and later, Major League Baseball commissioner) A. Bartlett Giamatti described the irresistible lure of the New World:

> Once immigrants had seen America, they were spoiled forever for the old life because now they knew a fantastic, open secret; life—even life tough and demanding in a strange land—can change. Change is possible . . . In America there was the chance for change. That story went back and millions came. The American dream be-gan with the dream of a land of change. It was the first dream not fated-to-be that anyone could remember. It was itself, like Amer-ica, a new thing. In the new century, they continued to come, now not driven by fate so much as drawn by the dream.

The Italian ports of Genoa, Naples, Messina, and Palermo became great human expatriation centers as peasants traveled from small villages across Southern Italy to await passage to America. Fourteen steamship companies offered direct service between Naples and New York City and a handful provided direct passage to Boston. Steamship companies were forbidden by the Italian government from advertising more than the bare details of sailing dates to discourage crowds from gathering at the docks. By 1905, Naples emerged as the leading European port in the number of emigrants departing for America. Heavy demand drove the price of steamship tickets from about fifteen dollars to twenty-eight dollars, which did nothing to diminish sales.

Even to reach the docks in the major cities, Italian farmers and peasants had made the epic decision in town after town throughout Southern Italy to abandon the familiar, often for the first time in their lives, to venture into the unknown. They walked, rode donkeys, or sometimes boarded trains to trek from rural villages to port cities. Years later, Italian writer Angelo Mosso described the scene as peasants departed a rural town in Sicily, bound for Palermo: "The locomotive whistled fitfully with a laboring hiss, but the disorder was so great that the engineer did not move the train. Despite the requests and the reprimands of the police, the crowd still clutched the train, embraced by the final grasps of good-bye. When the train moved, there was a heartbreaking cry like the anguished roar that bursts from a crowd at the instant of a great calamity. All the people raised their arms and waved handkerchiefs. From the window of the cars the leaning figures of the young men and women strained; they seemed suspended in air and kissed the hands of old people as the train departed . . . One woman [whose husband was already in America] broke away from the crowd and began to run alongside the train as it pulled out of the station, yelling out: 'Say hello to him [meaning her husband]; remind him that I am still waiting for him to send me money for the steamship ticket. Tell him I am waiting, and tell him . . . tell him . . . that if I have to stay here any longer I will die.' "

Travelers were heartbroken and frightened at the prospect of leaving their homes and families, but their decisions were final, and by now, few paused to look back. When they reached the embarkation cities, the chaos on the docks shook them, but, like my grandparents, they boarded steamships by the tens of thousands, desperate to escape the desolation of Southern Italy. One Italian author described the scene as emigrants boarded the *Galileo*, bound for America:

At last the sailors were heard shouting fore and aft, "*Chi non e' passeggero, a terra*"—"All ashore that's going ashore." These words sent a thrill from one end of the *Galileo* to the other. In a few minutes a whistle sounded and the ship began to move. Then women burst out crying and bearded men hitherto stolid were seen to pass a hand across their eyes. A few were talking in low tones. From the forecastle a voice called out in a sarcastic tone, "*Viva L'Italia*" and looking up I saw a tall thin man who was shaking his fist at his native country.

Emigrants would miss little about Italy's desperate poverty, but their final good-byes with relatives and friends who had accompanied them to the ships were filled with sorrow. Fearful and excited at the same time, amid tears and grief, departing emigrants and family members they were leaving behind embraced and kissed each other again and again on the docks, reluctant to let go for fear of never again seeing their loved ones.

In what became a popular farewell custom, to remain connected to relatives for as long as humanly possible, many emigrants brought balls of yarn on board ship, leaving one end of the line with someone on land. "As the ship slowly cleared the dock, the balls unwound amid the farewell shouts of the women, the fluttering of the handkerchiefs, and the infants held high," said one emigrant. "After the yarn ran out, the long strips remained airborne, sustained by the wind, long after those on land and those at sea had lost sight of each other."

PART 3

Arrival, Settlement, Discrimination

CHAPTER 8

In January of 1909, my grandparents baptized their second child, Accurzio, my uncle "Gus," at Sacred Heart Church on North Square. Their first son was also their first child born in the United States, and thus the only member of the family at that time who was an American citizen. The christening took place just yards from their Garden Court Street home at the church frequented by their *paesani* from Sciacca, Sicily. Saint Leonard's Italian parish was located just a short walk in the opposite direction, but my grandparents would not have dreamed of baptizing their infant son anywhere other than Sacred Heart. Though both Catholic parishes served Italian immigrants almost exclusively, Sacred Heart was "their" church, and the house of worship for *paesani* who lived in my grandparents' tight enclave in the North End.

My grandparents worshipped, lived, and socialized in Boston virtually the same way they did in Italy—with friends and family from the same hometown or region. Other Italian immigrants did likewise. Back home, they felt most comfortable with their *paesani,* whether huddled in their little fishing villages or nestled among the rolling hills of family farms that dotted the countryside. After months of unfamiliar and unsettling experiences—uprooting their lives in Italy, traversing the Atlantic aboard ships under miserable conditions, and holding their breaths with fear that they might be turned away at Ellis Island—the Puleos and thousands of other Italians reverted to the familiar as quickly as possible when they settled in America.

They did their best to re-create their Old Country experience by settling in American cities with the same friends and neighbors they knew so well in Italy.

Ellis Island immigration inspectors were first to notice the phenomenon. Of the twelve million immigrants who passed through Ellis Island's gates, nearly one-third were Italians. During the first decade of the twentieth century, Italians arrived in staggering numbers, more than two million between 1901 and 1910, with the total on some single days exceeding 15,000. In 1905, more than 316,000 Italians entered America, with 358,000 following in 1906, and nearly 300,000 in 1908. And the vast majority of them arrived en masse with *paesani,* friends and relatives from the same hometown. Emigration emptied village after village in Southern Italy and essentially transported them intact to America. On my grandparents' ship manifests, page after page lists "Sciacca" as the immigrants' hometown, and dozens of arriving passengers list Boston's North End as their final destination in the United States. So many consecutive people reported "Sciacca" as their home village and "Boston" as their destination that immigration inspectors used "ditto" marks to record this information.

Italians drew strength from *paesani* as they crossed an ocean and arrived in a hemisphere as strange to them as it was to fellow countrymen Christopher Columbus, Amerigo Vespucci, Giovanni Caboto (John Cabot), or Giovanni da Verrazano centuries earlier. At Ellis Island, especially, *paesani* helped each other through a process that was always chaotic, sometimes humiliating, and often frightening. "Here, only a mile of water separated them from the American mainland, but some would be rejected and never permitted ashore," wrote one author. "A cough, a limp, or slowness of speech might be enough to send a hopeful immigrant on the 3,000-mile journey back to Italy."

Friends and fellow townspeople calmed each other's fears as doctors inspected immigrants for diseases, especially the dreaded contagious eye disease called trachoma, which medical personnel checked for by using metal hooks to pry back the eyelids. *Paesani* buttressed each other's resolve as they struggled to understand questions from examiners—Where are you headed? Do you have a job? What kind of work can you do? Is anyone waiting to meet you? How much money do you have? Immigrants had to be especially careful when answering questions about job status. "If they said they had a job waiting for them, they could be considered contract labor and be sent back to Italy," one account noted. "If they said they had no job prospects, they could be rejected as potential public burdens. They rehearsed carefully [with *paesani*] answers such as: 'I have good job prospects,' or 'My cousin will help me find a job.'" And if the unthinkable happened, if a single family member failed to pass a test and was ordered back to Italy, *paesani* consoled and comforted his loved ones and promised to care for them in America.

Paesani shared the joyful moments at Ellis Island, too. Once immigrants made it through the inspections, the delousing, and the medical exams, they had passed the Ellis Island test. They were told to walk down a corridor to a door bearing the simple, yet emotionally charged sign: "Push—To New York." Together, they passed through the door, as described by one historian, most often to a cheering throng of waiting friends and relatives, more *paesani,* who had arrived in America before them.

From the destitute villages of Southern Italy to the embarkation ports in Italian cities, from the grueling Atlantic crossing to the Ellis Island waiting rooms to the door they "pushed" to enter New York and America, Italian immigrants relied on their *paesani* for support, comfort, and counsel.

Now it made perfect sense for them to settle near each other in unfamiliar American cities as they struggled with a strange language and sought work for which they were unsuited. By living close together, on the same block or in the same building, my grandparents and their neighbors drew strength from close friends they had known all their lives.

What better way for newcomers and foreigners to overcome obstacles they would encounter?

What better way to protect and care for each other?

The Italian immigration process in Boston and other American cities was characterized most dramatically by the development of these tight-knit enclaves. Italians from the same region or village relocated to America through a process called "chain migration" and settled on the same block, or even the same street, in New York, Boston, Philadelphia, Buffalo, St. Louis, Chicago, and San Francisco. Knowing little of the country to which they were migrating, immigrants from all countries generally followed the pathways of those who preceded them. With Italians, though, this tendency was more pronounced thanks to the general importance of family and village ties, especially to the Southern Italian culture.

Most often, men would come first, like my grandfather, and once settled successfully would bring over their wives and children, while encouraging other relatives and village neighbors to come as well. Virtually every block in the "Italian" sections of cities was inhabited by *paesani*. "In Little Italies of large cities, blocks were divided into sections of Sicilians, Genoese, or Calabrians," one historian noted. "Italians were surrounded, thus, with others speaking their own dialects. . . . Each colony sought to preserve its folkways, demonstrating a slight distrust of persons from different sections of Italy." In his study of Boston's North End settlement patterns, historian William DeMarco wrote: "The North End, as small as it is, has always been a community of neighborhoods. Persons were identified as being 'lifelong residents of North Street,' or from 'lower Prince Street,' or 'down on Salem Street.' These and other such designations not only identify a section of the North End, but usually tell the part of Italy from which a family came, which church it frequents, what its social status is, and what clubs its members belong to. From the Italian community's earliest days in the North End, these designations were determined by 'regional enclaves.' "

Boston Italians who settled outside of the North End also tended to cluster by region, even in areas where other nationalities settled in the neighborhood. In mixed ethnic neighborhoods such as the West End, Hyde Park, the South End, and Dorchester, the Italians who moved there tended to be *paesani* from the same village in Italy.

Peasants and laborers who emigrated from Genoa, Avellino, Naples, Sicily, Corsica, and Sardinia were referred to as "Italians" or "South Italians" by Americans, who perceived and identified them as belonging to a single national ethnic group. But the immigrants themselves did not share this identity, at least before about 1920. The political unification of Italy could neither wipe out centuries of separation, nor could it instantly supply a common identity for those who believed themselves to be different depending on the region in which they lived.

In the Old Country, people defined themselves by their association with their parents and their villages. They belonged not to Italy first, but to their families and then to their villages. Decades of exploitation by landowners coupled with the harsh realities of daily life led to a rejection by Southern Italians of the traditional social institutions of the larger society —churches, government agencies, fraternal organizations. These *conta-*

dini, or peasants, came to rely on family and close friends. As an Italian statesman said shortly after Italy's unification: "Although we have made Italy, we have yet to make Italians." Italians harbored no sense of nationalism, no national pride in being "Italian," and indeed, did not even consider themselves "Italians" until, ironically, they had sunk roots in America and found strength in such unity as a way to battle both economic hardship and discrimination. "It is a curious footnote to the history of immigration that many Italians became Italians only after first becoming Americans," one historian wrote. Instead, for the people of Southern Italy especially, it was their home village or region, not the country of Italy, that influenced their language and inspired their love and loyalty.

Southern Italians referred to this regional or village loyalty as the concept of *campanilismo,* which derives from the word *campanile,* meaning a church steeple or belfry, and denoted a way of life that defined Italian settlement patterns in the United States. Central to each of the scattered villages in the Italian countryside was the local church with its bell tower. The attachment the villagers felt to the bell was symbolic of their loyalty to their village and their neighbors. The sound of the bell defined the boundaries of the villagers; those who lived beyond, and thus could not hear the bell, were strangers not to be trusted, since the interests of these outsiders too often conflicted with those of the villagers. In their isolation, these individual village communities developed their own distinct customs, manners, and dialects.

Even villages that were only separated geographically by a few miles were, culturally, worlds apart.

It was no surprise, then, that when Italian villagers migrated to America, they were eager to seek out their *paesani* who had arrived ahead of them as soon as possible to begin reestablishing many of the village's customs and social relationships. My grandfather sought his brother-in-law and other Sciacca townspeople when he arrived in Boston. After 1900, the increasing Sicilian population, including my grandparents, occupied the length of North Street and Fleet Street, near the fish pier area. The community from the province of Avellino, also continuing to grow, inhabited the Sheaf Street-Copps Hill area, as well as North Square, according to historian

William DeMarco, and *Abruzzesi* settled near Endicott and North Margin streets. The Northern Italian Genoese community lived on North Bennett Street and Fulton Street (though by 1910, many Northern Italians left the North End and moved to Charlestown, uncomfortable that the neighborhood was, in their view, being overrun by Southern Italians).

These lines of demarcation were starkly defined and rarely crossed, and when they were, they could present cultural problems for immigrants. One immigrant from Sicily described "passing" as an *Avellinese* in Boston for many years. His wife was from Avellino and he had acquired her dialect. "This worked well," he explained. "I opened a barber shop which attracted Neapolitans and *Avellinesi*. With a wife who cooked *Avellinese*-style, and my speaking the dialect at the shop, everyone thought I was from Avellino. I passed as *Avellinese* for more than thirty years until a *paesano* arrived from Siracusa [Sicily] and told everyone I was Sicilian. By that time I was accepted by the *Avellinesi*, so it did not hurt my business. Twenty-five or thirty years earlier, who knows what would have happened!" Another man from Abbruzi said that while a few of his *paesani* lived near Copp's Hill, "this was the neighborhood of *Avellinesi*."

Even North End marriages followed the precepts of *campanilismo*. An astonishing 82 percent of the thousands of marriages celebrated at St. Leonard's and Sacred Heart Church between 1873 and 1929 were between individuals from the same province—men from Avellino married women from Avellino and so forth. Most of these marriages, perhaps 60 percent, were between men and women from the same village or town. "What could be more natural?" asked one immigrant. "They had everything in common."

The formation of these enclaves-within-an-enclave, these settlement and marriage patterns, assured for Southern Italians in America the continuation of the Southern Italian concept of *la via vecchia*, "the old way," which provided security and familiarity and asserted the importance of *la famiglia* in the New World. As DeMarco wrote: "In terms of subcultural neighborhoods, the North End resembled the Italian countryside by 1920. A community which had once been home to a variety of nationalities became home to a cross-section of Italian subcultures. By creation of these new villages, the old word *campanilismo* had been brought to Boston."

————

Campanilismo was a double-edged sword for Italian immigrants. By settling in American cities, maintaining friendships, and marrying in patterns that mimicked life in the *mezzogiorno*—indeed, by forming large Italian enclaves like the North End at all—Italians derived enormous benefits in their efforts to acclimate to their new country. Conversely, the enclaves also created lasting damage by hampering Italians' efforts to assimilate into, and advance within, American society.

On the plus side, the enclave served as a decompression chamber, in the words of one historian, "shielding its inhabitants from the uncomfortable pressures of a strange environment and allowing them to adjust gradually to its demands," and offering Italians an opportunity to make an easier transition from Italy to the United States. For those who were coming to America only temporarily, the enclave and sub-enclaves provided a secure, familiar setting without requiring returning "birds of passage" to make a heavy investment in assimilation; they did not need to learn English, for example. For those Italians who decided to remain, the enclaves provided a buffer against a harsh and strange American society. They helped ensure the survival of *la via vecchia,* which dictated a host of Italian family mores and social customs. These ranged from the responsibility of Italian men to provide for their families to the strength of the Italian wife and mother at home; she usually managed all financial affairs and held a position of respect unparalleled in the family. While the Italian husband and father was the "political" head of the household, it was the Italian mother to whom the family looked for emotional and spiritual strength and guidance.

The warmth and familiarity of the enclave also served as a buffer against an entirely new way of life; few Italian immigrants were prepared for the sights and sounds that awaited them in America. The new arrivals were awed by skyscrapers, bridges, and elevated trains. Most of these immigrants had spent their lives in pastoral settings, as farmers or fishermen; their first encounter with urban America clashed with their hopes and expectations. "Noise is everywhere," wrote one immigrant. "The din is constant and it completely fills my head." Others were shocked by dirty cities: "New York was awful," said one. "The streets were full of horse manure.

My little town in Italy was much more beautiful. I said to myself, 'how come, America?'" Upon his arrival in 1908, Bartolomeo Vanzetti, who would eventually live—and be arrested, imprisoned, and executed—in Massachusetts, wrote: "Until yesterday, I was among folks who understood me. This morning I seemed to have awakened in a land where my language meant little more to the native (as far as meaning was concerned) than the pitiful noises of a dumb animal. Where was I to go? What was I to do? Here was the Promised Land. The elevated rattled by and did not answer. The automobiles and trolley speed by, heedless of me."

Italians who were entranced by the strange sights also expressed their puzzlement. At the age of fifteen, the Italian "pick-and-shovel poet," Pascal D'Angelo, was startled, then fascinated, by the spectacle of a New York City elevated train rumbling around a curve: "To my surprise not even one car fell. Nor did the people walking beneath scurry away as it approached." Minutes later, while riding a trolley, D'Angelo was distracted by the sight of a father and son moving their mouths in continuous motion "like cows chewing on cud." He had never known of chewing gum and assumed "with compassion, that father and son were both afflicted with some nervous disease." Later, just before he and his immigrant companions reached their destinations, D'Angelo was surprised to note street signs with "Ave., Ave., Ave." printed on them. "How religious a place this must be that expressed its devotion at every crossing," he mused, though he could not understand "why the word was not followed by 'Maria.'"

Not all Italian immigrants settled in large enclaves. For example, a group of *Calabresi* settled in Boston's South End in the mid-1880s, surrounded by immigrants from other countries, as well as native-born Americans. Perhaps due to their exposure to other ethnic groups, these Calabrian immigrants married outside the Italian community more frequently and obtained their citizenship sooner, yet still traveled to the North End for baptisms and marriages. Eventually, they started their own Catholic church in the South End, called Our Lady of Pompeii. By the end of the first decade of the twentieth century, the small Italian community in the South End began disbanding as members moved to Dorchester, South Boston, and Hyde Park, and beyond to Malden, quickly assimilating into the American mainstream.

But, the Calabrians who settled in Boston's South End and lived among neighbors from many countries were the exceptions among Italian immigrants. And while it is not an exaggeration to state that the cohesiveness and strength of the neighborhood enclave was the single most important element in the Italians' transition from immigrants to Americans, the drawbacks of the Italian enclave were profound.

Though Italians acquired scraps of information about America during their forays into downtown areas, especially in a place like the North End, which bordered the business district, the enclaves' overall insularity prevented Italians from learning rapidly: to read and speak English; about Americans and their customs; or additional skills to improve their job prospects and their economic plight. This was particularly true of Italian women, most of whom did not work outside the home and thus had no jobs beyond the boundaries of the neighborhood to go to each day. One Boston Italian immigrant woman always said she was "going to America today" anytime she left the North End neighborhood.

Maybe more important, the fact that Italians so often were cloistered in enclaves prevented Americans from learning about *them*. This hindered their acceptance, prevented their advancement, and fueled discrimination so white-hot and intense that Italians were among the most vilified immigrant groups ever to arrive on America's shores.

CHAPTER 9

It was an angry James Donnaruma who wrote to his congressman in January of 1914, vehemently opposing a law Congress was considering that would require all immigrants over the age of sixteen to pass a literacy test before they were allowed admittance to the United States. "The idea is repugnant to all liberty-loving people and contravenes the spirit which gave initial impulse to the revolution of the colonists," Donnaruma wrote from his editor's desk of *La Gazzetta del Massachusetts* to Representative (and future Boston mayor) Andrew J. Peters. "There is no place in this land for bigotry and the underlying motive of this measure was born of race and religious proscription."

Donnaruma's ire flared for several reasons on this cold January morning. First, he opposed the literacy test on principle, believing it was anathema to American values. Next, a similar bill had been vetoed less than a year earlier by President William Howard Taft in one of his last acts before leaving office; Taft said immigrants were illiterate because they had been denied the opportunity for education, the very opportunity they sought in the United States. Taft's logic was similar to the arguments proffered by former president Grover Cleveland when he vetoed a similar literacy-test bill in 1897. Italian newspapers, including *La Gazzetta,* had praised Taft's actions, but in the intervening year restrictionist sentiments had deepened and were more widespread than ever, and the federal House of Representatives had taken up the bill again in December of 1913. The bill's goal was to "bring about an elimination of the most undesirable of those coming to our shores," wrote the House Committee on Immigration and Naturalization, "and at the same time not to strike down those who come to make their homes with us, to build up the moral and material prosperity of our country, and to become permanent citizens among us."

Donnaruma bristled over the resurrected literacy bill for one other important reason: its language made clear that it was primarily directed to-

James Donnaruma (right) with colleagues in the offices of *La Gazzetta del Massachusetts,* 231 Hanover Street, in 1913. *(Courtesy of Pam Donnaruma and the* Post-Gazette*)*

ward Italians, and he viewed the proposed legislation as yet another in a long line of vindictive anti-Italian measures, attitudes, and actions that had dominated the national landscape for more than two decades.

Who could argue with him?

The current bill wending its way through the House of Representatives, as well as the legislation Taft had vetoed a year earlier, had its genesis in the research and final report of the United States Immigration Commission, a body composed of senators, representatives, and economic experts appointed by Congress to study the problem of immigration. The commission conducted an exhaustive three-year study of immigration between 1907 and 1910 and published the forty-two-volume *Report of the Immigration Commission* in 1911. Headed by Vermont senator William P. Dillingham, an immigration restrictionist, the commission was weighted with men who favored limitations or restrictions against "new immigrants," particularly from Italy, Greece, and Poland. While much of the Dillingham Commission's statistical research and many of its findings were sound and valid, its editorial statements and conclusions were clearly biased against Italians and other southern and eastern European immigrants. The commission identified 1882 as a watershed year, when "the character of immigration had undergone a fundamental change for the worse." Much of the decline in the character of these "new immigrants" was due to their illiteracy, and their growing numbers were forming a "burgeoning, uneducated proletariat."

The new immigrant, the Dillingham Commission concluded, "could not be assimilated, lowered the American standards of living and diluted the Anglo-Saxon stock." In short, the new immigrant demonstrated an "irreversible inferiority."

With only one dissenter, the nine-member commission advocated that the United States restrict the entry of immigrants from southern and eastern Europe while keeping the country's gates open to northern and western Europeans. Literacy tests and quotas headed the Dillingham Commission's recommendations on how to deal with the "immigration question."

In December of 1910, Senator Dillingham visited Boston to appear before the North American Civic League for Immigrants to advocate for a literacy test, restriction of southern and eastern European immigration, and rapid assimilation for those already in the country. "All these immigrants need help," he said. "They need to be interested in American institutions, and it can only be done through a society of this nature, and by the cooperation of churches, societies, and individuals by teamwork." That same year, James Donnaruma was appalled when Massachusetts Republican senator Henry Cabot Lodge delivered a speech calling for a literacy test for immigrants. "Within the last twenty years, there has been a great change in the proportion of the various nationalities immigrating from Europe to the United States . . . the great growth in recent years in our immigration has been from Italy, from Poland, Hungary, and Russia and from Eastern Europe. There is a growing and constantly active demand for more restrictive legislation."

The current bill Congress was considering, and Donnaruma opposed, called for all aliens over sixteen to pass a literacy test in English "or some other language" before being admitted to the United States. Part of its argument was that a literacy test would "improve the class" of immigrants that entered the United States and thus reduce the number of criminals who entered the country. To Donnaruma, one of the most offensive passages from the proposed legislation quoted directly from the Dillingham Commission's report: "The proportion of the more serious crimes of homicide, blackmail, and robbery, as well as the least serious offenses is greater among the foreign-born. The disproportion in this regard is due principally to the prevalence of homicides and other crimes of personal violence among Italians..."

Donnaruma, now married and the father of four children, had spoken and written against literacy tests for years, using *La Gazzetta* as his forum. Since George Scigliano's death, his had been the clearest and strongest voice on behalf of Italian immigrants in Boston. He had watched as Boston Italians had purchased homes, started businesses, raised families, and, by 1910, solidified the North End neighborhood. In the pages of his newspaper he educated Italians on getting along in America; in his personal life he helped his countrymen obtain jobs, intervened on their behalf to prevent deportations, and provided financial assistance to Italian widows whose husbands' deaths had left their families destitute.

Donnaruma viewed the literacy test as more than a tool to prevent new Italian immigrants from coming to America; he saw it as an affront to Italians living here already. Most of the honest, hardworking Italians who had sunk roots in his city would have been barred from the country if a literacy test had been grounds for entry.

A man with a strong sense of his people's brief history and uphill struggle in the United States, Donnaruma looked upon the literacy test as yet another sign that discrimination against Italians was tolerated, acceptable, and even encouraged in their new land.

By the time James Donnaruma entered the fight against the literacy bill in early 1914, Italians had endured a quarter century of some of the most deepseated, visceral resentment, and blatant and brutal discrimination, aimed at any ethnic group in American history. The anti-Italian bigotry that George Scigliano had fought against in Boston had been widespread in the United States since the late nineteenth century; the scope and breadth of discrimination against Italian immigrants, and Italian Americans in general, were remarkable, ranging from physical mob violence to less overt, yet extremely damaging anti-Italian pronouncements and writings from respectable politicians and journalists. One of the little-known yet illustrative facts about the Italian experience is that Italian immigrants were lynched more frequently in America than any other group except African Americans.

The worst single day of lynchings in American history occurred in New Orleans in 1891, when eleven Sicilian immigrants, nine of whom had been acquitted and two of whom were awaiting trial, were dragged from their holding cells and killed by a mob in retribution for the murder of nationally prominent police chief David Hennessy. The vicious killings of the Italians sparked enormously serious repercussions nationwide, leading to the near impeachment of President Benjamin Harrison and bringing the United States to the brink of war with Italy. It also began a period of nearly forty years—bracketed by the trial, conviction, and 1927 execution of Nicola Sacco and Bartolomeo Vanzetti—of systemic discrimination against Italian immigrants and Italian Americans during the great immigration period. Perhaps most important, these events set the tone for anti-Italian sentiments and stereotypes that continued throughout the twentieth century and persist today.

The slaughter in New Orleans was the culmination of numerous violent incidents against Italians in the early immigration years, and it marked the beginning of more acceptable forms of institutionalized bigotry against Italians, from mob rule to police action to discriminatory writings. Two Italian historians maintain that the New Orleans violence following the murder of Hennessy "marked a turning point in nativist thought against Italians, for it encouraged the conviction that Sicilians had at last established in America their centuries-old criminal conspiracy, the Mafia, which now threatened to disrupt American society."

While the New Orleans lynchings marked the beginning of a dramatic increase in violence against Italians, more insidious and damaging was the manner in which "respectable" voices in America excused or even defended the mob's actions, blatantly demonstrating their anti-Italian bias. Writing in the *North American Review* in May of 1891, Massachusetts's own Henry

Cabot Lodge cited the New Orleans incident as an argument against un-restricted immigration. "What are the true causes of the events of the 14th of March at New Orleans? One, certainly, was the general belief that there had been a gross miscarriage of justice [i.e., the acquittal] in the trial of the accused Italians... The killing of the prisoners at New Orleans was due chiefly to the fact that they were supposed to be members of the Mafia... These dangerous secret societies spring up and commit murders... They come not from race peculiarities, but from the quality of certain classes of immigrants of all races." The *New York Times* editorialized on the New Or-leans lynchings by expressing vicious xenophobia toward the Sicilian vic-tims, claiming the New Orleans mob was compelled to use force to "inspire a wholesome dread to those who had boldly made a trade of murder... These sneaking and cowardly Sicilians, the descendants of bandits and as-sassins, who have transported to this country the lawless passions, the cut-throat practices, the oath-bound societies of their native country, are to us a pest without mitigation." Other editorial and magazine writers expressed similar sentiments, despite the fact that not a single accused Sicilian in the New Orleans case was convicted of any crime; most commentary about this episode leveled only cursory, if any, criticism against the mob that dragged the acquitted Italians from their holding cells and killed them.

The virulent anti-Italian tone of the writing surrounding the New Orleans incident opened the verbal floodgates from the popular press and literati alike, who declared open season on Italians in general. *Harper's Weekly* accused Italians of "piling up a record of crimes... unparalleled in the history of a civilized country in time of peace." In a separate piece, *Harper's* acknowledged that there were some good Italians, "but when he is bad he is bad in an underhand, violent, grand-opera way that is a scandal to our citizens." Author Henry James, who visited Ellis Island at its peak, worried that "Italians, of superlatively southern type and the swarming of a Jewry that had burst all bonds" could lead to an immigrant "conquest of New York." Novelist Jack London paired "Dagoes and Japs" as the enemies of true "Saxon Americanism." (Later in his life, London described how he learned his bias against Italians from his mother: "I had heard her state that if one offended an Italian, no matter how slightly and unintentionally, he was certain to retaliate by stabbing one in the back. That was her particular phrase—'stab you in the back.' ") In an article entitled "Pests Imported from Europe," *The Illustrated American* warned that "so many Italian immigrants have the idea that this country exists not for the *bona fide* American, but for the scum of the earth—which, thanks to our legislators, is allowed to be poured into it." Writing in *Century Magazine,* progressive intellectual and professor Edward Alsworth Ross declared, "The Italians are primitive in every way... and yet, to know them, to know their utter helplessness and unsophistication, is to have infinite pity for them... that the Mediterranean peoples are morally below the races of northern Europe is as certain as any social fact." *Life* magazine claimed Italians were poor material for citizenship: "They are intensely eager for citizens' papers and resort to all sorts of tricks to secure them."

Even John Foster Carr, founder of the Immigrant Publication Society, wrote in his *Guide for the Immigrant Italian* in 1911: "Italians are too ready to have recourse to violence in quarrels. If this habit could be given up, Italian immigrants would at once find themselves more welcome in America; for this is the one thing that makes them distrusted." Carr also admonished Italians: "The use of brute force is barbarous. Throw away all weapons you may have. Speak in a low voice. Try not to gesticulate, and do not get excited in your discussions... dress well and eat better."

Historian and author Dr. Frederick Bushee added his opinion of the Italians in Boston: "They show the beginnings of a degenerate class, such as has been fully developed among the Irish... If allowed to continue in unwholesome conditions, we may be sure that the next generation [of Italians] will bring forth a large crop of dependents, delinquents, and defectives to fill up our public institutions."

Physical attacks against Italians continued too. In 1893, an Italian was lynched in Denver, Colorado, and two years later in Walensburg, Colorado, six Italian miners under suspicion of murdering an American saloonkeeper were executed by a mob. Two hundred Italians were forcibly driven from Altoona, Pennsylvania, in 1894, three Italians were lynched in Hahnville, Louisiana, in 1896, and five met a similar fate in Tallulah, Mississippi. Violent incidents continued into the twentieth century, with mob actions and lynchings of Italians in Erwin, Mississippi (1901); Marksville,

Louisiana (1901); Marion, North Carolina (1906); Tampa, Florida (1910); Willisville, Illinois (1914); and Johnson City, Illinois (1915).

In 1914, the infamous Ludlow (Colorado) Massacre took place at the Rockefeller-owned Colorado Fuel and Iron Works near Pueblo. The immigrant tent colony there became embroiled in a demonstration about wages, hours, and working conditions, and mine operators called in the state militia to quell the strikers. Troopers raked the demonstrators with machine gun fire and burned the entire Ludlow tent camp to the ground; two Italian women and thirteen Italian children were burned to death in the melee. (Because of the nature of the tragedy, historian Andrew Rolle pointed out, President Woodrow Wilson was forced to intercede and the state of Colorado ultimately admitted partial responsibility for the deaths and paid damages to surviving family members.).

Most of this brutality was directed toward Southern Italians, who were viewed as inferior to the people of the North. The U.S. Bureau of Immigration reinforced these entrenched biases, classifying Italian immigrants as two different races—northern and southern. Southern Italians were viewed as a different race entirely, likely for many reasons: their darker complexions, their inability to speak English, their general illiteracy, and their unusual Catholic religious customs. In the "Race" column of their entry papers at Ellis Island, both my grandparents were listed as "Southern Italians."

In fact, implicit in the violence and criticism directed against Southern Italians was the comparison between them and African Americans; the two groups were viewed in ways that were strikingly similar during this time period. Discrimination against Southern Italians was as much racism as xenophobia. "Because of their swarthy complexions, Southern Italians were not considered members of the white race in some parts of the South," wrote one immigrant. "One Southern employer was quoted as saying, 'it makes no difference to me whom I employ—Negro, Italian, or white man.'" In some parts of the South, Italian children were forbidden by law to attend white schools.

In many communities, blacks and Southern Italians developed friendships, lived near each other, and worked together performing many of the same kinds of physical labor. Sicilians were so despised in New Orleans at the time of the mass lynching for, among other reasons, their close ties with blacks. Historian David Roediger describes a Mississippi town in which whites wrecked an Italian American's restaurant and drove away its owner after he defied Jim Crow laws by serving a black customer. After *another* Louisiana lynching, of three Italians in 1896, so many African Americans turned out to mourn that local whites fretted about the possibility of "interracial revenge." Three years later, the lynching of five more Italian Americans in Tallulah, Louisiana, resulted in part from their fraternization with blacks. Southern Italians, especially, "consistently expressed horror at the barbaric treatment of blacks," according to historian Rudolph J. Vecoli, in part because "[Southern] Italians were also regarded as an inferior race." Roediger points out that Italian American lawyer and activist Gino Speranza questioned how an Italian immigrant could place faith in "American justice when he . . . learns of it through the lynchings of his countrymen or the burning of negroes."

Northern Italians actually encouraged this separation and distinction from their Southern countrymen; they resented and were embarrassed to be associated with peasants and farmers from the South. The years of feuding between the North and South in Italy, far from being mended by the country's unification, simply carried over to the United States. Northerners who felt superior to southerners in Italy held similar feelings in America. Moreover, by the time of the great emigration from the South, northerners were beginning to establish themselves in the United States. Many had learned English, opened small businesses, or were professionals such as doctors or lawyers. They deeply resented the literally hundreds of thousands of swarthy, short-statured, unskilled laborers from the South who arrived in the United States each year and "represented the 'typical Italian' in the American mind." One historian described an intense "pizza versus polenta" rivalry that developed in America between Northern and Southern Italians.

Other writers, academics, and government officials seized upon this North–South split to support their own racial prejudices against Southern Italians and Sicilians. In his writings after the turn of the twentieth century, Henry Cabot Lodge was careful to exempt from his harshest criticism "the northerners who had German blood and belonged to a people of Western civilization." In the future, this "Teutonic Italian, with his higher standard of living and capacity for skilled work, was a racial entity, not to be confused with his southern relative." New York assistant district attorney Arthur Train also believed a distinct dichotomy existed within the Italian character: "Northerners, *molto simpatico* to the American character, displayed many national traits...singularly like our own and resemble Americans in being honest, thrifty, industrious, law-abiding, and good natured ...on the other hand, Southerners exhibit few of these good qualities," and were "apt to be ignorant, lazy, destitute, and superstitious. In addition, a considerable percentage of those from cities are criminal." American critic William Dean Howells wrote that Northern Italians "have an appealing lightness of temper," while southerners hailed from "half-civilized stock." Even British science fiction writer H. G. Wells referred to Southern Italians as a "racially different and astonishingly fecund" ethnic group, and "darker-haired, darker-eyed, uneducated proletariat."

Academics followed suit. Sociology professor Edward Alsworth Ross warned Americans of Southern Italians' inferiority in 1914, when he noted that "steerage passengers from a Naples boat show a distressing frequency of low foreheads, open mouths, weak chins, poor features, small or knobby crania, and backless heads!" Stanford University's first president, David Starr Jordan, whose writings on "biologically incapable" Southern Italians were reprinted in the *Congressional Record,* argued: "There is not one in a thousand from Naples or Sicily that is not a burden on America. Our social perils do not arise from the capacity of the strong, but from the incapacity of the hereditarily weak."

Official government reports also stereotyped Northern and Southern Italians. The Dillingham Commission declared that "North Italians are held in higher estimation by the natives than Italians from the Southern part of Italy...The South Italians are slow in becoming Americanized... They live in colonies, have very little association with natives, are suspicious of Americans, do not trust their money to the banks, and trade at American shops as little as possible...While industrious, they are said to be impulsive, erratic, and quick to leave their job if they see apparent advantage elsewhere...It seems generally agreed that the Sicilians are less steady and less inclined to stick to a job day in and day out than other races."

Writers and historians of the day even used the words of America's chief executive to support anti–Southern Italian sentiments. "I think we must agree with President [Theodore] Roosevelt, who in his message to Congress noted the need of distributing the desirable immigrants throughout the country and of keeping out the undesirables ones altogether," wrote Robert DeCourcey Ward, a founder of the Immigration Restriction League of Boston. "Most writers on this question have emphasized the need of scattering the undesirable [Southern Italians] who as President Roosevelt points out, should not be admitted at all." In 1902, a decade before he was elected president, Woodrow Wilson offered a glimpse of his restrictionist views in his five-volume *History of the American People,* in which he bestowed the status of a scholar's judgment on anti–Southern Italian bias: "These immigrants come from the lowest class of Italy... They have neither skill, nor energy, nor initiative, nor quick intelligence... The Chinese were more to be desired."

Southern Italians encountered great difficulties learning English, too, a burden that reinforced notions of their inferiority. Those who understood pronunciation at all could not fathom why so many consonants and even some vowels (particularly the *e* at the end of words like *cake*) were silent, or why certain letter combinations—*ou,* for example—carried so many different sounds (*tough, bough, though,* or *through*), and they struggled with pronunciations that had no corresponding cousin in Italian—the *th* sound in English, for example. One writer condescendingly described the "anxious moments and the near uproar" of a group of Italian men learning English in a Boston night school when they believed they heard the teacher called them "dagoes." The men had misunderstood, the writer noted; the teacher was merely "conjugating the 'go' verb—I go, he goes, we go, they go—the last of which they misconstrued as 'da-go.'" Apocryphal or not, the story touches on a source of ridicule of Italian speech patterns that continued for years, and even exists to the present day. Southern Italian immigrants were unable to pronounce the *th* in words such as *these* and *those*; thus, the children in their households grew up learning those sounds incorrectly, and these second-generation Italians were later labeled as ignorant, stupid, or even as criminals by non-Italians who sneeringly referred to them as "dese and dose" men.

Even the occasional writer who strained to discern the positive attributes of Southern Italians usually wound up damning them with the faintest of praise and patronizing them in the most offensive of ways. Consider the conclusion of one turn-of-the-twentieth-century writer who sought to "sketch an outline" of the general character of Southern Italians:

> They are shrewd, highly imaginative, voluble, and volatile, expansive and explosive. Over a trivial incident they grow excited, all talk at once, and bluster and gesticulate as if it were a matter of great moment. Morally much may be said in their favor. They are sober, industrious, and economical. To strangers they are uniformly polite. Their experience with Americans has taught them to be suspicious, but their confidence once gained they are affable and hospitable. All Italians are proud and high-spirited, and, when ill-treated, are defiant and revengeful. Emphatically, [Southern] Italians are not lazy and thriftless. I do not forget that they are dirty as well as economical, but I do not allow the dirt to hide their better qualities.

Writing decades later, historian Silvano Tomasi asserted that Southern Italian immigrants "were looked upon as being of such a stupendous ignorance [that it was] unequaled by any other class of people found in the civilized world."

Ethnic stereotyping and discrimination did not end with nativist attitudes toward Southern Italian adults. The combination of Italian immigrant illiteracy and Americans' perception of Southern Italians' inferiority profoundly affected the attitudes toward, and achievements of, Southern Italian schoolchildren. In many ways, Italian schoolchildren were penalized for their immigrant parents' illiteracy and negative attitudes toward formal education, as well as the insularity of the Italian family. The clash of cultures that took place on America's streets also played out in classrooms across the country.

Public school officials engaged in a startling level of anti-Italian bigotry when it came to their students. Teachers ridiculed Italian schoolchildren for their broken English, the clothing they wore, or their parents' inability to speak English or read at all. Teachers and administrators classified Italian children as "retarded" or "problem" children more frequently than those of any other ethnic group and often viewed Italian students as lost causes. Educators rarely made any effort to communicate with their students' Italian immigrant parents or include them at all in school affairs.

Most American teachers had little confidence in the abilities of the Italian American student and little patience as their pupils struggled to learn and assimilate. Scholar Gloria Speranza, who produced one of the most comprehensive studies of Southern Italian schoolchildren in Boston, noted the case of a North Bennett Industrial School teacher in the North End who reviewed a handbook of course objectives for vocational guidance. The book suggested that "learning to cooperate with others—to understand them and to be understood by them" was a key to a healthy school experience. In her own handwriting in the book's margin, the teacher added: "Not much real value here. Would be of little use in the Italian group." Another North End teacher infuriated Italians when she several times called an immigrant's daughter a "dummy" and a "wop" in the presence of other schoolchildren. The girl's mother protested and related the matter to Donnaruma, who published the story in *La Gazzetta*. In their response, school authorities asserted that the fifth-grader was "rather backward in her studies" and belonged to what the school called "a slow fifth." Another elementary school teacher wrote: "Italian children were usually more crude in manner, speech, and dress than non-Italian children... These children, especially the boys, were a source of constant irritation to teachers.... These children were disliked both by teachers and non-Italian pupils." Pioneering New York City Italian American educator Leonard Covello also pointed out that American teachers ignored Italian culture in the classroom: "Throughout my whole elementary school career, I do not recall one mention of Italy or the Italian language or what famous Italians had done.... with the possible exception of Columbus, who was pretty popular in America. We soon got the idea that Italian meant something inferior."

Schools, academics, and government officials generally ignored concerns of Italian parents, believing that their illiteracy and own lack of formal education made them ill suited to decide what was best for their children. Prominent writer John Watrous Knight publicly declared that Italians were a "lower form of life" and had "little appreciation for institutions of a free land in general and public schools in particular." In 1903, a group of eighty-five North End Italians petitioned the Boston School Committee to appoint a truant officer "who possesses knowledge of the Italian language and the customs of Italian people . . . we beg that this petition receive your earnest and careful consideration." The School Committee did not acknowledge the request for more than six months, according to Gloria Speranza, and then responded with a biting bureaucratic arrogance that would be difficult to imagine the committee using with any other ethnic group: "It is not expedient to add to the Truant Officers force at the present time. Therefore, we recommend that the petitioners be given leave to withdraw."

In some ways, Italian immigrants' attitudes toward school and education, which they carried with them from Italy, encouraged the prejudice they encountered in the United States. They put little faith in formal education or "book-learning," Speranza noted. "Books had been remote from their everyday life. Most Southern Italian peasants viewed reading as a pastime for people of the idle upper class." In the *mezzogiorno,* schools were remote, poorly maintained, and underfinanced. "Children were required to complete three years of school, and in much of the South, government ignored even these limited attendance rules," Speranza wrote. "As a result, government reinforced a certain reverence for book-learning among people of the North, and barely encouraged such learning in the South." Teachers in Southern Italy often discouraged peasant children from attending schools so they could focus time and attention on the few children of the elite. School supervisors, curricula, and teacher training all emanated from Rome, which caused Southern Italians to immediately distrust government schools; any institution that attempted to influence their children more than the family unit, especially when the organization's loyalty was rooted in the North, made Southern Italians fearful and wary. They carried these suspicions with them to America.

The Southern Italians' focus on work and family also hamstrung their children's educational progress and encouraged discrimination. Many Southern Italians saw no reason for their children to continue school past eighth grade; they felt it was more important to the family for children to work as soon as possible and contribute to the household income. Italians placed a high value on home ownership once they decided to settle in America and understood that they could achieve that aim with as many family members contributing to the cause as quickly as possible. This was borne out by drop-out rates among Boston's Italian communities in the North End and West End, which soared once students reached high school age.

All of this—immigrant illiteracy, blind bigotry, Italian attitudes toward formal education—led American educators to dismiss the potential of most Italian children, unless and until they renounced their parents' attitudes and behaviors. Total assimilation and Americanization were viewed as the only way to protect Italian schoolchildren from the backward views of their parents, according to public school dogma. "This led to a barrier between children of Italian origin and their parents," Leonard Covello wrote. "We were becoming American by learning to be ashamed of our parents."

In Donnaruma's eyes, the literacy bill he opposed was yet another tool the government could employ to stigmatize Italian immigrants who could not read, further institutionalize the discrimination they suffered, and more deeply ingrain the shame their children and others had in their illiteracy. His personal outrage fueled his desire to join an organized opposition effort spearheaded by the American Association of Foreign Language Newspapers (AAFLN). In working against the Dillingham bill, the AAFLN sought to "defend a class of people who cannot defend themselves, to defend people whose country and parents did not give them the privilege of an education . . . to deprive these people of the freedom of this country, if they desire to come here, is certainly very unjust and unfitting." Or, as the AAFLN president wrote to Donnaruma in January of 1914: "This is a grave matter, striking at the vital interests of every immigrant and at the foreign-speaking population of this country, of whom you are a champion."

It was the dual injustice of the literacy bill—both symbolic and practical—that drove Donnaruma's most fervent objections. While the measure applied only to new immigrants arriving at United States ports, he and other Italian leaders around the country believed that its negative stereotyping would harm those Italians who were already living, working, and raising children in America. The stereotype of the "dumb, ignorant, backward" Italian would persist and intensify once the United States Congress legitimized the image. This was untenable for Donnaruma, who, in the past ten years as editor of *La Gazzetta del Massachusetts,* had seen and helped his countrymen in Boston make remarkable progress. They had battled illiteracy, discrimination, poverty, health issues, the English language barrier, neighborhood congestion, and unfamiliar urban surroundings to establish households, businesses, neighborhoods, and lives in their new country. They had accomplished all of this drawing on the strength of their families, their capacity for hard work, and their willingness to sacrifice to save money.

The passage of a literacy bill would jeopardize the progress of Italians already living in America by virtually singling them out as inferior and isolating them in the eyes of the rest of the population; and it would deny new immigrants the opportunities their predecessors had to build a better life. Donnaruma had witnessed the advances and contributions many illiterate Boston Italian immigrants had made; it would have been shameful and tragic if the doors at Ellis Island had slammed shut on these people because they could not pass a literacy test.

New Italian immigrants deserved the same chance.

The Dillingham literacy bill was the most important piece of legislation affecting Italians in several years. As winter turned to spring in 1914, Donnaruma and Italians across Boston and America followed the progress of the bill through Congress. With their eyes on Washington, D.C., they likely cast little more than a glance toward the storm clouds that were gathering over Europe. Those clouds would darken in anger toward the end of June and, with the assassination of an Austro-Hungarian archduke by a Serbian nationalist on June 28 in Sarajevo, Bosnia, unleash a deluge that would eventually consume Europe, disrupt and all but halt immigration to America, and plunge the United States into war.

CHAPTER 10

On the eve of the First World War, James Donnaruma had every reason to be proud of the accomplishments Italians had made in his city and across the nation, and concerned that a literacy test would mark a symbolic setback in their progress.

With the influx of more than 376,000 Italians to the United States in 1913, the single greatest year for Italian immigration to America, the Italian populations of major East Coast urban neighborhoods swelled, and most Italians had made the decision to settle in the United States permanently. Italians now made up more than 10 percent of Boston's population, compared with less than 2 percent in 1900. Nearly thirty thousand Italians now lived in the North End, almost 95 percent of the neighborhood's population. In 1909 alone, the St. Leonard's and Sacred Heart Italian parishes performed a staggering 570 marriages and 2,300 baptisms between them, an average of more than eleven marriages and forty christenings per week. If marriage and child rearing are indicators of permanent settlement, Boston Italians made their intentions to stay resoundingly clear in the North End.

Italians now owned more than 25 percent of the real estate in the neighborhood, and Donnaruma's *La Gazzetta del Massachusetts* had expanded its circulation throughout and beyond the neighborhood. Italian immigrants were learning to read in their own language *and* in English, albeit slowly, usually taking reading courses at night after a day of exhausting labor. Donnaruma would have been pleased on both counts when the *Boston Herald*, in a 1911 article on foreign-language newspapers, called *La Gazzetta* "a clearing house for Italian thought in Boston," while describing the look of the paper as "so thoroughly Americanized that when viewed from a distance of 10 feet it looks like a pretty good small town newspaper fresh from the printing plant." (Donnaruma must have found the *Herald*'s compliments deliciously ironic as well; he had taken on the big Boston papers many times for their failure to accurately depict Italians or cover Italian issues, and in the inflammatory language of the day, one of his 1911 *Gazzetta* editorials had labeled that same *Herald* newsroom as "an asylum" and "a cage of jackasses.")

Italian-owned businesses were thriving in the North End as well. In addition to watching as the Pastene and Boston Macaroni companies expanded operations, Donnaruma and his neighbors saw Giuseppe Parziale introduce pizza to the Boston public in 1908 from his shop at 78 Prince Street; Louis Reppucci and his brothers launch Reppucci Construction in 1912; Biaggio Alba open the Red Lantern Restaurant around the same time; and Martin Adamo become the proprietor of a North End pharmacy in 1914. Boston Italians now worked as pushcart vendors, barbers, hotel porters, cobblers, cooks, carpenters, blacksmiths, stonemasons, and furniture finishers. "[Italians] are beginning to take their proportionate place in skilled trades, in commercial establishments, and in the professions," one Boston magazine writer noted. In 1910, the Boston Society for the Protection of Italian Immigrants, led by Reverend Gaettano Conte, began assisting immigrants in finding jobs.

Still, even as late as World War I—and despite some upward job mobility—a plurality of Boston Italians, perhaps as many as 40 percent, still worked as unskilled laborers, the "pick and shovel men" from Southern Italy and Sicily who built many of Boston's and other American cities' roads, bridges, tunnels, sewer systems, and skyscrapers in the early twentieth century. Hundreds of Boston's Southern Italians worked beneath ground to build the nation's first subway station at Park Street in the late 1890s, and thousands more followed, bowing their backs and straining their arms to dig the ditches, cut the stone, lay the pipe, and hoist the steel that Boston required to accompany her expansion during the first decade of the twentieth century. Earning pitifully meager wages, lower than those of virtually any other immigrant group, Southern Italians scrimped and saved at astounding rates. Children worked as soon as they were old enough to help make ends meet, and Italian families took in boarders to boost their income further.

Simple survival was their goal at first, followed closely by earning enough to escape the poverty that had dogged them since they left Italy.

But home ownership was their dream.

Owning a home underscored the Italian immigrant promise: "He who crosses the ocean buys a house." For Italian immigrants in America, owning a home had many meanings. It was an important step in becoming American, a tangible sign that they could overcome hostility and sink roots in their community and their adopted country. It was evidence that, with hard work, anything was possible in the United States, a message they could pass on with pride to their children. For Italian immigrants, home ownership *was* the American Dream, decades before the term described a growing, economically vibrant middle class. "[Italian immigrants] did not so much 'buy into' the American Dream of home ownership as help create it," David Roediger wrote.

And they knew that work—often backbreaking, dirty, degrading, and almost always sunup to sundown—was the path that led to the dream's fulfillment.

When Constantine Panunzio arrived in Boston in 1902 from the province of Puglia, he found lodging in a North End boardinghouse, where he shared a three-room apartment with thirteen other people. "At night the floor of the kitchen and the dining table were turned into beds," he wrote. He began searching for a job immediately, armed with advice from his fellow boarders that pick-and-shovel labor was practically the only work available to Italians. "[Pick and shovel] were the first two English words I had and they possessed great charm," he recalled. "Moreover... if this was the only work available for Italians, they were very weighty words for me and I must master them soon and as well as possible and then set out to find their hidden meaning. I practiced for a day or two until I could say 'peek' and 'shuvle' to perfection."

Panunzio then asked a fellow boarder to take him to 'pick and shovel' work to see what it was like, and his friend took him to Washington Street in Boston's downtown section, a ten-minute walk from the North End. "I did see, with my own eyes, what the 'peek' and 'shuvle' were about," he wrote much later, after becoming a professor of sociology in America. "My heart sank within me, for I had thought it some form of office work; but I was game and since this was the only work for Italians, and since I must have money... I would take it up."

Thousands of other Italians "took up" the pick and shovel along with Panunzio, hoping for a chance to earn *something*, perhaps to purchase a steamship ticket back to Italy, or to provide for their families in the United States. They helped build Boston as the city expanded, or they left the city each day or for the week to construct the sewer systems in nearby Brockton or Beverly, or dig the Northampton reservoir in the central part of the state. Americans came to associate brutally difficult, unskilled, manual labor with Italians. "The one-time conqueror of the world [Rome] is now its slave," declared one contemporary writer. Another, commenting on the large number of Italians who were unskilled laborers or farmers, claimed such occupations gave Italian immigration "an all but unique character in the world's history. The same individuals, had they lived two thousand years ago, would not have been harnessed to tasks materially different from those they toil at today." The grueling work Italians performed belied a common legend that had traveled from America to Italy, causing one immigrant to remark: "I came to America because I heard the streets were paved with gold. When I got here, I found out three things: first, the streets weren't paved with gold; second, they weren't paved at all; and third, I was expected to pave them."

From the beginning of their arrival in America, when they were forced to deal with the type of unscrupulous *padroni* that George Scigliano exposed, Italians faced daunting work conditions. *Padroni* duped them with promises of work, only to leave Italians abandoned miles from home in lonely and remote locations, minus the money they had paid for the alleged jobs. Employment agencies often worked in collusion with employers, who after a few weeks would fire the workers, hire a new crew, and share in the agencies' new "fees." Even then, those Italians who were abandoned and swindled were often the fortunate ones. Many men who were taken to real jobs never forgot the experience. Camille Tonatore remembered his early days in Louisiana as "the slaving times." He recalled seeing a man "harnessed to a plough like a mule, working for eighty-five cents a day," an instance of peonage that was not uncommon in Italians' early work experience. The nature of the work Italians performed meant that the great majority would not become financial success stories; they lived in poverty while working at whatever jobs they could get, even when working conditions were dangerous or unhealthy.

Yet, their capacity for hard work and their determination to work hard—at whatever the wages—created a demand for their services, particularly in the cities. The first stereotypes of Italians as shiftless and lazy had dissipated. Nearly 90 percent of the New York Department of Public Works around the turn of the twentieth century was composed of Italians who graded streets, laid sewer pipe, or built subways. "We can't get along without the Italians," a city official observed. "We want someone to do the dirty work; the Irish aren't doing it any longer."

Work was a family endeavor, and most Italians considered contributing to the family's income a priority. Men were the primary breadwinners, and while most first-generation Italian immigrant women did not work outside the home—the few who did most often worked within the enclave—some took in piecework or sewing to help make ends meet. Children, especially boys, were expected to contribute to the family income as soon as they were old enough. One Italian immigrant described the general attitude toward work among his *paesani:* "Everybody went to work upon arrival; women, children, old men. If school was obligatory there were ways of avoiding it. A boy would tell the principal of his school that his family was moving to another school district. The principal would fill out the transfer papers, telling the boy: 'You must present these papers to your new school.' Of course, the boy never did and he was free to get a job as wagon driver, delivery boy, bootblack, anything that would contribute to the family income." This emphasis on work by children helped the Italian family in the short term but certainly hurt Italians' long-term progress in America. By removing students from school as soon as they were able to work, by not placing a priority on education, first-generation Italian immigrants inadvertently hindered their children's economic and political growth. This was not done by design, of course; it was simply expected that everyone in the family would work to assure that food, clothing, and housing needs were met.

In addition, Italians often took in boarders, usually *paesani* who were recent arrivals in America, to help with domestic finances. No other immigrant group relied on boarders as much as Italians to boost family income, and Boston Italians took in boarders more than any other group in America.

This emphasis on work and on contributions from boarders and all family members helped Italians augment their paltry wages; this extra money plus their frugality made them among the best money savers of all immigrant groups as they pursued their dreams of home ownership. Italians were willing to rent cheap apartments and rooms, subsist on inexpensive foods, sew their own clothing, and reuse as much as they could to save money. Early in the first decade of the twentieth century, Walter Weyl wrote a vignette entitled "The Italian Who Lives on Twenty-Six Cents a Day." Weyl's piece featured a peasant named Pacifico who "secured his dollar and fifty cents a day, minus railway fare, minus the arbitrary charge for the doctor, minus the padrone's fee.... Pacifico, born in a bottomless poverty, was not spoiled, and he shrugged his shoulders at the hard work, the bad food, and the ceaseless extractions. The essential fact remained: he earned a dollar-and-a-half a day; he lived on twenty-six cents a day." When Pacifico began to earn more than $1.50 per day, Weyl maintained, he was able to save enough to marry, send his children to school, and become economically independent. "A bank account today is what a log cabin and a hundred-acre lot were a hundred years ago."

Other writers and economists also noted the extraordinary ability of Italians to save money. In 1905, statistician Eliot Lord noted: "The thrift of the Italian is so exceptional that even bootblacks and common laborers can sometimes save enough to figure as tenement landlords." Historian Luciano Iorrizzo added, "When all was done, the Italians saved more than any other immigrant group. From a monthly salary of $35, the Italians could save $25 or more." One Boston writer marveled in 1903, "Even microscopic incomes do not forbid Italians the practice of thrift."

For those Italians who wielded the picks and gripped the shovels, whose calloused hands cracked and bled from the winter cold, whose grimy sweat ran from their brows in the summer heat, whose backs creaked and forearms bulged as they strained to hoist stone and steel, whose dirt-caked clothing clung to their broad frames and hampered their movement, whose foremen spat at and cursed them to work faster, who departed for work in the silent darkness of early morning and trudged home long after sunset— for these Italians, home ownership made it all worthwhile.

And Italians were making remarkable gains.

While home ownership among Italian immigrants did not reach its peak until after the First World War, the importance Italians—especially Southern Italians—attached to it was evident from the moment they decided to stay in America, and the rate of property ownership grew enormously in the first decade of the twentieth century. "Nothing embodied the essence of community more than a home," historian Gary Mormino wrote. "Home ownership became the great trade-off, a capstone to the immigrants' relentless labors. No home, no community; no property, no dignity."

Prior to 1900, home ownership rates among Italian immigrants were low, but after the turn of the century, rates increased substantially. In 1904, Gino Speranza reported that New York Italians owned approximately four thousand parcels of residential real estate valued at greater than $20 million. (Another ten thousand stores in the city were owned by Italians at an estimated value of $7 million.) By the next year, New York Italians owned a quarter of the Elizabeth Street properties—the Sicilian section of Little Italy—and by 1925, they owned half the property on the street. Speranza noted that from a per capita standpoint, the value of property owned by Italians in New York was "much below that of the Italian colonies of St. Louis, San Francisco, Boston, and Chicago, but a fair showing for the great 'dumping ground' of America."

For Italians, home ownership was more important in the assimilation process—the process of becoming American—than occupational mobility, education for them or their children, or political power. "Italians preferred to invest their futures in property rather than career advancement," Mormino pointed out. "Housing represented a means to an end, an investment for family in community." Another historian wrote that the Italians she studied "apparently believed that family interests were better served by property ownership and financial security than by children's leisure and education." In her study of Sicilians, Donna R. Gabaccia added, "Sicilians had simple housing standards: They wanted above all to own a house ('As little as it is, so long as it's mine')."

The homes Italians owned were by no means luxurious. Most were tenement buildings whose apartments may have contained two bedrooms, a kitchen, and a small living room. Perhaps renters had a tiny storage space in a dark, dank cellar. Almost no one in Italian enclaves in the early years, landlords included, had their own bathrooms. Usually, bathrooms were shared and located off a common hallway, and even then, not all of them had showers; immigrants often had to shower in public bathhouses or the YMCA.

Still, owning a home represented the highest form of prosperity for Italians. It meant they could never be evicted by a dishonest or greedy landlord. It meant they had acquired an asset that would have been forever out of their economic reach in Italy. It meant they possessed a bulwark against the insecurity of irregular or seasonal employment or the very real danger of being injured, or even killed, on the job. "The desire to own a home can be seen as the wish of former peasants to possess—even at great sacrifice—something which had been denied to so many for generations," one historian wrote. "Land—a tangible asset—could proudly be passed on to the younger generation."

Italians believed that owning their own home was a sign of self-respect and independence. Despite performing the most menial of jobs, earning abysmally low wages, withstanding a barrage of ethnic bigotry, and settling in the poorest sections of most cities, Italians made home ownership a priority.

Illiterate, unskilled immigrant laborers struggled, earned, and saved enough to create their own version of the American Dream. This progress they had made, this toehold they had gained in the United States, had occurred with many thousands being unable to read or speak English. It was this fact that lay at the heart of James Donnaruma's opposition to the proposed literacy test law.

Such a law would deprive thousands of new immigrants of the opportunity to succeed by denying them entrance into a country where such success was possible.

Donnaruma's fears were allayed in January of 1915 when, after more than a year of Congressional debate and posturing on both sides, President Woodrow Wilson vetoed William Dillingham's literacy test bill. Wilson's veto came as a mild surprise; the president had espoused staunch immigration restrictionist views, and his anti-Italian writings were well documented. Perhaps President Wilson no longer saw the need for the bill now that war was raging in Europe and immigration to the United States had declined sharply.

"Restrictions like these [literacy], adopted earlier in our history as a Nation, would very materially have altered the course and cooled the humane ardors of our politics," the president explained when he vetoed the bill. "The literacy test...constitutes a...radical change in the policy of our Nation. Hitherto we have generously kept our doors open to all who were not unfitted by reasons of disease or incapacity for self-support...in this bill it is proposed to turn away from tests of character and of quality and impose tests which exclude and restrict."

And then Wilson addressed his conundrum, what he—and Italian leaders such as Donnaruma—saw as the fundamental flaw in the literacy bill, a proposed law that would mandate "that those who come seeking opportunity are not to be admitted, unless they already have one of the chief opportunities they seek—the opportunity of education."

It would not be the last time the literacy test bill was debated, or the last time Wilson would veto such a proposal. When Congress next took up the measure in 1917, however, America herself would be at war, and the calls for restrictions upon foreigners entering the country would grow louder and stronger.

PART 4

WAR, ANARCHISTS, ASSIMILATION

On September 10, 1915, James Donnaruma wrote to Felix Marcella, an attorney with offices in Pemberton Square and a candidate for the Massachusetts legislature: "It is the intention of this newspaper to publish in its coming issue a statement from each of the Italian candidates for the House of Representatives. The statement should contain no more than seventy-five words, and the question you should answer is why you should be elected as one of the members of the Legislature. Please see that the statement is in our office on Monday morning next."

Written in the terse and pointed style befitting a busy newspaper editor, Donnaruma's letter to Marcella nonetheless was one of many efforts made by the editor and publisher of *La Gazzetta del Massachusetts* to encourage and support Italians who had become American citizens to run for public office. Italian political voices in Boston had been few since George Scigliano's death nearly a decade earlier, a source of frustration for Donnaruma, who recognized the importance of political influence and power both to stave off discriminatory laws such as the literacy test bill and continue the progress Italians had made in Boston and other cities.

Now was the time.

With new immigration slowed to a near trickle due to war in Europe, Boston's established Italian neighborhoods in the North End and the contiguous West End and smaller, fledgling enclaves in East Boston, Roxbury, and Hyde Park were solidifying and becoming even more cohesive. Also, without the influx and influence of thousands of new immigrants, Italians in America, while maintaining strong family units and neighborhood ties, were able to hasten their assimilation and deepen their commitment to their new country. It was during this period, after the beginning of the First World War, that immigrants from Italy began to identify themselves as "Italians" to other Americans, rather than describing themselves as hailing from a particular province or region of Italy. (Among *themselves,* Italians continued to identify with their village or province of origin, to which they remained fiercely loyal.)

The North End, now fully developed as the nexus of Italian life in Boston, its population now approaching thirty-five thousand, pulsed with vitality, as hacks, pushcarts, delivery trucks, and people competed for right of way along the neighborhood's narrow streets. "There was a congestion the like of which I had never seen before," Constantine Panunzio wrote during this time. The Commercial Street waterfront area was among the busiest on the entire East Coast, as stevedores, longshoremen, and teamsters guided horse-drawn wagons loaded with beer barrels onto the docks or loaded and unloaded heavy wooden crates from the cargo holds of ships. The area promised to get busier and more congested: In the fall of 1915, workers for United States Industrial Alcohol were building a fifty-foot-tall steel tank on the waterfront that would hold more than two million gallons of molasses, which the company would distill into industrial alcohol to use in the production of munitions and high explosives for the European nations at war against Germany. Dozens of massive steamships, their holds laden with hundreds of thousands of gallons of molasses from Cuba, Puerto Rico, and the West Indies, would begin making Boston a port of call the following year. On the opposite side of the neighborhood, near Haymarket Square and Faneuil Hall, adjacent to downtown, Italian fruit and produce vendors gathered to sell their goods from pushcarts, aggressively negotiating prices of bananas, tomatoes, cucumbers, or green beans with their potential customers. "Around the entire neighborhood . . . a thousand wheels of commercial activity whirled incessantly day and night, making noises which would rack the sturdiest of nerves," Panunzio observed.

Even with the beehive of commerce buzzing with activity from early morning until after dark, the Italian neighborhood retained the unmistakable warmth and charm that comforted and united its residents. North End Italians gathered on street corners and in grocery stores to chat, shared a cup of coffee or a glass of wine at the kitchen table to discuss each others' families or news from the Old Country, called to each other from window to window or fire escape to street, and sat on their front stairs or on chairs along the sidewalk to gossip and debate the day's events. "Above the streets, the fire escapes of tenements were festooned with lines of drying laundry,

A common sight in Italian neighborhoods was laundry drying on clotheslines strung between tenements, as shown here in the Cleveland Place block of the North End in 1935. *(Courtesy of the Boston Public Library, Print Department)*

while housewives exchanged news and gossip with any neighbor within shouting distance," historians Jerre Mangione and Ben Morreale wrote. "The roofs became the remembered fields of Italy where residents could visit one another on summer Sundays while the young played in the tar-filled air." On those same summer Sunday mornings, the pleasant appetite-inducing aroma of simmering tomato sauce—or "gravy," as many Southern Italians and Sicilians referred to it—wafted through open windows in anticipation of the noontime pasta (or "macaroni," as Boston Italians called it in the early days) feast. All of these customs would continue for decades.

Without a doubt, Italians had ensconced themselves in the North End and embraced the neighborhood, and the city of Boston, as their home. From this standpoint, James Donnaruma's hope that their political fortunes could improve was well founded.

Italians were still slow to embrace American citizenship, however. The number of political candidates whose statements Donnaruma promised to publish was limited to a handful; one major reason was that citizenship rates among Italians in 1915 still hovered around only 25 percent. While

Italians enjoy the North End Park in the summer of 1908. *(Courtesy of the Boston Public Library, Print Department)*

Italians had long ago decided to remain permanently in America, the tug and memory of home were powerful, and obtaining American citizenship was regarded as a final renunciation of their beloved Italy. This, coupled with their continued and intense suspicion and distrust of government, meant that Boston Italians eschewed citizenship, disdained politics, and for the most part, maintained their aversion to civic activism. "As a nationality, Italians have not forced political recognition," immigrant leader Gino Speranza had written a decade earlier. "Though numerically strong, there is no such 'Italian vote' as to interest politicians."

Little had changed by 1915, a fact that put Italians at a disadvantage in acquiring municipal jobs or even controlling events in their own neighborhoods. It would take Italians some years before they would fully grasp this reality and overcome their reluctance to officially become Americans and embroil themselves in the political process; for now, most were content to follow the same settlement patterns of my grandparents, who, in 1915, had their fifth child—yet neither Calogero nor Angela Puleo had become citizens. Most Italians still dedicated themselves primarily to their immediate and extended families, felt most comfortable with and most trusting of their *paesani,* and, quite simply, paid little attention to civic affairs or politics.

There were many exceptions to this rule, of course, and most of those were honest, hardworking Italians, such as Donnaruma, who recognized quickly that citizenship and political influence were the keys to Italians' continued advancement and progress in America.

The most vocal activists, however, were also the most violent and destructive. Their actions over the next several years would periodically terrify large portions of the country, damage the reputations of law-abiding Italians, and intensify sweeping anti-immigrant fervor in America. Their stated and oft-repeated goals were the violent overthrow of the United States government and the capitalist economic system.

They were Italian anarchists—and by 1915, their national headquarters and center of operations was Boston's North End.

CHAPTER 12

Anarchists of all nationalities had frightened Americans since the late nineteenth century; indeed, the very word *anarchism* was popularly understood to mean the politics of terrorism and violence.

Americans watched from afar as anarchists drew blood on the world stage numerous times from the 1880s onward. Within the decade spanning the mid-1880s to the mid-1890s, anarchists had assassinated Spanish prime minister Canovas del Castillo, French president Sadi Carnot, Hapsburg empress Elizabeth, and Italian king Umberto I, and anarchist bombers killed dozens of Parisians in terror bombings throughout the 1890s. With these events, author Eric Rauchway pointed out, the "anarchist movement . . . announced its enthusiasm for terrorism." In the United States, the deaths of seven policemen in the 1886 bombings at Haymarket Square in Chicago had been blamed on anarchists, and in 1892, Russian Jewish anarchists Alexander Berkman and Emma Goldman conspired to assassinate Henry Clay Frick, chairman of Carnegie Steel, after the violent Homestead labor strike of 1892. Then, as the new century dawned, an American-born anarchist of Polish extraction, Leon F. Czolgosz (pronounced "Cholgosh"), assassinated President William McKinley on September 6, 1901, in Buffalo, New York. Americans were bereaved and frightened, as "the threat of violence hung over the citizens of the Western world," Rauchway writes. "Nobody knew when a bomb or a gunshot might burst from a crowd."

Since war had exploded across Europe in 1914, anarchists had reacted with renewed intensity and ferocity in the United States. Their activities became even more violent after the May 7, 1915, sinking of the British luxury liner *Lusitania* by a German submarine. More than 1,200 people, including 128 Americans, had been killed, and sentiment began building for the United States to enter the war against Germany, a sentiment and a war that anarchists vigorously opposed.

Throughout 1914 and 1915, a rash of bombings shocked New York City.

In one brazen attempt, a bomb was placed in the courtroom beneath the seat of magistrate John L. Campbell, who had convicted and sentenced an anarchist for inciting a riot. The judge was about to ascend to the bench when the bomb was discovered and disarmed. During November and December of 1915, suspicious fires and explosions rocked strategic manufacturing plants across the country. Fire destroyed the Bethlehem Steel Works in Pennsylvania, which was producing armaments for the Allies. A thunderous explosion tore through the du Pont Powder Mill in Wilmington, Delaware, killing thirty men. A man was arrested in Pittsburgh after threatening to blow up the Westinghouse Electric and Manufacturing Company plant and assassinate President Woodrow Wilson. Guards were doubled at principal government buildings in Washington, D.C., including the state, war, and navy departments, after numerous bomb threats and a bomb explosion destroyed a room in the Capitol in the summer of 1915.

And at the start of 1916, Bostonians saw the danger creep closer to home. On New Year's morning, a Massachusetts State House night watchman making his rounds discovered a wicker suitcase tied to the doorknob of the sergeant-at-arms's office. Suspicious, he called the state police to investigate. They discovered a pipe inside the suitcase filled with several sticks of dynamite—only a faulty fuse prevented the bomb from exploding. The next morning, an explosion ripped apart the New England Manufacturing Company in the Boston suburb of Woburn, and rumors quickly circulated that the company had received a letter two weeks earlier threatening to blow up or set fire to the plant unless it stopped producing goods and shipping them overseas to the warring nations in Europe.

All of these incidents were jarring to Boston Italians and Bostonians in general. Even more terrifying, though, were Boston police warnings issued in 1916 that the North End, home to more than thirty thousand hardworking and primarily law-abiding Italians, had also become the headquarters for some of the leading Italian anarchists in America, men whose primary persuasive tools were terror and violence. Years of poverty and government oppression in Italy incited their passion, shaped their revolutionary philosophy, and drove them to be among the most radical of all ethnic anarchists. Italian anarchists, more fervently than any other group, believed that capitalism *and* government were responsible for the plight of the working class and the poor, for "the poverty and squalor in the midst of plenty," in the words of Nicola Sacco years before his arrest. Historian Paul Avrich pointed out that Italian anarchists like Sacco were sure that "in the end, truth, justice, and freedom would triumph over falsehood, tyranny, and oppression. To accomplish this, however, would require a social revolution, for only the complete overthrow of the existing order, the abolition of property and the destruction of the state, could bring the final emancipation of the workers."

While the overwhelming majority of Boston Italians were apolitical and peaceful, the radical anarchists and their followers frightened residents and made them even more suspicious of the entire ethnic group.

Suspicion turned to fear and anger in Boston, when, as 1916 drew to a close, Italian anarchists made their presence known in the North End.

In the early morning hours of Sunday, December 17, 1916, a dynamite bomb explosion shattered the silence in the North End and interrupted the joy of the Christmas season in the Italian neighborhood. The blast ripped a gaping hole through the three-foot-thick brick wall of the Salutation Street police station, broke every window on one side of the building, blew out the window sashes, and split the window casings. Inside the station, floors and walls cracked, furniture splintered, and ceiling plaster showered down upon virtually everything. Authorities said the bomb had been placed in a jail cell in the basement of the station, directly under rooms in which three policemen were sleeping. They were fortunate to have escaped injury when the explosion blew outward against the station's lower wall, rather than upward toward the basement ceiling and the first-floor sleeping area.

Damage stretched far beyond the station house. The bomb's powerful explosion had smashed every pane of glass in the tenements across Salutation Street, from Commercial Street to Hanover Street, as well as those on Battery Street, Commercial Street, and North Street. Rubble and glass covered the pavements within a two-block radius of the police station. It was a stroke of fortune that the explosion occurred early on a Sunday morning; the streets surrounding the station were deserted and no passersby had crossed into the blast's direct path. State chemist Walter Wedger said later that eighteen to twenty sticks of dynamite had been used to fashion the massive bomb, and that the explosion could be heard and felt across the harbor in East Boston. "This is without any question the biggest explosion of this character which has ever happened in Boston," Wedger said.

Italian anarchists claimed credit for the bombing, a reprisal against Boston police for the arrests of several anarchists after a violent anti–military preparedness riot in North Square in early December. Boston newspapers called it the "liveliest riot" the neighborhood had ever seen. More than twenty shots were fired by police and protestors, though no one was hit by gunfire. Ten demonstrators were arrested, including Alphonsus Fargotti, who was charged with assault with intent to kill for slashing a police officer with a fifteen-inch knife blade. The Friday prior to the explosion at the police station, a judge bound Fargotti's case over for action by a Suffolk County grand jury, a ruling reported in Saturday's newspapers. Fargotti's allies made a bold and violent statement in response, striking at law enforcement's heart—a station house where police worked and slept.

Fargotti was a militant anarchist and a disciple of Italian anarchist leader Luigi Galleani. The demonstration in early December had been organized by the International Workers of the World (IWW), also known as the "Wobblies," who had engaged in violent protests across America, sweeping eastward from the Rocky Mountain states, demanding economic improvements for the country's lowest-paid workers. Their efforts began in Idaho, Wyoming, and Colorado, where they led strikes in mines, lumber camps, and textile mills. One of their goals was to organize workers into one massive union that would one day topple capitalism, a mission that aligned with the anarchists' radical desires.

Both the Wobblies and the anarchists believed that the war was producing exorbitant profits for business at the expense of downtrodden workers who struggled to make ends meet, particularly unskilled immigrant laborers. Though their agendas were not exactly the same—Wobblies favored a socialist form of government while anarchists believed in *no* government—their militant anticapitalist views made them practical ideological bedfellows. It was no surprise that anarchists and Wobblies joined hands in riots, strikes, and protest movements across the country.

The early December North End riot began with an IWW meeting

held in North Square, in front of Sacred Heart Church. Fearing inflammatory remarks that would incite the crowd, police officers warned IWW leaders not to speak and to refrain from distributing radical literature. When one police officer cautioned some crowd members to move along and clear the sidewalk, the riot began. Fargotti slashed at patrolman William Cogan with a butcher's knife, slicing the officer's overcoat and severing a tendon in Cogan's right hand. Close by, a few others in the crowd began shooting. One police officer wrested a .32 caliber pistol from a demonstrator. The sound of the riot was heard blocks away, and additional officers from the Salutation Street and Hanover Street stations arrived quickly, dispersed the crowd, and made arrests. Officers found a fully loaded pistol in Fargotti's pocket when they arrested him.

The North Square riot and the Salutation Street police station bombing were among the first incidents of Italian anarchist violence in Boston and in major eastern cities in general, but they would not be the last. Over the next several years, America's involvement in World War I, its expansion as an international force, and the growth of big business would fuel anarchists' anger and embolden them to follow a path that Galleani had laid out in his writings: "Continue the good war, the war that knows neither fear nor scruples, neither pity nor truce...When we talk about property, State, master, government, laws, courts, and police, we say only that *we don't want any of them.*"

Boston would serve as the Italian anarchists' headquarters for Galleani's war, even after Galleani himself was deported in June of 1917, just six months after the North End police station bombing. The anarchist mantle would be taken up by others, including two men, Nicola Sacco and Bartolomeo Vanzetti, whose arrest and imprisonment in the 1920s would create headlines around the world and focus more attention than ever on Boston's Italian population.

CHAPTER 13

Italians in Boston and across the United States who were viewing from afar their birth country's entanglement in Europe's Great War received a hard dose of the conflict's impact on America in January of 1917. They watched despondently as Congress delivered a blow as jarring in its own way as the North End police station bombing a month earlier. Undeterred by his literacy bill's defeat just two years earlier, Senator William Dillingham shepherded yet another piece of similar legislation through the upper chamber, this one calling for doubling the head tax (to eight dollars) for prospective immigrants to enter the United States and requiring new arrivals to pass a literacy test as a prerequisite for entering the country.

As he had in 1915, President Woodrow Wilson vetoed the bill, but this time he did so in the midst of a war overseas, anarchist activity at home, and the increasing fear that America would become embroiled in a world war. Anti-immigration groups accelerated their attacks, reminding Americans that immigrant customs, languages, and even differences in appearance were cause for suspicion and often a threat to national security. In the midst of this climate, Congress overrode Wilson's veto and the literacy bill became law; the dam was broken and from here on, the anti-immigrant wave, most especially against Italians from Southern Italy and Sicily, swamped any pro-immigrant sentiment in the United States.

His veto notwithstanding, Wilson did little to lobby against a Congressional override. The president had other problems and could not afford to expend political capital or energy on a knockdown fight on behalf of incoming immigrants. He and the country had been walking a neutrality tightrope since the outbreak of the European war, and Wilson was teetering on it to stay above the fray. On January 22, the president delivered a speech to the Senate calling for "peace without victory." Wilson argued that the war in Europe must be ended on terms that would establish "not a balance of power, but a community of power, not organized rivalries by a common peace." To achieve that end, the warring countries must agree to a "peace without victory.... victory would mean peace forced upon the loser" and would therefore "rest only as upon quicksand. Only a peace between equals can last."

Interventionists, including many Democrats, sharply criticized Wilson for a view that they considered at best naive, and at worst, a sign of American weakness. Republicans were most vocal with their criticism. "Peace without victory is the natural ideal of the man who is too proud to fight," thundered former president Theodore Roosevelt, who ridiculed Wilson as a spiritual descendant of the Tories of 1776 and the Copperheads of 1864, both of whom had demanded peace without victory. Massachusetts senator Henry Cabot Lodge rejected peace without victory, declaring that lasting peace "rests upon justice and righteousness."

Wilson's neutrality position was irrevocably undermined by the Germans when, in the afternoon of the last day of January 1917, the German ambassador to the United States delivered an official warning that, as of midnight, America's merchant ships traveling to Europe would be sunk on sight by German submarines. The opening of unrestricted submarine warfare against Allied and neutral shipping caused President Wilson to break off diplomatic relations with Germany.

As Wilson's second-term March 5 inauguration date inched closer, America inched closer to war. If and when it entered the conflict, it would do so on the side of its major European allies, including France, Great Britain, and Italy.

Italians, along with the rest of the country, watched and waited.

Any illusion that the United States could avoid war was shattered on March 1, 1917, when newspaper headlines around the country revealed the existence of the "Zimmerman Telegram," a communiqué from the German foreign minister to the German minister in Mexico that was intercepted by British intelligence. The message disclosed a plan for Germany to enter into an alliance with Mexico if the United States entered the European war. If Germany and her allies were successful, Mexico's reward would be the return of its "lost territories" of New Mexico, Texas, and Arizona. When the American people learned of Germany's treachery, public opinion surged toward war.

Wilson knew that the neutrality tightrope had snapped. "We are provincials no longer," he said four days later in his inaugural address. "The tragic events of the thirty months of vital turmoil through which we have just passed have made us citizens of the world. There can be no turning back. Our own fortunes as a nation are involved whether we would have it so or not."

Later in March, Wilson was horrified when several unarmed American merchant ships were sunk in the Atlantic by German submarines, and many crew members drowned. Hysteria gripped the country, and Wilson, desperate to avoid war but astute enough to realize that events had overtaken him, was forced to act. Before a packed and enthusiastic House chamber in the Capitol on the night of April 2, 1917, Wilson asked Congress to declare war on Germany to stop its "warfare against mankind." To thunderous applause, the president said: "The world must be made safe for democracy... We desire no conquest, no dominion. We seek no indemnities for ourselves, no material compensation for the sacrifices we shall freely make. We are but one of the champions of the rights of mankind."

Two days later, Congress voted overwhelmingly to declare war (82–6 in the Senate and 373–50 in the House). Wilson signed the war resolution on April 6.

The United States was joining the fight against Germany, the war to end all wars, the war that would, in President Wilson's words, make the world safe for democracy.

America's decision to enter the First World War affected the lives of Italians in Boston and around the country. In the weeks and months that followed, Italians enlisted, were drafted, kept anxious tabs on friends and relatives fighting in the Italian army, and pledged their loyalty to America. Italian immigrants living in the United States who had not yet become citizens, including my grandfather, were offered the option of serving in either the American or Italian armed forces if they enlisted or were drafted, since the two countries were allies. My grandfather, by now the father of six and the sole breadwinner for his family, never actually served but from the beginning declared that his desire was to become a member of the United States Army. Many Italians who filled out American draft registration cards listed their next of kin—parents, siblings, and sometimes wives and children—as living in Italy, further linking the two countries. Many Italians, perhaps as many as 60,000 to 70,000 immigrants and sons of immigrants, returned to Italy to join the armed forces of their homeland. Visiting Italy after war broke out, Boston's Constantine Panunzio saw the flags of his homeland and his adopted country flying side by side and described his feelings:

> Before my eyes the two national standards...were waving triumphantly in the stiff breeze sweeping over the mountain crest. One stood for Italy, both ancient and modern, which the world respects; for the Italy of my childhood, for all the memories of my youth, of loved ones, for all that had been beautiful and lovely in my boyhood; for the tender memories of loved ones, living and dead. The other stood for all the suffering of the years, for the awakening of manhood, for the birth of freedom, for the unfolding of life. I loved not one the less, but the other more!

When the United States first entered the war in April, only about 750,000 men served in the armed forces and national guard. President Wilson signed the Selective Service Act in May, requiring all men between the ages of eighteen and thirty-one, including noncitizens, to register with their local draft boards (in 1918, Congress expanded the ages to between eighteen and forty-five). By November of 1918, when the war ended, almost 4.8 million men and women served in the army, navy, and marine corps. An estimated 300,000 of those were Italians, including nearly 90,000 noncitizens. Between 7,000 and 9,000 Boston Italians served in the United States military during World War I. "Some [Italian] men, arriving in the U.S. on the eve of war, found themselves drafted into the military of a country whose language they could not read, write, speak, nor understand," one historian wrote. "Still they served their adopted country honorably, many of them paying the supreme sacrifice in defense of freedom and liberty." Italian American servicemen suffered about 32,000 casualties, including more than 11,600 deaths.

In Boston, most Italians, like most Americans, supported the war effort from the outset. In the week following Congress's April 1917 declaration, enthusiastic rallies and parades took place throughout the city, including one at Faneuil Hall, where Mayor Curley addressed mostly Italian fruit peddlers and meat packers. "It isn't necessary to talk patriotism to men who work within sight of the greatest beacon light of liberty this old world has ever known, Faneuil Hall," Curley said. He reminded the men that "the president of the United States has not asked for a declaration of war on the German people, but on the German government," a sentiment that drew a roar from the crowd.

In late June, Boston Italians reacted with pride when the Italian War Mission, an envoy of delegates dispatched by the king of Italy, visited the city in a gesture of diplomatic unity. Mayor Curley and James Donnaruma exerted intense influence to convince both the U.S. State Department and the Italian ambassador to the United States to approve the commission's stop in Boston. "The City of Boston contains more than 50,000 persons . . . of Italian birth, who will extend you, mutually with the residents of Boston, a splendid welcome," Curley wrote to Italian ambassador Count V. Macchi di Cellere on May 16, 1917. When press reports indicated in early June that the Italian War Mission might skip Boston, Curley, with lobbying from Donnaruma, wrote to U.S. secretary of state Robert Lansing that the decision would be "most regrettable" and that "in the name of the fifty thousand . . . Italians in Boston, I firmly protest." Lansing replied promptly by Western Union telegram, explaining that the Italian envoy had developed a "high fever and is in bed and under a doctor's care" and that his travel had been "temporarily suspended." The intention of the Italian envoy was to visit Boston, Lansing said to Curley, and "you will be wired when you might submit a program for approval."

When Curley received word that the visit would finally take place on Monday, June 25, he wrote to members of the Boston welcoming committee, including Donnaruma, requesting that the group report at 7:30 A.M.— "in frock coat, silk hat, grey tie, grey gloves, and grey trousers"—to the Copley Plaza Hotel, where automobiles would take them to South Station to greet the visitors. The Italian envoy was treated to a whirlwind tour of the city, including a meeting with the governor and legislature at the State House, a visit to both the Charlestown Navy Yard and the Fore River Shipbuilding plant in Quincy, an inspection of Boston art exhibits at the art museum, a visit to the Boston Public Library, and a trip to the Boston Common for a series of speeches. A dinner, "followed by addresses, concert, and dancing" back at the Copley Plaza, closed out the day's events.

By all accounts, the visit to Boston by the Italian delegation was a rousing success and left the city's Italian population filled with pride at Boston's magnanimous and enthusiastic welcome. Mayor Curley offered his "sincere thanks" to Donnaruma days later for the newspaper editor's "generous and intelligent service" in connection with the visit. "The reception from every standpoint reflects great credit upon the Italians of Boston." Curley added that an official in the Massachusetts secretary of state's office called the city's response to the Italian War Mission's visit "the most enthusiastic reception accorded the envoys of any foreign government."

If Boston's Italians were flush with patriotism and pride over America and Italy's alliance against Germany, and the role they played balancing their dual loyalties, they continued to be dismayed at the actions of anarchists whose behavior fostered fear and suspicion about the entire ethnic group.

Within days of American's entry into the war, Boston's district attorney warned the city against potentially violent anarchist activity, declaring that Boston was in "grave danger from disturbances by anarchist bands who are holding nightly meetings, planning what they can do to tear down the structure of Government while the country's eyes are fixed on danger from without." DA Joseph Pelletier, no doubt recalling the destruction of the North End police station less than six months earlier, urged that additional guards be stationed in every bank and that manufacturing companies increase precautions. "A few hand grenades, effectively used, would put Boston in darkness for six months," he warned. Pelletier called for a "thorough survey" of Boston, "that we may get the names and addresses of all who are not citizens. Then we must learn what these people are doing. We must know their purpose in being in the city." Pelletier did not mention Italians specifically, but their high percentage of noncitizenship, coupled with the "nightly meetings" that Italian anarchists were holding in the North End, made it clear that they were the primary targets of the DA's warning.

Over the next several days, Pelletier's warnings appeared prophetic, as a series of activities in other cities, though not Boston, were blamed on an-archists. The Capitol police presence was bolstered in Washington, D.C., after the Secret Service relayed a tip that anarchists were planning to dy-namite the Capitol building, a report that proved to be false. In Pittsburgh, authorities blamed anarchists for an arson fire that destroyed a portion of the Aetna Chemical Company, one of the country's largest munitions manufacturers. And in the most tragic event in the late spring of 1917, 116 workers, many of them teenage girls, perished in a massive explosion at the Eddystone Ammunition Corporation in Chester, Pennsylvania. The explo-sion occurred in the pellet room of the shrapnel building, where the girls worked polishing shells. Officials believed that "foreigners" working in the factory planted the bomb, taking their own lives in the explosion.

"It is very difficult to have five thousand people working in a muni-tions factory and not have some foreigners employed," lamented the fac-tory manager.

With war overseas, violence at home, and the recent Bolshevik Revolution in Russia fanning a "Red Scare" and fear of radicalism in the United States, President Woodrow Wilson's Justice Department targeted socialists, the IWW Wobblies, and anarchists as primary enemies of America, with an-archists bearing the brunt of the government's increased enforcement. "Their [anarchists] uncompromising opposition to the war brought down on them the full panoply of government repression," historian Paul Avrich wrote. "Throughout the country, anarchist offices were raided, equipment was smashed, and publications were suppressed."

Law enforcement efforts reached a peak on June 15, 1917, when three of the leading anarchist leaders in America were arrested.

In New York, federal agents broke into the offices of the radical publi-cation *Mother Earth* and charged Emma Goldman and Alexander Berk-man with conspiracy to interfere with the draft. They were convicted and sentenced to two years in prison.

Boston-area Italian anarchist Luigi Galleani was the third prominent figure arrested on the same day. By this time, the Justice Department con-sidered him "the leading anarchist in the United States" and described his radical newspaper, *Cronaca Sovversiva* (Subversive Chronicle), as "the most rabid, seditious and anarchistic sheet ever published in this country." On June 15, following an editorial critical of draft registration, federal agents raided *Cronaca's* offices in Lynn, Massachusetts, and arrested Galleani at his home in Wrentham, Massachusetts—southwest of Boston—where he lived with his wife and five children. He was charged with conspiracy to obstruct the draft, entered a plea of guilty, and was ordered to pay a fine of $300.

Galleani's arrest led to police actions against other Italian anarchists in Boston and elsewhere. Some were arrested and threatened with deportation for starting a defense fund for Galleani and his colleagues. Others found themselves tossed in jail for insulting the American flag or failing to register for the draft. Still others, including Boston's Sacco and Vanzetti, fled to Mexico, where for several months during 1917, they conspired to retaliate against what they regarded as repression in the United States through the use of bombings and other violence. A Justice Department agent later speculated that this group had gone to Mexico to receive instructions on the use of explosives. By the fall of 1917, most of these comrades had returned to the United States. For the next several years, they would live an underground existence and employ bombs as their primary weapon against government authority. They would, as the title of a previously published collection of Galleani's articles suggested, go *faccia a faccia col nemico*—"face to face with the enemy."

By their violent actions, they damaged the reputation of honest, hardworking Italians, particularly in Boston, where the anarchists were so active. Boston Italians had made important economic strides in the last decade, and—despite tougher and more restrictive immigration laws—had thus begun to blunt some of the more hostile discrimination against them.

Now, the violent activities of the anarchists threatened that progress by providing an excuse for law enforcement officials and ordinary Americans, in a time of war and intense xenophobia, to tar all Italians with the same brush, something Italians deeply resented. They had battled such generalizations a decade earlier when the influence of such criminal organizations as the Black Hand and *La Camora* was at its height, and they were refighting those battles to avoid being stereotyped as anarchists.

It would be puzzling and ironic, therefore, when several years later, even as Boston Italians still fought to separate themselves from the anarchists in the public mind, they would embrace the cause of two of these loyal and avowed Galleani followers, Sacco and Vanzetti.

Thousands of law-abiding Italians would suggest that injustice against the two anarchists was an egregious affront to all Italians, that their fates were interwoven and inseparable.

CHAPTER 14

"You may be pleased to know that a number of prominent Italians in this State . . . [have] unanimously agreed to support you for President of the United States," James Donnaruma wrote to Henry Cabot Lodge, the Republican U.S. senator from Massachusetts, on July 18, 1919. "I hope that you will give us the opportunity to do so."

The letter represented a complete turnabout for Donnaruma in his feelings for Lodge. A decade earlier, the two had clashed bitterly about Lodge's support for an immigrant literacy bill, and Donnaruma was equally aware of Lodge's previous track record of anti-Italian statements and sentiments, dating back to the 1891 New Orleans lynching. However, unhappy with President Woodrow Wilson since he was elected to his first term in 1912, Donnaruma had begun cultivating a relationship with Lodge, one of the senior Republican voices in the Senate. Impressed with Lodge's tough isolationist positions, and his anti-Wilson rhetoric, Donnaruma forged an even stronger bond with the senator in the latter stages of the Great War and after the armistice of November 11, 1918. The two became close friends. Donnaruma corresponded regularly with Lodge, published numerous favorable articles about the senator in *La Gazzetta,* and whenever possible attempted to persuade Italians—who, if politically inclined at all, tended to support Democrats—that the Republican senator better served their interests. "If the election of the president of the United States [in 1920] will be left to the Italian people to decide, I wish to assure you that you will have no dissention in any city or town in the United States," Donnaruma assured Lodge. "Italian people certainly love you, and we would feel highly honored to vote for you."

Never pleased about the restrictionist Wilson's election, Donnaruma had grown increasingly frustrated in recent years, believing the president concentrated too much on foreign affairs to the neglect of economic issues at home, and frowning on what he believed was Wilson's shabby treatment of Italians, immigrants in general, and working-class Americans in the wake of the World War. The euphoria that had accompanied the armistice in November 1918 had dissipated, and Bostonians and other Americans struggled to make sense of a nation that seemed to be spinning out of control in 1919, a condition that Donnaruma laid at Wilson's feet.

"Mr. Wilson should pay more attention to America and its people than mingle himself up with the situation in Europe," Donnaruma declared in his letter to Lodge.

Since the *Boston Globe*'s front page proclaimed, WHOLE WORLD IN DELIRIUM OF JOY on November 11, 1918, and its editorial effused, "it is victory, victory at last . . . a new day dawns," Bostonians in general, Boston Italians, and other Americans had had little to celebrate—though certainly not all of the bad news could be blamed on Wilson.

Even the war's end, which Boston historian Francis Russell proclaimed was "the beginning of the new, the bright promise of a future," came on the heels of a dreadful autumn in which Bostonians and the rest of the world battled a deadly influenza epidemic that, in just over two months, wreaked havoc of biblical proportions. When it was over, more than 500,000 Americans lay dead, and estimates ranged from 20 million to 100 million deaths worldwide. More than 25 percent of the United States population became ill, and an estimated 18,000 servicemen died of the virus. Hundreds of Italian families in the North End and East Boston were affected by the flu; many were devastated.

In Boston, the horror started in late August when sailors aboard a training ship at Commonwealth Pier came down with the flu, and by early September, thousands of soldiers at Fort Devens had contracted the disease. The army camp became a scene from hell. One doctor wrote: "Camp Devens has about 50,000 men, or did, before this epidemic broke loose . . . One can stand to see one, two, or twenty men die, but to see these poor devils dropping like flies gets on your nerves. We have been averaging about 100 deaths a day, and still keeping it up."

By October the flu was rampaging through Boston. Officials shut down theaters, clubs, and other gathering spots. Boston schools were ordered closed when the death toll in Boston climbed to more than two hundred victims. Boston historian Thomas O'Connor noted that, with the death toll rising so fast and gravediggers becoming scarce, circus tents were used to cover stacks of unburied coffins in local cemeteries.

The alarming death rates hit the congested Italian neighborhoods particularly hard. By now, the North End and the contiguous West End housed nearly 50,000 Italians, and nearly 20,000 more had established residence in East Boston, accounting for all but a few thousand of the 77,000 Italians in Boston. The large number of people living in such a small space and a lack of fresh air in tenements all added to the rapid spread of the flu.

Italians suffered heartbreaking losses. The Reverend Vittorio Gregori, pastor of Sacred Heart Church in the North End, submitted a report to Cardinal O'Connell describing the distribution of $500 in church funds to families devastated by the flu:

> To Emilia Ristaino, 37 Sheafe St., whose husband, Antonio, died of influenza, leaving her 6 small children, $10; To Michelina Semenza, 180 North St., whose husband, Angelo, died of influenza, leaving 5 children, the oldest of which is 11 years old, $10; to Salvatore di Basile, 15 Margaret St., whose two children died of influenza, $5.00; to Nicola Giangrande, 108 Webster St. in East Boston, whose wife just died at the hospital and 7 of whose 8 children are sick with influenza, $5.00; To Maria Girelli, 6 Hanover St., whose husband died of influenza, leaving her with 6 small children, $10.

Father Gregori also reported distributing $69.50 "among 17 needy families, whose pride did not permit them to ask openly for charity, whose names they request be not published." At O'Connell's suggestion, Gregori also donated $50 to the pastor of St. Lazarus Parish in Orient Heights, East Boston, to distribute among Italian parishioners in that neighborhood, and another $50 to the pastor of St. Anthony's Italian parish in nearby Somerville. For Father Gregori, the influenza epidemic must have tempered any joy he and his parishioners experienced just two years earlier when the Sacred Heart mortgage was paid off (although even then Cardinal O'Connell had denied the pastor's request to celebrate by "burning mortgage papers").

By late October, the epidemic began to subside, though doctors attributed a small recurrence in November to the number of people who crowded onto the city's subway trains. In the North End, the pastor of St. Leonard's Church, "out of gratitude for the great blessing Almighty God had bestowed on us in preserving us from the Spanish influenza" asked O'Connell's permission to celebrate a "high mass in Thanksgiving" followed by a Sunday afternoon public procession. "Besides being an occasion of showing gratitude to God, it shall, we trust, revive the faith of many of our lukewarm parishioners," Rev. A. Sousa wrote. Cardinal O'Connell's secretary wrote back promptly with word that the archbishop approved the mass of thanksgiving, "but that he does not grant the permission for the public procession in the afternoon for reasons best known to himself."

North End Italians were disappointed in O'Connell's decision, and perhaps word got back to him. In what appears to have been a conciliatory gesture and an acknowledgment of the neighborhood's suffering during the flu epidemic, O'Connell granted permission in January of 1919 to Father Gregori of Sacred Heart to spend $2,700 to purchase and install a new organ in the church. He also wrote to Gregori that he was "glad to be of assistance during these terrible days" of the flu outbreak.

Grand parades and celebrations at the end of the Great War temporarily lifted the spirits of Bostonians, and Americans generally, but by the beginning of 1919 a grim pall hung in the air, and things would get worse as the year went on. Many events during this watershed year affected Italians directly.

Tragedy struck the North End on January 15, when the molasses tank on the Commercial Street waterfront collapsed, sending a wave of 2.3 million gallons of molasses crashing in all directions. The tragedy killed 21 people, injured 150, caused enormous property damage, and, because initial inaccurate reports blamed the disaster on Italian anarchists' planting a bomb at the site, sparked further anger against Italians.

The molasses flood seemed to set the tone for Boston and the country in 1919. The flood was later attributed to the tank's shoddy construction, improper testing, and complete lack of oversight—in essence, the fault of executives of the company that owned the tank, United States Industrial

Alcohol. James Donnaruma believed many other problems plaguing the country emanated from a leadership vacuum in the White House, one that was likely to continue with *any* Democrat after the 1920 election. His entreaty to Lodge to become a candidate for president was in large part based on the editor's belief that Wilson had either exacerbated the nation's problems or was ineffectual in dealing with them; Donnaruma expected such ineptitude to continue whether Wilson himself chose to seek an unprecedented third term or another Democrat was elected. He had become a staunch Republican and would support the GOP candidate in 1920.

The year 1919 began with returning soldiers and sailors flooding the civilian labor market even as government war contracts were being cancelled. Further, with the wartime shortages of labor in 1917 and 1918, blacks from the South had migrated to northern industrial cities seeking jobs, a practice they continued after the war ended. Now, blacks, whites, immigrants, and returning veterans were battling for fewer jobs, all in the midst of rising prices and a soaring cost of living.

As a result, labor unrest was sweeping industry and government from coast to coast, including strikes and work stoppages. The public's attention and its fear were focused on domestic radicals such as socialists, Wobblies, and anarchists, who were often blamed for the unrest. In mid-February, the Bureau of Immigration deported between seven and eight thousand aliens, including Italians, "as rapidly as they can be rounded up and put on ships." The mayor of Seattle toured the country after sixty thousand workers struck and paralyzed his city, warning of the Red menace in the United States. The Lawrence, Massachusetts, Citizens Committee vowed to "wage war on Bolshevism" and root out labor agitators. A radical labor leader was arrested in Cleveland in connection with a conspiracy to kill President Wilson.

All of this domestic tension affected international diplomacy as well. President Wilson, after negotiating the Treaty of Versailles and arguing strenuously for a League of Nations, faced strong opposition on the League from Republicans in the Senate, led by Lodge. GOP senators believed that the League would jeopardize American sovereignty and become an "impediment to the independence of this country." Lodge and other Republican senators wanted the Treaty and the League of Nations severed in their ratification discussions; President Wilson believed that they were inextricably linked.

One other position Wilson held during the peace talks infuriated Italians in Boston and across America. At treaty discussions in Versailles, Italian premier Vittorio Emanuele Orlando laid claim to the Adriatic port city of Fiume, home to many Italians, arguing strongly that the city was promised him as part of his agreement to desert the Central Powers (Germany and Austria-Hungary) and join forces with the Allies. After the war, the Italians eagerly anticipated expanding their northern border and adding lands on the eastern shore of the Adriatic Sea. Wilson reluctantly agreed to the northward Italian expansion but was firmly opposed to Italy's absorption of Fiume, arguing that such an acquisition ran counter to his deeply held principle of national self-determination. Italian delegates protested Wilson's stance by walking out of negotiations and remaining absent for two weeks. Wilson was unmoved and the Fiume issue continued as a source of bitterness between the two nations. Virtually the entire Italian American community also supported Italy's demand for Fiume, alienating them from Wilson. The president further angered Italian Americans when he issued a statement that "if the Italians were going to claim every place where there was a large Italian population, we would have to cede New York to them because there are more Italians in New York than any Italian city." Of Wilson's stance and subsequent statement on Fiume, Donnaruma complained to Lodge: "His action at the Peace Conference showed that he is not reliable, and has created distasteful dissention, even among the people of a certain allied nation . . ."

Events closer to home also called Wilson's leadership ability into question in the eyes of Donnaruma and his fellow Italians. His support of the Prohibition amendment, which was ratified in January, was seen as an affront to Italians, for whom wine was a staple for virtually all ages at mealtime. "The present administration, while they are preaching humanity, democracy, and freedom, have deprived the United States of beer and wine," Donnaruma wrote to Lodge, "thus making this country the laughingstock of the whole world." In addition, Donnaruma was rankled by a bill Wilson supported that would regulate the publication of foreign-language newspapers that incited radical behavior. "Statistics show we have at this time more radical newspapers printed in english [*sic*] language than in all other languages combined," Donnaruma asserted. "If the foreign language newspapers would permit themselves to publish some of the articles which are printed in the American press, I am positively sure that the editor would be sent to jail."

Fiume, Prohibition, regulating foreign-language newspapers—all of these were important to Donnaruma and Italians. Yet, they paled in comparison to the most troubling and frightening crisis America faced in 1919, one that profoundly and adversely affected Italians: the increasing brazenness and violence of the anarchists, and Wilson's response to them. Without question, Donnaruma detested the anarchists for the shame and scorn their actions brought down upon the overwhelming majority of law-abiding Italians, an editorial and personal opinion he expressed multiple times. Yet, he believed Wilson's mishandling of the economy added the gasoline that fueled the anarchists' fiery rhetoric and violent actions. "The present administration is allowing the capitalists to starve the people," wrote Donnaruma, who himself was a capitalist with conservative leanings. "A man who is earning $30 per week cannot support his family, and conditions are still growing worse. Mr. Wilson should devote himself to straightening the present conditions instead of trying to suppress newspapers printed in [a] foreign language." Donnaruma also objected to sweeping raids that rounded up scores of innocent foreigners, often Italians, along with anarchists.

The anarchists' boldness in 1919 had its genesis in Taunton, Massachusetts, where Italian anarchist Luigi Galleani, himself awaiting deportation, delivered an incendiary speech. The next evening, in the nearby town of Franklin, four Italian anarchists, all ardent supporters of Galleani, blew themselves up in what police believed was a botched plot to destroy the mill of the American Woolen Company, where they worked and where a strike was in progress. Federal authorities arrested three other men in the conspiracy on March 1. President Wilson's newly sworn-in U.S. attorney general, A. Mitchell Palmer, promised a nationwide crackdown on "aliens and Bolsheviks, radicals, and anarchists" who were "roaming the country, disrupting its peace, and terrorizing its people."

The battle lines were drawn.

As May Day approached, anarchists, angry about Galleani's impending deportation, mailed package bombs to some of the nation's most prominent and influential citizens, most especially those who had spoken out against aliens, radicals, and labor leaders. On April 28, a bomb sent to the home of Georgia's former senator, Thomas Hardwick, cosponsor of a 1918 deportation bill, found a target, exploding as the Hardwicks' maid opened the package, blowing off both of her hands.

The Hardwick bombing made headlines across the nation, and on April 30, postal inspectors intercepted thirty-four "May Day" bomb packages already in the mail system. They were addressed to people such as Attorney General Palmer, Postmaster General Albert Burleson (who had banned radical literature from the mails), Supreme Court justice Oliver Wendell Holmes (who had written and spoken on immigration restriction), commissioner general of immigration Anthony Caminetti, and multimillionaire businessmen John D. Rockefeller and J. P. Morgan. None of these bombs reached their targets, and the Hardwick maid was the only person to suffer injury, a fact that Postmaster Burleson attributed to the vigilance of his department's employees.

Americans were outraged and newspapers clamored for action. The *New York Times* called the "mailbox bombs" the "most widespread assassination conspiracy in the history of the country." Police and citizens, including ex-soldiers and ex-sailors, rousted radicals who gathered to commemorate May Day in New York, Cleveland, and Boston. The worst of these incidents occurred in Boston, where parading radicals in Roxbury—including many Italian followers of Galleani—were set upon by indignant bystanders and "chased through the streets, beaten, trampled, and kicked," according to historian Paul Avrich. Shots were exchanged, a police captain died of a heart attack during the melee, and 116 demonstrators were arrested. Fourteen demonstrators were found guilty of disturbing the peace by the Roxbury Municipal Court and sentenced to several months in prison. After sentencing, Judge Albert F. Hayden blasted "foreigners who think they can get away with their doctrines in this country...if I could have my way I would send them and their families back to the country from which they came."

About one month later, on June 2, Hayden's Roxbury home was virtually destroyed by a bomb that had been placed against a main support column. No one was home, but the judge's son, Malcolm, was just moments from entering the house and was nearly struck by the car that carried the bombers as they fled the scene.

The next day, Hayden and the rest of the country awakened to shocking headlines proclaiming that the Roxbury dynamite bombing was part of an organized anarchist conspiracy unleashed in Boston and six other cities, including Washington, D.C., where powerful bombs exploded almost simultaneously, all going off within an hour of midnight, all planted at the homes of prominent persons who were involved in anti-radical or anti-anarchist activities. This included Attorney General Palmer, whose home in the fashionable northwest section of Washington, D.C., was bombed while he and his family were in their bedrooms on the second floor. The bomb, planted under the steps of Palmer's house, destroyed most of the dwelling and smashed in windows of houses as far as a block away but miraculously did not injure Palmer, who was reading at a front window of an upstairs bedroom and was showered with glass, or his wife, asleep in a rear bedroom.

While searching the scene around Palmer's house, police made a remarkable discovery: the bomb had blown to bits the man who had planted it. They believed the bomb had exploded prematurely, before the bomber could make his escape. An intact Italian–English dictionary was discovered near Palmer's house, and while police never positively identified the dead bomber, historian Avrich concluded that the evidence pointed to Carlo Valdinocci, a dedicated Galleanist. Avrich also surmised that militant anarchists Sacco and Vanzetti were involved in the conspiracy as well.

At each bomb site—Boston, Washington, New York, Cleveland, Philadelphia, Pittsburgh, and Paterson, New Jersey—police also found leaflets signed by Italian "anarchist fighters." The message of the text was plain enough and sobering: "There will have to be bloodshed; we will not dodge; there will have to be murder; we will kill, because it is necessary; there will have to be destruction; we shall not rest until your downfall is complete and the laboring masses have taken possession of all that rightfully belongs to them. . . . Long live social revolution! Down with tyranny."

The outrageous nature of the June 2 bombings sent another wave of fear and anger across the nation, particularly after the Secret Service announced that they believed the same group of anarchists, mostly Italians, had sent the May Day bombs through the mail. Nor did federal spokesmen allay the panic. The Department of Justice declared the bombings to be part of an organized, nationwide conspiracy to overthrow the American government. A campaign had been launched, as one official put it, to start a "reign of terror in the United States." Attorney General Palmer, who had narrowly escaped death, said those "who can not or will not live the life of Americans under our institutions... should go back to the countries from which they came... we are determined now, as heretofore, that organized crime directed against organized government in this country shall be stopped."

On Wilson's orders, Palmer wasted little time. He beefed up the Justice Department, especially the Bureau of Investigation, whose General Intelligence Division was supervised by J. Edgar Hoover. This would set the scene for the notorious "Palmer raids" during the fall of 1919 and winter of 1920, in which more than three thousand aliens would undergo deportation proceedings, and eight hundred, including many anarchists, would be evicted from the country. While the raids were sweeping, often included abuses, and were carried out with "indifference to legality," according to Avrich, most Americans supported them. Bostonians concurred, especially when Boston police announced that the city was the nation's "Bolshevist headquarters" and that several Boston Italian anarchists were involved in the June 2 explosions in the other cities. Prior to the majority of the raids, though, in late June, anarchist leader Luigi Galleani was deported to Italy as scheduled, along with eight associates. The anarchist leader had escaped arrest when federal agents, after questioning other men, were unable to prove their suspicions that Galleani had orchestrated the June bombings.

Donnaruma condemned Wilson's poor decision making, from Fiume to Prohibition, plus his seeming inability to deal with the national unrest and violence, as detrimental to Italians and Americans in general. Lodge, though approaching seventy, presented an attractive alternative with his tough, plainspoken style, especially since Donnaruma had helped the senator mend fences with Italians.

"I do not agree with your statement . . . that you are too old to become a president," Donnaruma wrote to Lodge. "Your brains, your activity, your action, and your firmness [do] not prove that. It is the consensus of opinion that you are the brains of the United States Senate, and as long as we are of that opinion, why not then be the standard bearer of your party in order that all the people in the United States will be able to receive justice, and the long-advocated democracy?"

CHAPTER 15

Early on the morning of April 4, 1920, James Donnaruma boarded a train at Boston's South Station for a ten-day trip to New York City. Barely recovered from a heavy cold that he attributed to an exhausting schedule, Donnaruma believed his attendance at the Inter-Racial Council's National Conference on Immigration was far more important than a few extra days of recuperation to regain his full health.

He was not alone in his assessment. In a letter to Donnaruma, Coleman du Pont, the chairman of the council's board, said the conference's agenda items, including "present immigration and naturalization laws, the shortages of labor, the repressive and denunciatory attitude toward the foreign born, and economic questions," were all so vital that Donnaruma "cannot afford to be absent," especially when conference attendees would also discuss "the welfare of your race in America and abroad." W. H. Putnam, vice president of the American Association of Foreign Language Newspapers, wrote to Donnaruma to urge his attendance in New York, declaring that "your absence from this conference would be nothing short of a calamity." The Inter-Racial Council described itself as an influential group of "industrial, mercantile, and banking firms and corporations; members of racial groups; and individuals interested in immigrants and their adjustment to America."

As usual, Donnaruma had spent the previous months working to improve the welfare of Italians in Boston, following a harrowing second half of 1919. First, Henry Cabot Lodge had politely declined his invitation to run for president, a disappointing, though not unexpected response. "I quite appreciate your feelings in regard to the President [Wilson] and fully agree with you that he could have been of more real service by remaining in the United States and devoting some of this time at least to the many great domestic problems which confront us," Lodge replied to Donnaruma. While the senator was "greatly indebted" to Donnaruma's flattering invitation, and appreciated "all you so kindly say," Lodge said he was not a candidate for the presidency "and in fact, never have aspired to that high office."

Lodge's rejection signaled the beginning of a string of bad news in the months that followed. On September 9, the national spotlight again focused on Boston when nearly 1,400 Boston police officers went on strike after the 5:45 P.M. roll call, angry that their wage demands had not been met. That night, riots broke out across the city, and mobs smashed windows, looted more than fifty stores, and threw stones at picketing police officers. WAVE OF CRIME SWEEPS CITY, the *Boston Herald*'s headline shouted the next day. During a second night of rioting, three men were killed and another fifteen injured. In all, eight people died during the strike, seventy-five were injured or wounded, and an estimated $300,000 worth of property was stolen or destroyed. Mayor Andrew Peters called in the State Guard to restore order in downtown Boston and surrounding neighborhoods.

The unprecedented strike of public safety officers shocked the nation and drew angry denunciations. Massachusetts governor Calvin Coolidge blasted the striking policemen, saying "No man has a right to place his own ease or convenience or the opportunity of making money above his duty to the state." Speaking in Montana, an outraged President Wilson said that for the police force of a great city to go on strike, "leaving the city at the mercy of thugs, was a *crime against civilization.* The obligation of a policeman was as sacred and direct as the obligation of a soldier."

The Boston police walkout acted as a catalyst for steelworkers, who, on September 20, declared strikes against the major steel companies. More than 300,000 workers in Pittsburgh, Chicago, Cleveland, and Youngstown, Ohio, demanding higher wages and better working conditions, struck against Carnegie, Bethlehem, and U.S. Steel. Riots and violence broke out at several locations.

Then, in December, at about the same time renowned anarchists Emma Goldman and Alexander Berkman were being deported by the Justice Department, the U.S. Congress revived several pending bills designed to regulate the content of foreign-language newspapers. A concerned Donnaruma was assured by Frances Kellor, president of the American Association of Foreign Language Newspapers (AAFLN), that "none of these bills is to be passed." Still, to be on the safe side, Kellor added: "Nothing would make the foreign language press so strong as for them to voluntarily submit a bill for their own regulation and protection. Have you any suggestions along this line, as to the kind of provisions that might be included?"

Donnaruma, who argued against *any* censorship or regulations governing the foreign-language press, did not answer Kellor's letter, but likely questioned the strength of AAFLN's commitment to its membership.

The turbulence that shook Boston and the country during 1919 calmed in the early months of 1920, and Donnaruma plunged into his work on *La Gazzetta* while continuing to exert his leadership on causes to benefit Italians. Still irked that Prohibition had taken effect on January 17 after a one-year grace period since ratification, he channeled his energy into events he *could* control.

In March, he worked closely with the Instructive District Nursing Association (IDNA) on a fundraising effort to improve prenatal care for Italian women and reduce the high infant mortality rate in places such as the North End. IDNA volunteers collected money door to door in Boston neighborhoods and also collected at department stores, hotels, and North and South Stations. Donnaruma gathered a list of all doctors in the city who were either of Italian heritage or treated patients in the North End, urging them to contribute to a worthy cause and to spread the word about the IDNA initiative. He even threatened to quit the health effort if doctors did not participate. To Dr. Geraldino Balboni, he wrote: "You should take much more interest in the proposition than you have shown in the past. Unless you can show some interest in the matter and do part of the work, I shall be obliged to wash my hands of the whole matter . . . I am very busy and will not undertake to do the work alone."

Just as he departed for New York City and the immigration conference, Donnaruma received a request for more of his time and energy. The board of directors of the recently opened, archdiocese-managed Home for Italian Children asked Donnaruma to head up its fundraising campaign. The facility was established as an orphanage for Italian children who lost parents during World War I or in the influenza epidemic. Located on Centre Street in Jamaica Plain, the orphanage described itself as the "only monument of charity erected by Italians in Massachusetts." One fundraising letter said, "None can ever replace a father or mother, but the Franciscan Sisters come nearest to filling the vacancy left in the hearts of these orphans." Another slogan for the home stated: "Give until it hurts was a war-time slogan—Let us use it in peace-time for these little Victims of Fate." Donnaruma was forced to decline the early-April invitation to lead the fundraising, especially due to his involvement in the immigration conference, but he would continue his financial and editorial support of the Home for Italian Children for years to come. (Later, this facility would be renamed the Italian Home for Children to reflect its mission to serve children of all nationalities.)

His fight against regulations for foreign-language newspapers, the IDNA initiative to improve prenatal care among Italian women, the Inter-Racial Council's immigration conference, the request to lead fundraising for the Home for Italian Children—all of these consumed Donnaruma's time and energy, and illustrated his commitment to his people and their heritage. It was also his way of taking constructive action rather than allowing the destructive behavior of the anarchists, whose goals and tactics he fiercely opposed and resented, to define all Italians for the American population. The actions of a few anarchists increasingly influenced the government's and the elite's response to Italians in general. Congress continued to debate ways to make immigration even more restrictive, citing the rash of violence during the past several years.

News by and about anarchists continued to plague Italians. At around the same time that Donnaruma was helping IDNA's prenatal care effort among Italians, an anarchist named Andrea Salsedo, a Galleanist behind the rash of bombings in June of 1919, was arrested. Donnaruma could not know it in March, but Salsedo would be held and questioned for nearly two months by government agents. Incredibly, when agents left him alone for a few moments in early May, Salsedo would jump to his death from a fourteenth-story window. His fellow anarchists would protest and argue that Salsedo had first been beaten for information and, after he had divulged all he knew, had then been hurled from the window.

For Donnaruma, it was yet another example of anarchists in the news whose words and actions besmirched the reputations of honest, law-abiding Italians.

———

A week after the immigration conference, while Donnaruma was still enjoying a few days in New York, another crime took place in Massachusetts, this one in South Braintree, just a few miles south of Boston. On April 15, 1920, two employees of the Slater and Morrill Shoe Company were shot dead and robbed of the company's payroll in South Braintree. Two men armed with handguns did the shooting, and the killers were picked up by colleagues in a getaway car, escaping with more than $15,000.

Donnaruma was back in Boston on May 5, when police arrested the two anarchists Nicola Sacco and Bartolomeo Vanzetti for the murders. The pair gave false or evasive answers about their political beliefs and their whereabouts at the time of the shootings; both later protested vociferously that they believed they had been arrested for deportation purposes and had no inkling of the seriousness of the charges against them.

Nor did they or anyone else have an inkling of the uproar their arrest would cause. It would set in motion a series of events that would touch closely virtually every Italian in Boston and thousands of others around the world. It would also, in large measure, influence the Italian experience in America for years to come.

CHAPTER 16

On a chilly March 1, 1921, the SS *Cretic* steamed into the Port of Boston after a two-week voyage originating in Naples. Among the hundreds of passengers on board was my maternal grandfather, David Raffaele Mini-chiello, three months shy of his twenty-first birthday and less than one year after his discharge from the Italian army. Born and raised in the town of Grottaminarda in the province of Avellino, David Minichiello arrived in America with forty dollars in his pocket, literate in his own language and declaring his intention to remain "always" in the United States. He listed "laborer" as his occupation when questioned by immigration officials, and he told them he was planning to join his cousin in the North End once he entered the country.

My grandfather was one of more than 220,000 Italians who entered the United States in 1921, by far the largest number since 1914, and the last year Italian immigration would reach six figures. During the war, immigration declined each year, from 283,000 in 1914 to just below 50,000 in 1915, and all the way down to 5,200 in 1918. In 1919, the first postwar year, Italian immigration reached just 1,884 people. The following year, the number of arrivals from Italy rebounded to 95,000.

The large number of Italian immigrants in 1921 was not an accidental occurrence. Word had gotten back to Italy that the United States was preparing to impose strict and permanent country-by-country quotas; Italians feared that the doorway to America would either slam closed or remain open just a crack, which would mean lengthy waits as they tried to enter the country. Americans were weary of war, anarchist violence, the Red Scare, labor strife, and overcrowded urban neighborhoods (the 1920 census had confirmed that for the first time in American history greater numbers of people lived in cities than in rural areas), and their tolerance for an open immigration policy had reached its nadir by 1921.

In December of 1920, Senator Dillingham, now in his twilight years, had rejuvenated his proposal for national-origin quotas by introducing a bill to limit immigration to 3 percent of the number of each nationality in residence in 1910. When my grandfather arrived in the United States on March 1, the bill was being debated in Congress—it would pass overwhelmingly in May and be signed into law by newly elected president Warren G. Harding. Dillingham had presented his bill as a temporary one-year measure meant to curtail immigration to avert an oversupply of labor to America's depressed postwar industries. But the die had been cast, and the quotas had permanently reversed American immigration policy. As one historian described it: "America no longer welcomed 'huddled masses yearning to breathe free.' Instead, Progressive-era concepts of race, expounded in the Dillingham Commission's contention that national-origin predetermined the ability to assimilate, had been incorporated into law."

Moreover, he noted, the new quota laws were directed primarily toward Italians and other southern and eastern European immigrants, "the carriers of the contagion of radicalism."

Dillingham had filed his bill just two months after another shocking anarchist attack had struck the heart of a great American city.

After years of anarchist violence, and the previous year's arrest of Sacco and Vanzetti, America's patience for unrestricted immigration expired on September 16, 1920, when an anarchist bomb exploded at noontime on Wall Street in New York City. The blast killed forty-two innocent people and injured more than two hundred, mainly office workers who were streaming into the streets at lunch hour. More than $2 million worth of property was destroyed. The explosion originated on the north side of Wall Street in front of the Subtreasury Building and the U.S. Assay Office, directly across the street from the banking house of J. P. Morgan and an excavation site where the U.S. stock exchange was building an annex.

"[There was] a deafening blast," the Associated Press reported. "A moment later, scores of men, women, and children were lying prostrate on the ground and the streets were covered with debris from thousands of broken windows and torn facades of adjacent buildings. Ten minutes later, the stock and curb exchanges, the financial pulse of the world, had closed. Panic and confusion reigned in the heart of New York's financial district."

Thousands of office workers fled in terror from adjoining buildings; scores fell and were trampled in the rush. The noise of the explosion had been heard throughout lower Manhattan and across the river in Brooklyn "and brought thousands of the curious to the scene." Downtown hospitals went on full alert and makeshift medical stations were set up in the lobbies of nearby buildings, where nurses and doctors treated the less seriously injured.

Overnight, authorities launched a widespread investigation extending into every section of the country. Attorney General A. Mitchell Palmer called the blast "part of a gigantic plot" to overthrow the capitalist system. Extra guards were placed at all government buildings in Washington, D.C. William J. Flynn, chief of the Bureau of Investigation, went to New York the next day to oversee the investigation. He told the press that his agents had collected convincing evidence that the bombing was planned by a group of anarchists who perpetrated the "bomb outrages" of June 1919. The motive, Flynn believed, was revenge for the prosecution of Sacco and Vanzetti and for Salsedo's death earlier in the year, which Italian anarchists still insisted was not a suicide.

Among the evidence Flynn cited were several circulars found by a letter carrier in a mailbox on the corner of Cedar Street and Broadway, a few blocks from the scene, with the following message printed in red ink:

Remember. We will not tolerate any longer.
Free the political prisoners
or it will be sure death
for all of you.
American Anarchist Fighters

The message and signature convinced Flynn—most likely correctly—that Galleanists had been behind the Wall Street bombing. Later, Flynn announced that the anarchists had left the bomb in a horse-drawn wagon that they had hitched to a pole on Wall Street "with the timing device set a few minutes ahead." Three minutes later the bomb exploded. The horse and wagon were blown to bits.

A massive manhunt ensued. Detectives and federal agents visited nearly five thousand stables along the eastern seaboard in a vain effort to trace the horse, according to Paul Avrich. Police did find the maker of the horseshoes, a blacksmith in Manhattan's Little Italy section, "who recalled that the day before the explosion a [Sicilian] man had driven such a horse and wagon into his shop and had a new pair of shoes nailed to the hooves."

Though the bomber was never found, historian Paul Avrich has surmised that the Wall Street explosion was the work of Galleanist anarchist Mario Buda, a close comrade of Sacco and Vanzetti—"the best friends I had in America"—who believed he was striking a blow against America's financial power structure in retaliation for the September 11 murder indictments of his friends for the South Braintree killings. "[Yet] the victims of the blast," Avrich noted, "far from being the financial powers of the country, were mostly runners, stenographers, and clerks. Buda was surely aware that innocent blood might be spilled. He was a man, however, who stopped at nothing."

Avrich traced Buda's movements from New York to Providence, where the anarchist secured a passport from the Italian vice consul; a few weeks later he sailed back to Italy. By the end of November, he was back in his native Romagna, "never again to return to the United States."

Several days after the Wall Street bombing, Boston mayor Andrew Peters received a threatening letter, mailed from New York, accusing him of having the "blackest and yellowest" government in the country and warning him that he was being watched, and that a "better job" would be done in Boston than was done in New York. The letter was signed "The Reds." Peters turned the letter over to police but said he intended to take no special precautions to protect himself.

However, in Boston's financial district, Secret Service agents guarded federal buildings, including the subtreasury, the post office, the federal reserve bank, and the Internal Revenue offices. "The financial section of Boston is plentifully supplied with plainclothesmen and a large number of uniformed men are patrolling the streets of that district as a precautionary measure against attempted repetition of the New York bomb outrage here," the *Boston Herald* reported. Police officials gave orders for officers to act against "loiterers or suspicious looking persons or vehicles" and to examine any vehicle, "motor drawn or horse drawn that may have a suspicious aspect." Guards were also placed around the perimeter of the Massachusetts State House on Beacon Hill. Like New York, Boston was a city on alert against an enemy that was difficult to identify and one that could strike from almost anywhere, at any time.

The audacious midday Wall Street attack, the contempt for law and order, the brazen follow-up threats by the bomber, and law enforcement's conclusion that Italian anarchists had perpetrated the bombing all combined to convince Americans that tough new immigration restrictions were the only answer to stop the terror. It was the only way to properly screen who entered the country, and it was the best way to ensure that those immigrants already in the country would assimilate into American life without influence from new arrivals who might tempt them to revert to the old ways.

Two months after the Wall Street bombing, Americans also made it resoundingly clear that they wanted a new party occupying the White House.

My maternal grandfather arrived in the country just a few days before Republican Warren G. Harding delivered his inaugural address on March 4, 1921, flush from an overwhelming victory the previous November. Proving the pundits correct, Harding and his vice-presidential running mate, Massachusetts governor Calvin Coolidge, had swept into office, burying their Democrat opponent, Ohio governor James M. Cox. Harding amassed 404 electoral votes and won thirty-seven states, compared with Cox's 127 electoral votes and eleven states. The popular vote margin was even more impressive, 61 percent to 35 percent (Socialist Eugene V. Debs garnered 3 percent of the popular vote).

Moreover, Harding's coattails were long and their fabric sturdy. Republican congressmen and senators were elected across the country, and the GOP piled up a 150-vote majority in the House and a 22-vote majority in the Senate. "The Republican wave, still rising, has invaded rock-ribbed Southern and border States..." the *Boston Globe* reported. "It's an avalanche to Harding." The *Boston Herald* said the election returns "accentuate the stupendous overturn in government." Women, voting nationwide for the first time following the passage of the Nineteenth Amendment in

August of 1920, cast their ballots overwhelmingly for Harding, who was elected on his fifty-fifth birthday.

In Massachusetts, the Harding victory was even more impressive, thanks in part to the influence of the popular Coolidge, who won the admiration of voters for his leadership during the Boston police strike. Cox, the Democrat, carried only two small towns in the Bay State. Nearly 90 percent of Massachusetts's voters went to the polls, a full third of them women, and political experts estimated that about three-quarters of women voted for the Republican ticket. More than sixty thousand women cast ballots in the city of Boston alone, and Harding and Coolidge carried the capital city by a plurality of thirty thousand votes, the first time Boston had given a Republican a plurality since William McKinley in 1896.

To James Donnaruma's delight, Italians in Boston followed the state and national trends. Harding received 54 and 70 percent of the vote in East Boston and the North End, respectively, a backlash against the Democrats for Woodrow Wilson's failure to support Italy's claims on Fiume at the Paris peace conference.

In general, the stunning GOP victory was seen nationwide as a repudiation of Woodrow Wilson's policies and politics—especially his unflagging attempts to draw the United States into a League of Nations and his inability to stop anarchist violence. After eight years, America was experiencing fatigue with Democrat Progressives.

During his thirty-seven-minute inaugural address, Harding, the country's twenty-ninth president, spoke first on the topic closest to the hearts of most Americans: the sovereignty of the United States. He justified the country's decision not to participate in the League of Nations, which had become so closely associated with his predecessor, and which finally came into being without U.S. support on January 20, 1920.

Later in the speech, he addressed the violence America had experienced within its borders:

> I wish for an America no less alert in guarding against dangers from within than it is watchful against enemies from without . . .
> If revolution insists upon overturning established order, let other peoples make the tragic experiment. There is no place for it in

America…when revolution threatens we unfurl the flag of law and order and renew our consecration. Ours is a constitutional freedom where the popular will is the law supreme and minorities are sacredly protected. Our revisions, reformations, and evolutions reflect a deliberate judgment and an orderly progress, and we mean to cure our ills, but *never* destroy or permit destruction by force.

Four months later, on Thursday, July 14, 1921, at just before 8 P.M., the twelve members of the jury sitting in Dedham, Massachusetts, indicated to Judge Webster Thayer that they were ready to deliver their verdict in the case of the two anarchists charged with murder, Sacco and Vanzetti. In the six weeks that they had heard evidence on the South Braintree murders, jury members had developed a sense of camaraderie that would bind them together for the rest of their lives.

On this day, they would deliver a verdict that would resound across the world.

"Guilty to murder in the first degree," croaked the jury foreman when Thayer asked him for the verdict on first Sacco and then Vanzetti.

When he heard the words, Sacco shouted out: "*Sono innocente! Sono innocente!* They kill innocent men! Don't forget. Two innocent men they kill!" Vanzetti said nothing as he was led away by police officers.

The conviction of the two Italian immigrant anarchists, which could carry a death sentence, would spark a six-year global cause celebre that included mass demonstrations, letter-writing campaigns, political pleas, and legal appeals that would fill law libraries. Were Sacco and Vanzetti the deceitful, stone-cold killers the prosecution described, who were willing to resort to any crime to advance their anarchist beliefs and cause? Or were they two innocent men whose Italian immigrant status and anarchist activities made them easy targets for authorities looking to sate the passions of an inflamed public? Or was one guilty and the other innocent?

Boston Italians, who for the most part despised anarchists, overwhelmingly supported Sacco and Vanzetti during their lengthy appeals process between 1921 and 1926; they did not sympathize at all with the two men's anarchist cause, but they believed the convicted murderers sat on death row primarily because they were Italians. More than thirty years after the New Orleans lynchings, Italians saw the Sacco and Vanzetti case as the bookend example of unjust persecution against their countrymen.

For the most part, James Donnaruma disagreed with the majority of his fellow Italians on this issue. Despite the level of support for Sacco and Vanzetti, including the establishment of their defense fund in Boston, most of the articles he published in *La Gazzetta* were neutral reports on the developments of the case, with little commentary at first. When Donnaruma *did* begin editorializing on the front page, it was near the end, as Sacco and Vanzetti neared execution. Then, Donnaruma did not focus specifically on the justness of the verdict or the sentence, but criticized the turmoil caused by Sacco and Vanzetti's advocates; their behavior, Donnaruma argued, harmed and jeopardized the well-being of law-abiding, hardworking Italian Americans. Even anarchist violence abroad in support of Sacco and Vanzetti would hamper the progress Italians had made in the United States.

As Donnaruma explained in *La Gazzetta* in February of 1927, six months before Sacco and Vanzetti were executed: "Repetitions in European and South American countries of attacks upon official representatives of the United States by anarchists and fanatics who have seized upon the Sacco-Vanzetti case as an excuse for violence, may endanger the standings which law-abiding and respectable Italians have attained in America."

CHAPTER 17

On July 11, 1925, upon the dimly lit altar of Sacred Heart Church, the Reverend A. Lazzarin baptized my paternal grandparents' tenth child and their sixth boy, my father, Anthony, who was born on May 7. That the christening did not occur until a full two months after his birth was attributable to the continued large number of baptisms both Sacred Heart and St. Leonard's were performing on the children of immigrants, and in some cases on the grandchildren of immigrants. Combined, the two churches performed more than 1,500 baptisms in 1925, or nearly 30 per week—not as many as during the peak immigration years around 1910, but a substantial number nonetheless. A United States citizen at the moment of his birth, my father was the child of parents who had yet to seek citizenship despite nearly two decades in America, as was the case for more than 40 percent of the Italian born residents of Boston by the late 1920s. My paternal grandfather would declare his intention to become a citizen just two weeks after my father's baptism, yet five more years would elapse before he formally petitioned for citizenship in the two-step process, and another year would pass before he became a citizen in January of 1931.

Still, by the mid-1920s, my grandparents, their *paesani,* and Italians throughout Boston had developed strong commitments to their adopted homeland. Neighborhoods like the North End and East Boston still defined the Italian experience, to be sure—strength of family, devotion to religion, a priority on work—but residents were gradually learning to enjoy their Italian heritage within the context of being American. While the rate of citizenship hovered around 50 percent, for example, it was still significantly higher than the 38 percent level in 1920 and the 20 to 25 percent level ten years before that. Generally, the later Italians arrived in the United States, the quicker they applied for citizenship. My paternal grandfather, Calogero Puleo, who arrived in 1906, had not formally broached the issue of citizenship by the time of his tenth child's birth; my maternal grandfather, David Minichiello, who arrived in 1921, declared his intention to become a citizen on May 19, 1925, and obtained his citizenship on August 8, 1927, approximately one month before he married my grandmother, Rose Teta, at Our Lady of Mount Carmel Church in East Boston. My grandfather had promised my grandmother, who was born in America, and her family, that he would become a citizen before the marriage took place.

The general prosperity that followed World War I (except for the recession of 1920–21) and continued until late 1929 also bolstered the confidence of Italians as their economic status improved. By the time he applied for his citizenship in 1925, my grandfather Minichiello had become a talented shoemaker, just four years after describing himself as an unskilled laborer when he entered the country. My grandfather Puleo worked as a laborer for more than twenty years in America, yet when he petitioned for citizenship in 1930, he was an entrepreneur, a fruit dealer, working for himself, selling tomatoes, bananas, cucumbers, and other produce from his own pushcart. My grandfathers' experiences were typical of Italian heads of household during the 1920s; the North End and other Italian enclaves were still considered poor and their gains modest, but economic conditions had improved dramatically when compared with the period prior to the Great War. While a full 50 percent of Italians worked as laborers as the war began, that number dipped to about 30 percent just fifteen years later. By the late 1920s, Italians worked in increasing numbers as chauffeurs, clerks, mechanics, carpenters, painters, plasterers, and masons.

Other changes were afoot among Boston Italian families, and many of those were driven by the children of immigrants. Unlike their mothers, for example, the daughters of Italian immigrants began entering the workplace in large numbers in downtown Boston, particularly in the garment district, where they worked as seamstresses. During the 1920s, according to one historian, Italian women became the largest single group in the "needle" trades, having displaced Jewish women. Young Italian women also began to take part in North End library clubs, where they would read, discuss American civic affairs, learn needlepoint and pottery, and occasionally study music. While just under one in five Italians living in the North End by 1925 still could not speak English, more and more Italian immigrants were enrolled in English classes; in a shift that epitomized the increasing

A view of the North End from the Custom House Tower (1930). *(Photo by Leslie Jones. Courtesy of the Boston Public Library, Print Department)*

Americanization of Italians, Donnaruma introduced two English pages to *La Gazzetta* during the mid-1920s when he expanded the paper from four to eight pages.

Not all the changes were without tension. The 1920s saw a shift in attitudes within Italian families, as the oldest children of immigrants often clashed with their parents. In many cases, in the words of Leonard Covello, children were ashamed of their parents' Old Country customs, their struggle to speak even passable English, their outmoded dress, their desire to preserve *la via vecchia*—the old way—even as they assimilated into American culture. As late as the 1920s, many Italian parents still insisted that their children drop out of school once they reached the compulsory age of fourteen so they could work and contribute to the family income. In Boston, school attendance among Italian students plummeted as children grew older, according to scholar Gloria Speranza. Through eighth grade, about 85 percent of Italian children attended school; by age sixteen, Italian school attendance dropped off to only about 16 percent. As one Italian woman described it: "I had just completed the eighth grade at Paul Revere School when my parents decided it was time I quit school. I just cried when they told me. I loved math and reading and was an honor student." Italian immigrant children, who were often subjected to ostracism and discrimination, knew that being forced to drop out of school would only isolate them more, make them seem more "different" in the eyes of American children.

Older children of immigrants, now young adults themselves, also rebelled to some extent; most respected their parents but many believed the older folks hindered their acceptance into American society. Some, certainly not all, changed names by shortening them or eliminating vowels. Others Anglicized both first and last names. "Tommassini became Thomas and Lombardi became Lombard," historian Andrew Rolle noted. In his novel *Family on Vendetta Street,* novelist Lucas Longo described an Italian American doctor who changed his name from Bentolinardo to Bentley when he received his medical degree, and the pained reaction of his father:

> Doctor Bentolinardo. How many years his father had waited for his son to gain that title. All his life he had worked with one [building contractor] firm . . . he used to arrive early on the job, a half hour before, so that the bosses would never find fault, never fire him, and always send him out on the new jobs. He needed the money to pay for his son's education. Sacrifice was his daily bread —but he did it willingly, to work to save a few pennies. Some on the job—not Italians—seeing the oil seeping through his brown paper lunch bag, called it dago grease . . .
>
> Bentley. When the old man saw that gold-lettered shingle hanging out off the building . . . his whole being buckled. Dr. Bentley! He couldn't read English, but that betrayal he could read. All the letters weren't there . . . He wept like a baby, and called his son a traitor. He returned [to] his street crying. Some, trying to ease his ache, lied, saying: "The printer is to blame . . . the stupid printer who made the sign is to blame . . . not your boy . . . your boy, the doctor, he loves you . . . but that printer—how does he know to spell these long involved Italian names . . .

His son the doctor called on a patient who lived on [his father's] street. "I don't want to hurt my father. But he's unreasonable. I had to change my name to feel right...I know he's my father, but I can't live the way he has lived.."...

He didn't trust anyone any more, that poor old man. He ripped his name out of the mailbox. He never opened a window. Missed Mass. Did not care what happened...shut himself off completely. "Sick I went to work. With fever. I saved every penny. For him. My Ralph. And how does the traitor pay me back? With a new name. I am Bentolinardo. This new Bentley—who knows him? God, do you?"

This natural conflict occurred as the children of immigrants sought to get ahead. In seeking advancement, they became active outside the Italian ethnic group. They developed interests their parents did not accept or understand. Many refused to learn Italian, and others became hostile or indifferent to virtually everything else their parents held dear. "Too often the acquisition of American ways bred in the second generation a contempt for Italian origins that brought sadness to parents," wrote historian Alexander DeConde. "Sometimes the children came to despise the ways of their fathers, to lose any love of Italy they might have had, and to abandon their pride in being Italian." Anglicizing their names and repudiating their Old Country heritage, DeConde contends, helped second-generation Italian Americans avoid discrimination "and gain acceptance in the larger American community."

As Italian immigrants began to feel more comfortable in America and as Americans, and their children sought *la nuova via*—the new way—as a means of establishing their own identities, each group coped and often thrived without the pressure of additional waves of immigrants flooding their neighborhoods and enclaves. The immigration restrictions the country implemented in 1921 became even more stringent with the passage of the Johnson-Reed United States Immigration Act of 1924.

Whereas the 1921 law set the European quotas at 3 percent of a given nationality as of the 1910 census, Johnson-Reed reduced them to 2 percent

A youngster enjoys a five-cent hot dog at the corner of Hanover and Blackstone streets in the North End in 1937. *(Photo by Leslie Jones. Courtesy of the Boston Public Library, Print Department)*

of a nationality's foreign-born population as recorded in the census of 1890, a time when the United States had far fewer foreign-born residents from the "new immigrant" countries such as Italy and Greece. "It is true that 75 percent of our immigration will hereafter come from northwestern Europe; but it is fair that it should do so, because 75 percent of us who are now here owe our origin to immigrants from those same countries," wrote Republican senator David A. Reed of Pennsylvania, one of the bill's cosponsors, in the *New York Times*.

Italian advocacy groups, including the Boston Committee Against Unfair Restricted Immigration, fought tirelessly against Johnson-Reed to no avail. In his letter to James Donnaruma asking for his support in opposing the new quota law, the committee chairman, attorney Saverio Romano of Hanover Street, wrote: "The propaganda against Italian immigrants has been carried on for so long, and so persistently, and it has been so vile, that it is absolutely incumbent upon us at this time to reject the insults heaped upon our race, and that should be done in such a manner that they will never forget it." The Boston organization launched a petition drive aimed at Congress and invited Donnaruma to meet with groups of senators and representatives in Washington, but nagging health problems prevented Donnaruma from making the trip.

In its February 4 report on the trip, the committee recognized the futility of its Washington lobbying efforts: "The consensus of opinion . . . was that our mission was doomed to failure, and that the . . . bill was bound to be enacted into law." This despite the fact that Massachusetts senator Henry Cabot Lodge "admitted that, from outward appearances, it seems as if [the bill] intended to discriminate against Italians . . . the Senator assured us that he would call the Immigration Committee's attention to that feature." The Boston visitors were appeased by Lodge's reassurances that "he did not understand the injury [this] bill would cause us," reporting that the "cordiality and warmth of the reception" Lodge gave them "created in us a feeling that the justice of our cause has been recognized by the most important personage in Washington, excepting the President."

On May 26, 1924, Johnson-Reed passed overwhelmingly, and it also preserved previous immigration laws; all immigrants would have to be eligible not only under the quota law, but under all earlier legislation. The net result was the end of open-door immigration to America. Italian immigration dropped from just over 56,000 in 1924 to a mere 6,200 in 1925 and 8,200 in 1926.

Johnson-Reed defined America's new immigration policy and would govern the admittance of immigrants to the United States for the next forty years.

The passage of Johnson-Reed was part of a two-year roller-coaster ride for James Donnaruma. He had begun 1924 digging his way out of financial difficulty, the result of his constant assistance to Italians who had run afoul of the law, coupled with his sponsorship of an unsuccessful wrestling match between two Italian fighters. "I have had an immense lot of trouble," he wrote to his friend Jerry Longobardi. "[I was] very much convinced that I was to make no less than $10,000 profit. Everybody, both Americans and Italians, believed the very same thing." Instead, Donnaruma said, he had lost nearly $2,000 on the match, new debt piled atop of $5,000 he already owed for helping "many friends who happen to be in the toils of the police," men who were out on parole or needed bail money, mostly for nonviolent or petty crimes. In May of 1923, he was "without a cent to get along with," he lamented to Longobardi, though by mid-July he had "reduced a certain amount of expenses" and believed that within the next six months he would "be in a better position."

A month later, on August 2, 1923, Donnaruma and the rest of the country learned that President Warren Harding had died at the Palace Hotel in San Francisco, a president whose health and administration had been debilitated by the Teapot Dome scandal. Donnaruma reacted to Harding's death with appropriate reverence but made no pretense of his disappointment in the failures of the man he had supported for president. In addition to the scandal, the Harding administration had all but turned its back on Italians on the important issue of patronage jobs. "Not a single position of any importance [has been] given to any man or woman of Italian extraction," Donnaruma complained to Henry Cabot Lodge. Even Woodrow Wilson, whom Donnaruma disliked intensely, "played the game very well by recognizing the Italian element."

Harding's vice president, former Massachusetts governor Calvin Coolidge, a friend of Donnaruma's, assumed the presidency in August of 1923 and on November 4, 1924, was elected president in his own right. His trouncing of Democrat John W. David of West Virginia and Progressive Robert LaFollette of Wisconsin took some of the sting out of the passage of Johnson-Reed earlier in the year. Donnaruma urged his Italian readers to vote for Coolidge, citing his support for business and continued economic prosperity, arguing that a Republican administration would be most likely to overturn the hated Prohibition amendment, and reminding readers again that it was a Democratic president who had refused to place Fiume under Italian sovereignty at the end of World War I. Yet, despite Coolidge's overall easy victory—he won 382 electoral votes and 54 percent of the popular vote compared with Davis, his closest opponent, who garnered 136 electoral votes and 29 percent of the popular vote—Italians did not heed Donnaruma's call. Coolidge won only 33 percent of the Italian American vote in East Boston and just under 39 percent in the North End, a reflection of Italians' disappointment in the Harding years, and a harbinger of their strong future support for Democrats.

Though disappointed with the Italian vote, Donnaruma was pleased with Coolidge's election. However, his elation was dampened just five days later, when his friend, Senator Henry Cabot Lodge, died in Cambridge, Massachusetts, at the age of seventy-four. Though much of Lodge's influence had waned by 1924, his friends and colleagues remembered him for his lengthy public service and his vast contributions to the Republican Party. Twenty-four states sent delegates to his funeral at Mount Auburn Cemetery in Cambridge. "He was not loved, as a general rule, but he was respected for courage and large ability," noted one obituary writer. "He was a force—greatly dangerous or greatly helpful, as the view went—as well as a figure. He was individual. He was Henry Cabot Lodge."

Donnaruma does not record Lodge's 1924 death in his personal papers, but, as the *La Gazzetta* editor turned the page on his fiftieth birthday, it is not hard to imagine that the combination of his financial difficulties and health problems, coupled with the loss of his friend, produced a sense of melancholy and wistfulness about his own future and his own mortality.

CHAPTER 18

Charles Lindbergh's remarkable solo flight from New York to Paris and Yankee Babe Ruth's stunning drive toward sixty home runs in a single season captivated Americans in 1927; sandwiched between these two unprecedented achievements was the powerful international uproar generated by the impending doom of two anarchists imprisoned in Boston.

After seven years with the world's eyes trained upon it, Boston's Italian community held its collective breath and prayed for a miracle in the Sacco and Vanzetti case as midnight drew nigh on August 22, 1927. Boston's Charlestown prison, surrounded by eight hundred police, its walls and catwalks lined with machine guns and searchlights, was eerily silent shortly after 11 P.M. The streets around the prison had been roped off for a half mile and those who lived within the area were ordered to stay indoors.

Across the Charles River, crowds gathered on the Boston Common across from the State House, their eyes focused on the lights burning in the governor's office.

Inside the prison, the warden walked into the death house, where Nicola Sacco was writing a letter and Bartolomeo Vanzetti was pacing in his cell. "I am sorry," the warden said, "but it is my painful duty to inform you that you have to die tonight." Vanzetti whispered in reply: "We must bow to the inevitable."

A seven-year legal battle to stop Sacco and Vanzetti's execution had failed. In May of 1926, the Supreme Judicial Court of Massachusetts upheld their convictions and denied their motions for a new trial. Just two weeks earlier, on August 10, 1927, U.S. Supreme Court justice Oliver Wendell Holmes denied a request that he stay the executions, ruling that the case was a state, not a federal, matter. The Supreme Court denied a final petition on August 20.

Earlier this day, demonstrations protesting the executions had taken place across the country and in cities around the world. More than a hundred armed police officers surrounded the U.S. Capitol building in Washington, D.C., guarding against violence. In Worcester, Massachusetts, sixty miles west of Boston, a courthouse in which Sacco-Vanzetti trial judge Webster Thayer was presiding over an unrelated criminal case was patrolled by armed troopers. In Paris, a general strike had halted traffic and the American embassy was ringed with tanks to protect it from rioters. Large protests had also taken place in England, Switzerland, Germany, Italy, Portugal, Australia, Argentina, and South Africa, all to no avail. The overwhelming majority of Italians in Boston and across the United States supported the two condemned men.

But there would be no miracles on this night.

Shortly after midnight, Massachusetts governor Alvan T. Fuller left the State House, unswayed by a bombardment of last-minute pleas to intervene and spare the two Italian anarchists, including a long, tearful visit by Sacco's wife and Vanzetti's sister. "Good night, gentlemen," he said as he passed through the group of waiting newspapermen gathered outside a now darkened State House. Fuller's decision not to intervene meant that the execution could not be stopped—Sacco and Vanzetti were now out of options.

At half past midnight, the morning of August 23, 1927, Sacco was strapped into the electric chair in the Charlestown prison, shouted, "Long live anarchy!" and then said quietly, "Farewell, my wife and child and all my friends." The warden nodded and electricity surged through Sacco's body.

Moments later, Vanzetti was led into the death chamber. He said softly: "I wish to say that I am innocent. I have never done a crime, some sins, but never any crime. I am an innocent man." With that he shook hands with the warden and the guards and took his place in the chair. "I now wish to forgive some people for what they are doing to me," Vanzetti said. He was dead minutes later.

The next afternoon, medical examiner Dr. George Burgess Magrath performed the legally required autopsies on Sacco and Vanzetti. For several days, the bodies of the two anarchists lay in state at the Langone Funeral Home in Boston's North End, where thousands of people, Italians and non-Italians alike, visited to offer their respects.

On Sunday, August 28, thousands more congregated in the North End Playground on Commercial Street to take part in an eight-mile funeral procession across the city to Forest Hills Italian Cemetery. More than 200,000 people thronged the route to pay tribute to the two Italian anarchists, "one of the most tremendous funerals of modern times—a gigantic cortege that marched over streets strewn with flowers," reported the *Boston Globe*. "Never in this history of Boston has there been a demonstration quite like it." The funeral dwarfed that of George Scigliano two decades earlier.

Sacco and Vanzetti were cremated shortly afterward, and with a few isolated exceptions, the anarchist movement in Boston, and in America, died with them.

But, convinced that the two men would have been spared had their ethnic backgrounds been different, Boston Italians would honor their memories for years to come.

Pallbearers prepare for the funeral of Sacco and Vanzetti, whose funeral procession on Sunday, August 28, 1927, began at the Langone Funeral Home in the North End. The two anarchists had been executed days earlier, after their conviction for the 1920 murders of two payroll employees of the Slater and Morrill Shoe Company in South Braintree, Massachusetts. *(Courtesy of Pam Donnaruma and the* Post-Gazette*)*

———

While the Sacco and Vanzetti case drew international attention and news coverage to Boston and its Italian community, the 1920s marked a period of events and changes that occurred with somewhat less fanfare but carried great importance for Italians.

In the first year of the decade, charismatic and colorful con man Charles Ponzi bilked Italian and non-Italian investors out of millions of dollars before he was caught; he garnered headlines across the city and his "scheme" would become forever ensconced in the parlance of American financial circles to describe a scam or swindle.

In 1923, more than ten thousand people witnessed the opening of a new commercial airport in East Boston that would transform Boston into an international aviation and economic center. Years after it was named for a prominent Boston soldier, Lieutenant General Edward Lawrence Logan, the airport, in addition to promoting commerce and passenger travel, would also generate enough noise, congestion, and controversy to disrupt and mobilize the nearby Italian community as they sought to maintain their quality of life.

And in April of 1925, the judge hearing the enormous civil lawsuit in the case of the Commercial Street molasses flood found the company that owned the steel tank liable and awarded damages to 119 Italian immigrants and Irish city workers who were injured, and to the families of those who were killed. The landmark decision was the first of its kind against a large industrial corporation, and its repercussions would ripple across the nation. The case apparently served as a wake-up call for Italian immigrants to seize control of their own neighborhood; applications for citizenship increased dramatically after the Great Boston Molasses Flood class-action suit was decided.

Each of these events generated headlines, and each affected Italians in Boston. Ponzi, Logan Airport, and the molasses flood would become meaningful pieces of Boston Italian history in the 1920s, and they would influence Italian political and social behavior for many years.

Yet none of these would compare with the impact of another major de-velopment in the 1920s, one spawned, fed, and bloated by two seemingly unrelated developments: Prohibition and Mussolini's rise to power in Italy.

It would attach itself like a cancer to Italian American communities across the country for decades, even to the present day, always lurking, threatening to tear down and devour the reputations of the millions of decent, honest, hardworking people who formed the vast heart and soul of one of America's major ethnic groups.

This development was the meteoric rise of the organized crime syndicates, which would later become better known to Americans as *la cosa nostra* (translated as "our thing") or, simply, the Mafia.

Organized crime had existed in America's Italian community for years, most notably *La Camora* and the Black Hand organizations that George Scigliano had railed against during his lifetime. In Boston, Gaspare Messina started the first "crime family" in 1916, controlling a number of black-market and other illegal activities.

Yet, it was not until the unlikely combination of Mussolini's Fascist crackdown against Mafia chiefs in Southern Italy in the early 1920s and the passage of the Prohibition amendment in the United States that Italian organized crime gained the momentum it needed to thrive. Mafia dons fled to the United States, and often brought their lieutenants with them. The United States's prohibition against legally producing and selling alcohol provided these men with an easy way to raise enormous sums of money on the black market, and do it with a product that Americans demanded. Bootleggers and rum runners were technically criminals but few Americans viewed them as such, which made their movements and activities all the more difficult for law enforcement officials to stop. Add to this the sea of cash that was available for payoffs and bribes of police and politicians, and it is not difficult to understand why the syndicates grew so powerful during the 1920s.

Of course, not all organized crime was controlled by Italians. In Boston, in fact, by the time Sicilian immigrant Filippo "Phil" Buccola succeeded Messina as the kingpin of the Italian crime family, the Irish and Jewish mobs were also fighting for control over bootlegging, as well as gambling, loansharking, and prostitution. Frankie Wallace ran the Irish underworld in South Boston with an iron fist, and Charles "King" Solomon reigned over the Jewish rackets, managing perhaps the largest liquor, vice, and narcotics smuggling syndicates in New England. Buccola's men assassinated Wallace in the North End in 1931, and Irish gangsters took credit for gunning down Solomon outside Boston's Cotton Club two years later. This cleared the way for the Italian mob to gain the upper hand and expand and prosper over the next several decades.

Nationally, during the 1920s and 1930s, many non-Italians controlled organized crime syndicates, men like Meyer Lansky and Benjamin "Bugsy" Siegel, yet it was the Italians who seemed to capture more imaginations and headlines by the sheer force of their personalities, gangsters like Al Capone in Chicago and Frank Costello and Charles "Lucky" Luciano in New York. Even after Prohibition ended in 1933, the Italian-run syndicates more than made up for the millions of dollars that no longer flowed in from the sale of illicit liquor by profiting from gambling, loansharking, racketeering, and the expansion of narcotics trafficking. "During the 1930s, when the nation as a whole suffered the effects of the worst depression in its history, the syndicates operated on a business-as-usual basis," one historian noted.

The rise of the Italian Mafia and the publicity it received perpetuated the stereotypes that had plagued law-abiding Italians since their arrival in the United States. An American public that identified them as criminals during the Black Hand's heyday in the first decade of the twentieth century, and as violent radicals when the anarchist movement reached its peak in 1919, once again questioned the honesty of ordinary Italian Americans. In her master's thesis, Sara Jean Reilly noted the dilemma of the "ninety-nine percent of the Italians" during the 1920s who were "obedient, laborious, and the best of citizens" but who were "trapped" by the perception of an American public that both glorified and feared Italian gangsters and "ignored the law-abiding Italian."

Like the anarchists before them, the gangsters helped stall and stunt the full acceptance of Italians into American society, even as the 1930s approached.

CHAPTER 19

The worst kind of tragedy that parents can suffer struck James and Florence Donnaruma in late February of 1928—the death of a child.

Donnaruma's second son, Arthur, died at age twenty at the Massachusetts Homeopathic Hospital on Harrison Avenue, after a long illness that his father does not specify in his letters to friends. Arthur's death devastated James Donnaruma and paralyzed him with grief. "The loss has been such a severe shock for me that I cannot get over it very easily," he wrote to his friend Frank Dane, who was serving time in a Virginia jail for organizing an illegal boxing exhibition. Donnaruma had spent time in Washington, D.C., trying to secure Dane's release, but Arthur's death forced him to suspend his efforts. "It has taken away from me all my fighting spirit and I am not in a position now to start the proper work in your behalf," he said. "I will, however, perform my duty just as soon as I shall be myself again." Arthur's death came on the heels of additional financial troubles for Donnaruma, "placing me in a position where I have been unable to move," he wrote to Dane. "Why I didn't have a breakdown is surprising to me."

Throughout the 1920s, Donnaruma helped others, extending himself emotionally and financially, using his influence and reputation to help Italians obtain citizenship and avoid deportation, secure jobs, avoid prison, and obtain parole or pardons if Donnaruma believed they were innocent or their sentences too harsh. He wrote feverishly to city and state officials, the governor, and parole boards on behalf of friends and colleagues. He spent his own money, sometimes to his detriment, to assist fellow Italians who lost jobs or encountered bad luck, or whose families suffered illnesses and needed a doctor's care or hospitalization. Donnaruma undertook and accomplished all of this without missing a single issue of *La Gazzetta*.

But Arthur's death broke his heart and his spirit. With the exception of a few exchanges with Frank Dane, he remained subdued and relatively silent for the remainder of 1928, even insofar as the November presidential election was concerned. While *La Gazzetta* supported Republican Herbert Hoover, there is scant evidence that Donnaruma became involved on a personal grassroots level.

Had he done so, he likely would have expressed great frustration with his fellow Boston Italians. Nationally, Hoover trounced Alfred E. Smith of New York, the first Roman Catholic to be nominated for president by a major party, by a total of 444 electoral votes to 77, garnering nearly 60 percent of the popular vote, to that point one of the biggest majorities in the history of the Republican Party.

Among Boston Italians, though, Smith's Catholicism was an attribute too endearing to resist. He carried nearly 93 percent of the East Boston vote and almost 95 percent of the North End, among the highest vote totals he received anywhere in the country.

On January 26, 1931, nearly a full quarter century after he passed through the gates of Ellis Island, my paternal grandfather, Calogero Puleo, became a United States citizen. The forty-eight-year-old fruit dealer, married and the father of ten children, was listed as five feet, five inches tall and weighing 145 pounds. His "race" was identified as Southern Italian. A court officer had written "lacks education in English" in purple ink across his certificate of citizenship. Two North End *paesani,* Nicola Cesso, a street cleaner, and John Raso, another fruit peddler, served as my grandfather's witnesses, each swearing that they had known him since 1920. This concluded the citizenship process that he had begun with the filing of his declaration of intention in July of 1925, two months after his tenth child, my father, was born.

In the spring of that year, to mark the pride of the occasion, all twelve members of the Puleo family posed for a photo in a studio on Little Prince Street; my father, then six, clutched a small American flag and huddled close to my grandfather, the new citizen.

Also that spring, on May 19, my maternal grandparents, David and Rose Minichiello, celebrated the birth of their second child, another daughter. My mother, Rosina, or Rose, was born six weeks premature in the home her parents rented in Everett, a small city near Boston. But my grandparents' joy was short-lived and quickly turned to heartrending loss.

Certificate of citizenship for the author's paternal grandfather, Calogero Puleo.
He became a citizen in 1931, twenty-five years after his arrival in the United States
from Sciacca, Sicily. (*Courtesy of the author*)

My mother was a twin, born first; her sister, named Christine after my
grandmother's mother, followed shortly after, struggled for each breath
once she arrived in the world, and died less than twenty-four hours after
her birth. My mother's older sister, Mary, then not yet three years old, remembered years later Christine's small white coffin that sat atop my grandmother's sewing machine table during the brief, but sorrowful, home wake
that followed. Neither of my grandparents spoke much about their daughter's death in the years that followed. It was yet another of life's hardships
to overcome and move beyond.

Angela and Calogero Puleo and David Minichiello had cleared many
other hurdles to make America their home: leaving their beloved small
towns in Italy, enduring the misery of a transatlantic passage in steerage,
suffering the pain of stereotyping and discrimination, engaging in backbreaking labor, carving out a life in an unfamiliar and crowded urban set-

ting. Yet, they and thousands of other Boston Italians also experienced the contentment of sharing their new life with *paesani,* the warmth of the neighborhood enclave, the pride in saving money, starting a business, or buying a home.

America was hard, but she offered something Italy never could—the hope, perhaps even the promise, of a better future.

As 1931 drew to a close, the Puleos, the Minichiellos, and all Boston Italians would find their faith in that promise severely tested. If they believed they had survived all the hardships and cleared every hurdle America had placed in their path, they were mistaken.

With little warning or time for preparation, Boston Italians and Americans of all nationalities and geographic regions were about to come face to face with the Great Depression.

PART 5

BECOMING AMERICANS: *The* GREAT DEPRESSION *and* WORLD WAR II

In December of 1931, charismatic Boston mayor James Michael Curley presided over an unusual ceremony on the waterfront. To promote the city's efforts to provide relief to the legions of Boston's unemployed through an emergency assistance fund, Curley ordered his minions to place an effigy labeled "General D. Pression" in a coffin, and paraded it through Boston streets to Battery Wharf. There, "to the accompaniment of tap-dancing chorus girls and a brass band blaring 'Happy Days are Here Again,'" the coffin was lowered into a ferry boat for "burial" in Boston Harbor. As Curley pushed the boat from the wharf, the mayor declared that General D. Pression was "well buried for all time."

Boston residents must have viewed Curley's publicity stunt as an act of desperation. The Depression was now entering its third winter. While the stock market crash of October 29, 1929, "Black Tuesday," had not caused the economic blight that was devouring the United States, it had marked the beginning of the downward spiral that had sown fear in the urban neighborhoods, the mill towns, and the family farms across America. The numerous macro forces that had conspired to bring on the Depression—the crash of the equity markets, speculative investments, overextension of credit, unequal distribution of wealth, a poorly managed banking system, overproduction, the collapse of the farming apparatus—were now extending their choking tentacles into the kitchens and living rooms of ordinary Americans. "In towns and cities across the country," one historian wrote, "haggard men in shabby overcoats, collars turned up against the chill wind, newspapers plugging the holes in their shoes, lined up glumly for handouts at soup kitchens." Tens of thousands of displaced workers, whose factories or manufacturing plants had closed, took to the roads or the rails, hitching west, or huddling in boxcars traveling south or east, wherever there might be a job. "Those who stayed put," one writer noted, "hunkered down, took in their jobless relatives, kited the grocery bills at the corner store, patched up their old clothes, darned and redarned their socks, tried to shore up some fragments of hope against the ruins of their dreams."

In the eleven months since my Grandfather Puleo became a United States citizen, in the six months since my mother's birth, economic conditions had become frightful. Steel makers, automobile manufacturers, and mining companies had laid off thousands of workers, and thousands more who remained on the payroll saw their hours cut drastically. Nearly thirty thousand banks had failed since 1930, credit dried up, farms collapsed, police and firemen endured payless paydays. By the end of 1931, unemployment had climbed to eight million, and in a few months, that number would rise to twelve million, more than 20 percent of the American labor force, figures never before (or since) approached in American history. "In the minds of the average American," historian Gerald W. Johnson wrote, "1931 was the year of the Great Depression, for it was in the past 12 months that it really affected us who are just ordinary people." Up until then, the economic woes had been mainly limited to "international bankers, financiers . . . great executives . . . and derelicts who are chronically on the verge of unemployment in all years." Even those "great executives" who were too rich to be harmed by economic hardship experienced some of the fear of the financial ruin around them; J. P. Morgan, for example, decided to keep his yacht docked for a while. "It seems very unwise to let the *Corsair* come out this summer," he wrote to a friend in October of 1931. "There are so many suffering from lack of work, and even from actual hunger, that it is both wiser and kinder not to flaunt such luxuriant amusement in the face of the public."

If Morgan fantasized about hordes of the poor and the destitute storming the *Corsair,* he needn't have worried. Up until this point, Americans, though fearful and worried, were "by no means in despair," Johnson observed. "We do not believe for a moment that the hard times are going to continue . . . Nineteen thirty-one was a hard year, but it saw no bayonets, heard no firing in the streets, afforded no hint of the dissolution of our institutions . . . under the most terrific strain to which it has been subjected since Gettysburg, the Republic stands unshaken." Other historians also offered voices of hope. "I do not wish to minimize the extreme seriousness of the present situation," wrote James Tuslow Adams in the October 1931 issue of *Reader's Digest*, "but . . . when we compare the situation today . . . in relation to previous great depressions, I think we may say that, instead of giving way to despair, we have considerable cause for thankfulness."

Even as Adams wrote, cities were depleting their relief money and families were running out of food. Jobs and paychecks were disappearing, and in immigrant enclaves in cities across the country, "communities so shallowly rooted in American soil," such as Boston's North End and East Boston, "the Depression struck with especially harsh fury," wrote historian David Kennedy. "The frail institutions so painstakingly erected by the first immigrant generation simply fell apart." Banks serving immigrant neighborhoods were among the first to close when panic intensified. Mutual benefit societies and religious welfare organizations, "with which immigrants had tried to defend themselves against the abundant uncertainties of everyday life, collapsed under the weight of the demands now put upon them."

By early 1932, Americans in cities and rural areas alike were looking in vain to Washington, at least for relief for the unemployed. President Herbert Hoover remained philosophically opposed to the federal government undertaking such a widespread and all-encompassing effort. Private charities and local relief efforts, like Mayor Curley's Boston relief initiative, were Hoover's idea of assisting the poor and unemployed, not new federal programs. In addition, Hoover continued to espouse faith in the private economy's resilience and predicted a rebound that would pull the country out of depression.

Meanwhile, in New York State, Governor Franklin Delano Roosevelt had publicly endorsed government-sponsored unemployment insurance and old-age pensions. He declared that relief "must be extended by Government, not as a matter of charity, but as a matter of social duty." Roosevelt told New Yorkers that "the State accepts the task cheerfully because it believes that it will help restore that close relationship with its people which is necessary to preserve our democratic form of government."

In adjacent Massachusetts, as in states and cities across the country, even as they struggled to feed their families and keep a roof over their heads, even as inaction seemed to paralyze President Hoover, Italians and Americans of all nationalities heard Governor Roosevelt's pronouncements.

As the nation's economic crisis deepened and 1932 wore on, they continued to listen to his message.

With help from Boston Italians, Democrat Franklin D. Roosevelt overwhelmed Herbert Hoover in the November 8, 1932, presidential election, winning 472 electoral votes to Hoover's 59, and capturing 57 percent of the popular vote. Only Connecticut, Delaware, Maine, New Hampshire, Vermont, and Pennsylvania voted for Hoover; the other forty-two states went for Roosevelt. While James Donnaruma again supported the Republican candidate, there is little in his personal papers, or in the pages of *La Gazzetta,* to suggest that he did so enthusiastically. It mattered little; East Boston's Italian Americans cast nearly 95 percent of their ballots for Roosevelt, while just over 93 percent of North End Italians voted for FDR. The Republican campaign-button slogan "Play Safe with Hoover" must have seemed a cruel hoax to Americans standing in bread lines, while Roosevelt's "Happy Days Are Here Again" captured his spirit of confidence and provided voters with a glimmer of hope.

Bostonians and their fellow Americans had grown weary of Hoover throughout 1932. His stubborn resistance to providing federal relief to the unemployed isolated him from the people. "Cartoonists . . . routinely caricatured him as a dour, heartless skinflint whose rigid adherence to obsolete doctrines caused men and women to go jobless and hungry," wrote David Kennedy. Tarpaper hobo shantytowns became "Hoovervilles" and pulled-out empty trouser pockets became "Hoover flags." A joke circulated that when Hoover asked for a nickel to make a telephone call to a friend, an aide flipped him a dime and said, "Here, call them both." The issue of direct federal unemployment relief dogged him throughout the 1932 campaign, and a man who had only a few years earlier been one of the most admired people in America was now vilified in virtually every quarter. As Kennedy observed: "The Great Humanitarian who had fed the starving Belgians in 1914, the Great Engineer [for his leadership in the rebuilding of the lower Mississippi River region after the great flood of 1927] so hopefully elevated to the presidency in 1928, now appeared as the Great Scrooge, a corrupted ideologue who could swallow government relief for the banks but priggishly scrupled over government provisions for the unemployed."

Perhaps the final nail in Hoover's political coffin was the expulsion of the "Bonus Army" from Washington, D.C., in late July of 1932. Thousands of unemployed World War I veterans petitioned Congress for an early cash payment of the war service bonus due them in 1945. When the Senate refused to pass the bonus bill, many left the capital disappointed, but thousands more remained and set up an encampment on Anacostia Flats on the outskirts of the district. Hoover called in federal troops to contain the World War I veterans, but the commanding officer, General Douglas MacArthur, exceeded his orders. He drove the protesting veterans out with tear gas and burned down their shacks and tents. "The spectacle of the United States Army routing unarmed citizens with tanks and firebrands outraged many Americans," Kennedy noted. What was worse for Hoover, the Bonus Army episode "came to symbolize Hoover's supposed insensitivity to the plight of the unemployed."

After the Bonus Army debacle, Hoover was a beaten man, months before the election results in November would make it official. The election of Franklin Roosevelt closed the book on Hoover and infused Americans with a sense of optimism.

Still, notwithstanding Roosevelt's confidence, innovative New Deal programs, and uncanny instincts for connecting with ordinary people, America was in for a terrible time.

Franklin D. Roosevelt would be inaugurated on March 4, 1933, but six weeks earlier and half a world away, another leader assumed power, one whose reign would change the course of history. He promised to rebuild his country's battered economy, rearm its military after a humiliating World War I treaty had forbidden it from doing so, and restore his nation to its rightful place of prominence on the international stage. He also pledged to eradicate Marxism, remove Jews from his country, and conquer "by the sword" the land his nation needed for its "living space."

Adolf Hitler became Reich Chancellor of Germany on January 30, 1933, appointed by Reich president Paul von Hindenburg after much political wrangling following the strong performance by Hitler's Nazi Party in Germany's November elections. Wildly cheering crowds accompanied Hitler after his appointment. "Now we've got there," Hitler declared, as he enthusiastically shook the hands of his supporters. On the night of his appointment, Hitler swore to carry out his obligations "without party interests and for the good of the whole nation," according to biographer Ian Kershaw. He also pledged to uphold the constitution and respect the rights of the German president.

Yet, almost overnight, the German people would realize that this was no ordinary transfer of power. "Those who had misunderstood or misinterpreted the momentous nature of the day's events would realize how wrong they had been," Kershaw wrote. "After 30 January 1933, Germany would never be the same again."

Perhaps most prophetic and biting were the words of Erich von Ludendorff, who foresaw disaster when he wrote to his wartime colleague Hindenburg: "You have delivered up our holy German Fatherland to one of the greatest demagogues of all time. I solemnly prophesize that this accursed man will cast our Reich into the abyss and bring our nation to inconceivable misery. Future generations will damn you in your grave for what you have done."

CHAPTER 21

"We should have more newspapers in this country in the position to tell the truth to the people who are worried not knowing where they will get their next meal," wrote James Donnaruma to Carl Dreyfus, editor of the *Boston American,* in April of 1935. "Conditions are fearfully bad."

Donnaruma was writing to congratulate Dreyfus for a series of editorial cartoons and columns (including a column by William Randolph Hearst) critical of the Roosevelt administration for massively spending federal funds without achieving commensurate improvements—and for permission to reprint them in *La Gazzetta.* The Depression was in its sixth year, and for most people conditions were, indeed, fearfully bad.

It had been more than two years since Roosevelt took office, two years since his uplifting inaugural speech in which he reassured Americans that "the only thing we have to fear is fear itself—nameless, unreasoning, unjustified terror which paralyzes needed efforts to convert retreat into advance." He had brimmed with confidence, radiating optimism even while he acknowledged the reality facing most Americans. Yes, he said, "a host of unemployed citizens face the grim problem of existence, and an equally great number toil with little return," but "we have still much to be thankful for. Nature still offers her bounty and human efforts have multiplied it." Roosevelt stressed the importance of realizing "our interdependence on each other... [that we are] willing to sacrifice for the good of a common discipline" without which "no progress is made, no leadership becomes effective." If the people could provide him with this reassurance, Roosevelt pledged in return to do "my constitutional duty to recommend measures that a stricken Nation in the midst of a stricken world may require."

And the new president did just that, undertaking a massive "New Deal" legislative agenda in the first hundred days designed to put the unemployed to work, rebuild and then stabilize the country's shattered banking system, bring about economic recovery, make another depression less likely, and restore confidence in people whose faith in themselves, their elected leaders, and their nation had all but eroded. During his 1932 election campaign, Roosevelt said that the American people were demanding "bold, persistent experimentation," and that is what he would give them.

The president had little choice. By his March 4, 1932, inauguration day, author Jack Beatty pointed out, thirty-eight of the forty-eight states had been forced to close their banks to prevent panic runs. In New York, the stock exchange shut down. The Chicago Board of Trade closed for the first time since 1845, followed by the Kansas City Board of Trade. In Boston, a third of the labor force was jobless, four thousand transients were among the city's welfare recipients, and seven thousand citizens faced the loss of their homes for nonpayment of taxes. In the Italian North End, the unemployment rate hovered near 50 percent. "This nation asks for action," Roosevelt had promised in his inaugural, "and action now."

His first action was the government-supervised reopening of the banks on Monday, March 13, 1933, a critical step that he preceded with his first "fireside chat" on Sunday evening. He told the American people that "it is safer to keep your money in a reopened bank than under the mattress." Calmly, reassuringly, he told millions of Americans glued to their radios that the country's banking system was safe. Roosevelt's ability to instill confidence in the people and his ability to connect on a deep, personal level were borne out the next day when deposits and gold began flowing back into the system, and the banking crisis ended. "The common people of the country sent their congratulations," David Kennedy wrote, noting that 450,000 Americans wrote to their new president in his first week in office. "Thereafter mail routinely poured in at a rate of four to seven thousand letters a day." The White House mailroom, staffed by a single employee in the Hoover administration, had to hire seventy people to handle the flood of correspondence.

Roosevelt's immediate success at handling the banking crisis, and the outpouring of faith and support from the American people, buoyed him with the political capital he needed to begin the economic turnaround— to launch an era of unprecedented federal intervention in the welfare of individuals and the intricacies of the national economy. The act establishing the Civilian Conservation Corps (CCC) provided one of the New Deal's most popular and memorable programs. Young men, ages seventeen to twenty-four, from families on relief found work at camps managed by the United States Army. They earned $30 per month (as well as food, clothing, and shelter) to plant trees, clear brush, repair national park facilities, and build reservoirs and bridges. The Federal Emergency Relief Act, which created the Emergency Relief Administration (ERA), provided $500 million in grants to states to help the unemployed. And the National Industrial Recovery Act (NIRA), probably the most broad-based and far-reaching piece of New Deal legislation, "thrust the federal government directly into the workings of the corporate world," one author noted, by encouraging fair labor standards (including minimum wages), guaranteeing workers the right to organize for collective bargaining and choose their own unions, and appropriating a massive $3.3 billion to construct highways, public buildings, and other facilities.

Such sweeping government intervention in the economy angered and alarmed many conservatives, but as author David Burg noted, "so eager was the entire nation to overcome the depression that the vast majority, even among those who disagreed philosophically with New Deal policies, welcomed the Roosevelt administration's initiatives as acceptable, desirable, necessary." After the president filed his legislation, even bulwarks of business sensed a shift in the mood of the nation toward hope and optimism and urged the people to act on that hope. "President Roosevelt has done his part; now you do something," said Charles Edison, president of Thomas Edison Inc. in West Orange, New Jersey, to his employees. "Buy something—buy anything, anywhere; paint your kitchen, send a telegram, give a party, get a car, pay a bill, rent a flat, fix your roof, get a haircut, see a show, build a house, take a trip, sing a song, get married. It does not matter what you do—but get going and keep going. This old world is starting to move."

Roosevelt's first one hundred days were impressive by any standards. His New Deal policies had halted the banking panic, earmarked billions of dollars for federal relief to the unemployed, created new agencies and laws to protect the country's financial infrastructure, and authorized the greatest public works projects in the nation's history. He even passed legislation to tax beer and wine sales once the disastrous experiment called Prohibition was finally repealed by the twenty-first amendment to the

Constitution later in the year. When President Roosevelt signed the bills that Congress had passed in June of 1933, he declared that "more history is being made today than in [any] one day of our national life."

While the spring and early summer of 1933 likely marked the lowest point in the Depression from a macroeconomic standpoint, conditions had not improved markedly for individuals by the time James Donnaruma wrote to the *Boston American* editor in 1935. Public employment and relief assistance provided a safety net that had never before existed; but bread lines, food shortages, poverty, startling unemployment—more than 25 percent of the total population—and fear of the future continued nonetheless.

In the words of David Kennedy, by the middle of the 1930s, the Great Depression "still hung darkly over the land."

"Now, about the unemployed themselves; this picture is so grim that whatever words I use will seem hysterical and exaggerated," wrote Martha Gellhorn in November of 1934 from her Massachusetts hotel room. "I find them all in the same shape—fear, fear driving them into a state of semi-collapse; cracking nerves; and an overpowering terror of the future."

Gellhorn's discouraging words were penned to Harry Hopkins, President Roosevelt's confidante and the director of the federal Emergency Relief Administration (ERA). Hopkins sent out sixteen "reporters" in the fall of 1933 to investigate social and economic conditions across the country. "I don't want statistics from you," he told them. "I don't want the social-worker angle. I just want your own reactions, as an ordinary citizen. Go talk with preachers and teachers, businessmen, workers, farmers. Go talk with the unemployed, those who are on relief and those who aren't. And when you talk with them don't ever forget that but for the grace of God you, I, any of our friends might be in their shoes. Tell me what you see and hear. All of it. Don't ever pull your punches." With these words, Hopkins hoped to get beyond the sheer data and numbers of the Depression and "touch the human face of the catastrophe, taste in his own mouth the metallic smack of fear and hunger of the unemployed," David Kennedy wrote.

Gellhorn's report, covering her ten-day swing through Boston, Lowell, Brockton, Lynn, Oxford, Fall River, and Lawrence, Massachusetts, is filled with candor, pathos, and frustration. "I saw...mill owners, shoe factory presidents, union leaders, public health commissioners, public welfare nurses, doctors, and the unemployed themselves," Gellhorn reported to Hopkins. "The picture is grim." Gellhorn sketched a portrait of despair on many fronts: relief funds were inadequate, business was so poor that employers still could not hire, and the administration of public welfare programs suffered from slipshod, or even criminal, management.

Traveling through Massachusetts, Gellhorn reached the conclusion that "relief is [at the] bare subsistence level, and covers nothing but food (and that inadequately). Result: no clothing or home equipment can be bought. Rents are paid at the sacrifice of nutrition; often they cannot be paid and evictions are frequent." Further, she noted to Hopkins, most business owners with whom she spoke would not be increasing employment during the winter of 1935–36. "If possible, they will avoid dropping workers by curtailing hours still further," she wrote.

In the midst of this strife, Gellhorn reported, Hopkins should be aware of the multiple problems that were occurring in the administration of the relief programs, "administration which is so infinitely bad" that neither the recipients nor taxpayers trusted the system. "Incompetence has become a menace," she wrote. "The unemployed are suffering for the inadequacy of the administration." In short, patronage was hampering relief efforts. "The administrator is a nice inefficient guy who is being rewarded for being somebody's cousin," Gellhorn stated. In some cases, these clerks "are more than pitiful; they are criminally incompetent." Such a management structure engendered suspicion about the entire relief program; unemployed people who applied for aid often conveyed to Gellhorn that "political graft" was the currency that greased the system, that "pull and bribery will get you work, but need won't." As a result, "the public at large is contemptuous and mistrustful of relief; simply on the grounds that it is a political plum—and the idea, after all was to feed the needy."

Further, Gellhorn complained to Hopkins, to prove their eligibility for relief, potential recipients were subjected to formal and rigorous questioning, "when common sense and better trained administrators" could perhaps obtain the needed results without dehumanizing the applicant. "I can't see that these questions do anything very completely except hurt and offend the unemployed, destroy his pride, make him feel clearly that he has sunk into a pauperized substrata," Gellhorn wrote. "Politics is bad enough in any shape; but it shouldn't get around to manhandling the destitute."

Dire economic conditions were also taking a psychological toll on people across Massachusetts, especially those in urban areas with large families. "They know what they are going through," Gellhorn informed Hopkins. "I haven't been in one home that hasn't offered me the spectacle of a human being driven beyond his or her powers of endurance and sanity." Most heartbreaking for the breadwinners in these families was "watching their children grow thinner and thinner; fearing the cold for children who have neither coats nor shoes, wondering about coal," and this from people whose destitute condition was forcing them "to be beggars asking for charity... their pride is dying, but not without due agony."

While noting that men over fifty "have given up hope; for them there is no future," Gellhorn was most frightened about the impact that abject poverty was having on young adults and children. Those between the ages of eighteen and twenty-five were "apathetic and despairing; feeling there is nothing to look forward to, sinking into indifference." And Gellhorn feared for the "physical condition of small children. I just don't want to think what they're growing up to be... I could go on and on. It's hard to believe that these conditions exist in a civilized country." In her concern for young people, Gellhorn's words echoed those of First Lady Eleanor Roosevelt, who had written six months earlier in the *New York Times:* "I have moments of real terror when I think we might be losing this generation. We have got to bring these young people into the active life of the community and make them feel that they are necessary." In Boston, 42 percent of sixteen- to twenty-four-year-olds were out of work, and the unemployment rate of sixteen- and seventeen-year-olds approached 70 percent in Massachusetts. Mrs. Roosevelt's public visibility on this issue prompted thousands of children and young adults to write letters seeking her help, either for themselves or their parents.

Hopkins himself was overcome with concern about the elderly, who, he concluded, "through hardship, discouragement, and sickness as well as advancing years [have] gone into an occupational oblivion from which they will never be rescued by private industry." This was one line of thinking that would lead to Roosevelt's landmark legislation in the following year, the Social Security Act of 1935.

Through all of this hardship, Gellhorn observed that the "foreign born (or one generation American) reacts better. . . . than the native, perhaps because he has less to begin with." While "demoralization and nervous breakdown" were prevalent among the native born, "the foreigner attempts still, despite hopelessness and poverty, to maintain his home; and the women somehow keep alive their pride in what few possessions remain."

Gellhorn was not the only reporter Hopkins dispatched to Massachusetts. Robert Washburn, who was also there in November of 1934, spent virtually all of his time in Boston. Though he expressed concerns similar to Gellhorn's, he was not nearly as strident or pessimistic, even opining, in contradiction to Gellhorn, that many Bostonians possessed a "sanguine confidence in the future . . . the idea has never entered their heads that perhaps this [Depression] is semi-permanent." Despite his point of view, Washburn also pointed out that among Italians in the North End, the Depression had cut so deep that it had eaten away at their prideful aversion to applying for or accepting relief. "There is a large section of the population here where the old abhorrence . . . of 'going on the Welfare' has died out," Washburn wrote.

His observations were echoed years later by Boston city councilor Frederick Langone, whose father, Joseph, owned the North End funeral home where Nicola Sacco and Bartolomeo Vanzetti had lain in state in 1927 and was also a state senator during the Depression. Italian immigrant parents who had resisted assistance for years, "who were ashamed to go on welfare or seek government assistance," now sent their children for government-dispensed milk, butter, Maine potatoes, or Argentine canned beef. "I remember . . . as times got harder, people would come to my parents' house over the funeral parlor . . . early in the morning," Fred Langone wrote. "When I woke up to go to school, the kitchen was already full of people waiting for help . . . from government relief agencies. We couldn't even have breakfast in our own house . . . the two flights of stairs to our apartment were lined with people from East Boston, the North End, and

During the Great Depression, Boston Italians, like Americans everywhere, performed any tasks they could to survive. This couple sells vegetables on the corner of Prince and Salem streets in the North End in 1935. *(Courtesy of the Boston Public Library, Print Department)*

other parts of the city." Nor were Langone's morning visitors limited to Boston residents. "They even came from Medford, Somerville, Chelsea, and Revere," Langone said. "The people could barely afford the penny ferry from East Boston."

Langone's parents would take care of as many as two hundred needy people a day with emergency relief. Thanksgiving and Christmas were "the saddest time of year" for these families, Langone remembered. His mother would make the rounds of North End merchants to collect food and assemble holiday baskets for the poor, but "unfortunately, there wasn't enough for everyone and someone would always be left out."

Still, a large majority of Boston Italians did not seek government relief. They relied on meager savings, contributions from older children who scrapped for work, and rent from boarders to make ends meet. Families helped each other out whenever possible. Those who had food shared it with those who did not. If a mother fell ill, neighbors would look after her children. Families passed on the clothing their older children had outgrown to neighbors with youngsters. The settlement pattern of Boston Italians— chain migration by *paesani*—became even more supportive during the Depression years.

For his part, James Donnaruma spent a portion of the Depression struggling to keep *La Gazzetta* afloat. He reduced advertising rates, reminded potential advertisers that his paper had a greater circulation than all the other Italian-language newspapers in New England combined, and enlisted agents in New York City to seek advertisers with Boston branch offices or stores. In 1938, he borrowed $700 to pay *La Gazzetta's* expenses, putting the newspaper and its equipment up for collateral, and repaid the personal property mortgage in full eighteen months later. Combined, these tactics and efforts were remarkably successful. During the worst economic downturn in America's history, *La Gazzetta* never missed an issue.

Despite his own financial struggle, Donnaruma also found time to advocate on behalf of Boston Italians who sought the scant jobs available, mostly in the public sector. "He is a veteran being [*sic*] overseas, and has dependents. He was NEVER ARRESTED [Donnaruma's emphasis] in his life, which makes him a desirable person," he wrote in March of 1934, describing one candidate, Raffaele Mirra, for a job with the Metropolitan District Commission. "He would certainly be a perfect man for State work, being willing at all time[s]. He wishes to work not having in mind to be helped by either the Soldier's relief or the Boston Welfare Department." A subsequent letter from the commission had Donnaruma direct Mirra to "report to the Charles River Basin office on Friday morning so that he may go to work."

Thanks to Donnaruma's influence, Mirra was one of the lucky ones. Italians and Bostonians of all nationalities struggled mightily, often desperately, during the Depression, clinging to each other and to hope that conditions would improve soon. Martha Gellhorn noted the irony surrounding the crumbling of the shoe industry in Boston, Lynn, and Brockton. "It fills the workers and the unemployed with astonishment that there is nothing for the shoe factories to do; but none of them have shoes to put on their feet and are facing the winter with husks of shoes bound up with rags."

She concluded her report to Hopkins: "I'm not thrilled with Massachusetts... Sorry about these reports, but it is impossible to gloss over conditions."

CHAPTER 22

Even as the struggle continued during the Great Depression, progress by Boston Italians was visible in their neighborhoods. Boston's population, slightly over 560,000 in 1900, had swelled to 817,000 by 1935—the largest its population would ever be—of which nearly 100,000 were Italians. East Boston's Italian population of more than 50,000 now exceeded the 43,000 Italians jammed into the North End (most of the remaining Italians resided in the West End, Roxbury, and Hyde Park), and Italians were now firmly ensconced as Boston's second-largest ethnic group. Though the Irish controlled Boston's elected political structure by this time, Italians had made both economic and grassroots political strides, and their enclaves were beneficiaries of some of the Depression-era public works projects.

The biggest of these was the Sumner Tunnel, whose construction between 1931 and 1934 physically linked by roadway the Italian neighborhoods of East Boston and the North End, enclaves that had enjoyed social and cultural links for years. The tunnel, which burrowed under Boston Harbor to connect East Boston and the airport with the mainland, first augmented and then replaced the ferry service that had carried passengers between the two neighborhoods. While the tunnel work forced disruption and demolition on both commercial and residential areas, especially on East Boston's Porter Street to make room for the tunnel's toll plaza and entrance, Italians did benefit from the construction jobs that the massive project required.

Less extensive, but prominent nonetheless, was the creation of the now-famous Prado, between the North End's Old North Church and Hanover Street in 1933. Architect Arthur Shurcliff laid out the open space surrounded by brick walls containing mounted plaques that recounted the history of the North End. The Prado, which eventually would be anchored by a large statue of Paul Revere, replaced Webster Street, a North End alley that was one of Boston's narrowest and most crowded lanes, lined with

Italian men gather in 1954 for cards and conversation at "the Prado" between the North End's Old North Church and Hanover Street. *(Photo by Leslie Jones. Courtesy of the Boston Public Library, Print Department)*

tightly packed wood-frame houses, according to historian Anthony Sammarco. The Prado not only was a vast physical improvement to the neighborhood, it quickly became a social gathering place, where Italian men would congregate to enjoy card games in the springtime, or women would sit and chat on the plaza's stone benches.

Hard work and the willingness to take risks also helped the Italian people move forward, especially in the latter half of the 1930s. Italian entrepreneurship continued even during the worst economic years, especially in the pushcart fruit and produce trade and the fishing industry, which Italians dominated, and in the barbershop business; by 1930, more than half of the barbers in Boston were Italians. Though he lived in adjacent Everett by this time, my Grandfather Minichiello acted on his entrepreneurial impulse and desire to own a business. In 1935, by now the father of three daughters, including an infant (he and my grandmother would have their fourth child and only son in 1940), my grandfather opened his own

An Italian fisherman coils his line on the fish pier (1940) *(Photo by Leslie Jones. Courtesy of the Boston Public Library, Print Department)*. Italian fishermen prepare their catch (1930) *(Photo by Leslie Jones. Courtesy of the Boston Public Library, Print Department)*.

cobbler shop on Bow Street. An enormous risk during the heart of the Depression, he viewed it as the best way to improve his economic situation. In
the early years, when cash was difficult to come by, he often bartered with
customers, exchanging his careful, precision, custom work for government-
relief butter, flour, or beef. He heated the small shop with a wood-burning
stove, fueled with firewood that he often collected in empty lots or along
the roadside. Here, in a store filled with the commingled smells of fresh
leather and burning wood, surrounded by soles, heels, nails, and the sharp
metal tools of the cobbler's trade, my grandfather was his own boss, and the
fruits of his talent and his labor would benefit his family. Owning a business, working for himself, providing for his family—only fourteen years
after he arrived in America virtually penniless and unable to speak English—was a source of immense pride to my grandfather.

The Puleo family also progressed in the midst of the Depression. In
1937, after the worst years had passed, my grandfather moved his family
from their tiny flat on Garden Court Street to a five-room, three-bedroom
walk-up at 246 North Street. With money he earned as a fruit peddler, and
help from the older children now contributing to the family income, he
was able to afford an apartment that contained a rare, notable, and prized
amenity among North End units—a full bathroom, complete with tub.
For the Puleos, the days of sharing a hallway bathroom with dwellers in
other apartments were over; the fact that five brothers (one son had married and moved out by this time) shared one bedroom and four sisters another (for a short time—my aunt Angie would marry and leave the Puleo
home in October of that year) proved little hardship in the midst of this
luxury.

Slow and steady economic improvement was accompanied by small political steps among Boston Italians during the 1930s. They never came close
to the accomplishments of their New York counterparts, whose mayoral
votes in 1933 made Fiorello LaGuardia the most important Italian American elected official in the country (it would be another sixty years before
Boston elected its first Italian American mayor). LaGuardia was the most
notable Italian to hold public office but he was not the first Italian American to become mayor of a major American city. That distinction was held

by Angelo Rossi, who became mayor of San Francisco by appointment in January of 1931 (when he was named by the Board of Supervisors to fill the unexpired term of the incumbent mayor, who resigned to become governor of California), and then won election in his own right later in the year. And in 1936, another Italian American, Robert Maestri, became mayor of arguably America's most important port city, New Orleans. Thus, from 1936 to 1943, Italian Americans guided the affairs of three of the largest and most important cities in the United States, a development that, according to historian Humbert Nelli, reflected a shift in party alignment that was taking place during the Depression years of the 1930s and the war years of the early 1940s. Rossi and Maestri were Democrats, Nelli noted, "while LaGuardia was a nominal Republican who was generally at odds with the party... the relief programs of Roosevelt's New Deal convinced the urban masses that the government cared about their welfare and helped pull Italians and members of other ethnic groups into the Democratic party."

In Boston, the political gains were much more modest among Italians during the Depression, which was the true beginning of the Irish Democrats' political heyday in Massachusetts. The Depression era featured three successive Irish mayors—Curley, Frederick W. Mansfield, and Maurice J. Tobin—plus a single "one and done" term for Curley as governor of Massachusetts. The one anomaly of this era was the election of Yankee Republican Leverett Saltonstall as governor in 1938, and even then Saltonstall jokingly attributed his high vote totals in Irish districts to his "South Boston face."

In 1936, in the midst of this Irish dominance, Boston University law professor and future state superior court judge Felix Forte was the Republican nominee for Massachusetts attorney general, becoming the first Italian American nominated for statewide office. Yet, the most influential Italian politician elected during the Depression was state senator Joseph Langone, who built his name recognition as the North End's most respected undertaker (the term "funeral director" was not part of the lexicon) and truly came to prominence when he oversaw the public spectacle that was the funeral of Sacco and Vanzetti. He was the first Italian American state senator to represent overwhelmingly Italian districts in Boston, and his election in 1932 broke decades of Irish domination of these areas.

Impulsive, combative, candid, controversial, gregarious, and often acerbic, Langone angered the establishment media and party leaders, while building a reputation as a defender of the little man. "Browsing through the North End you will find two sets of opinions about him," wrote one reporter describing the senator who represented the North and West Ends, Charlestown, and East Boston. "The man in the street swears by Joe Langone; the man in the bank, the newspaper office, the business house is inclined to swear *at* him." Langone ignored the disparaging nicknames the press attached to him, such as "Boston's Human Firecracker" and the "Bay State's Slapstick Senator," and spent his time working and speaking daily on behalf of his constituents. "Among the avenues and alleys of the North End, he is the hope of the hopeless, the friend of the friendless," one account read. "It is characteristic that he chose the chairmanship of public welfare as his particular function . . . he continually harps on his interest in the poor."

His rise to prominence made him a force on Beacon Hill ("like it or lump it," one reporter wrote in a profile of Langone), often to the chagrin of Democratic Party colleagues, one of whom shuddered at his "bull-in-the-china-shop tactics" in the senate chamber. The sheer force of his personality helped him become a leader without portfolio, another observer noted, a man who "is taking over the Democratic leadership of the Senate, although he is not the leader selected by his fellow Democratic members."

Of medium build, with dark complexion and clear blue eyes, Joe Langone was "hearty of greeting, [but] not too sure of himself with the English language," in the words of one profiler, a result of learning "his father's tongue first." Married and the father of six children, Langone lived on North Street, where his constituents called him Joe and "he [knew] them by their first names, too." Langone's personality swings were legendary; the most gentle of men when he cuddled his four-year-old daughter, Rita, he was often transformed into a raging bully during political debate, often with little provocation. He drove one woman, a Boston property owner who lived in Gloucester, to tears during a Senate hearing, threatening to "kick her all around town and push her off the wharf if you ever come into my district," after she disagreed with Langone's proposed bill to increase pay for Boston police and firemen. "You high-binders keep out of my dis-

trict or we'll back you off Rowe's Wharf at 3 A.M.," Langone barked. After
the encounter, Lillian McLellan sobbed: "I am a lady. I think some gentle-
man should have stopped him." Later a friend of Langone's cracked: "If he
would only count to 100 before he opens his mouth to speak, Joe Langone
would go far."

Typical of the fiery political advocacy that endeared Langone to his
constituents was his call for an investigation into Boston's welfare department, which he declared a "pretty sweet racket" for municipal administrators, whom he accused of not paying out benefits properly. He demanded
"all the records [and wanted] to know how many families you are helping,
and how much you give to families of various sizes." Langone insisted the
department was receiving enough federal funds to increase benefits to the
needy. "I don't think a man can support a wife and kids on $48 a month,"
he said.

Langone received plaudits from the Boston Italian American community for other reasons, too. He filed a bill requiring the teaching "of any foreign language" in the public schools, with a goal of providing Italian
American students the opportunity to learn Italian. He publicly chastised
the chairman of the Democratic state committee for "selling out the Italians of Boston" by using his political influence to block the appointment
of an Italian American as a municipal court judge. In 1934, he vigorously
supported the appointment of Vincent Brogna as Massachusetts's first Italian American superior court judge, and took full credit when Governor
Joseph Ely appointed him. Even then, Langone did not accept Brogna's
historic appointment graciously. "While this action . . . is comforting to the
Italian race, it deceives no one as the Governor was forced by my campaign
of the last fourteen weeks to make recognition of my people," Langone declared in his press release.

And in the summer of 1939, Langone and sociologist William Foote
Whyte organized a march on city hall by North End residents demanding
more city services for the neighborhood, including more timely garbage
collection and hot water at the public bathhouse. "In a district where only
12 percent of the flats had bathtubs, this was a matter of serious moment,"
Whyte wrote later. Boston's daily newspapers carried major stories on the
demonstration, crediting organizers with rounding up anywhere between

three hundred and fifteen hundred marchers. "The fellows happily accepted the figure of fifteen hundred, but I suspect three hundred was closer to the truth," Whyte recalled. The day after the demonstration, engineers were examining the boilers in the bathhouse, and in less than a week, "we had hot water," Whyte said. "The street-cleaning and garbage collections also seemed to be pepped up, for at least a short time." Whyte recounted both the demonstration and his three-year residence in, and study of, the North End in what later became *Street Corner Society,* a neighborhood study that became an academic classic. Years after the book was published, he revealed the real-life characters behind the pseudonyms he used in the study; "George Ravello" was state senator Joe Langone.

For the most part, James Donnaruma and *La Gazzetta* supported Langone, despite the difference in party affiliations. When a man named John Langone (no relation) announced his candidacy for state senate against incumbent Joseph Langone, Donnaruma warned him that he "could not win" and would split the Italian vote, thereby causing Joseph Langone's defeat. Donnaruma published a statement from John Langone once (and was criticized for it by state senator Joseph Langone), but when the challenger's supporters requested additional publicity, Donnaruma declined. "I shall not be a party to defeat Italian candidates," he stated in an explanatory letter to Joseph Langone. "I have been running an Italian newspaper for the interest of the Italian people. I shall continue along that line." Donnaruma added that he rejected further statements from John Langone "solely to keep an Italo-American in office."

Joseph Langone's historic and boisterous political career ended in controversy years later, after he had left the state senate and was appointed to the Boston Election Commission. In June of 1946, Langone, his son, Joseph III, and two others were indicted in an election ballot scandal. Prosecutors told the grand jury that Langone's funeral parlor on Hanover Street was used as a place for Langone and the other indicted men to "write the names of voters on nomination papers until a sufficient number were obtained." The *Boston Globe* asserted the obvious: "The law requires that the individual voter sign papers." Two days later, accompanied by huge headlines in the *Boston American,* Langone resigned as an election commissioner, "refusing to comment on his reasons for quitting the $5,100 post."

Despite his lack of public utterances, it is not a stretch to imagine Joseph Langone sharing with friends his belief that the indictment was just another example of the Boston political establishment's never-ending attempts to silence him.

Local and state politics were important, but Boston Italians joined Americans everywhere in keeping a close eye on national and international politics during the Depression. Italians became concerned about Italy's increased belligerence outside of her borders under Mussolini's Fascist regime. Most Italians initially supported *Il Duce* as he improved an ailing Italian economy, imposed order in an Italy beset by civil unrest, and aggressively targeted the Mafia in Southern Italy. Now, Italians questioned Italy's invasion of Ethiopia in 1935 in defiance of League of Nations sanctions, and its support, with men and materials, of Spanish general Francisco Franco during that country's civil war in 1936. What was most disconcerting about Mussolini's support for Franco was his collaboration with his Nazi ally, Adolf Hitler. Italian Americans grew increasingly disillusioned as Italy drew diplomatically closer to Nazi Germany.

Meanwhile, in the summer of 1936, Hitler's intention was to showcase the might of the Nazi regime during the Olympics in Berlin. Although African American sprinter and long jumper Jesse Owens's four gold medals thwarted Hitler's efforts to use the Olympics to prove his theories of Aryan racial superiority, the Berlin games were an enormous propaganda success for the Nazi regime. Hitler, now elevated to Fuehrer, attended almost every day, underscoring the significance of the games, and the crowd rose in salute each time he entered the stadium. More important, as journalist William Shirer noted, the lavishness with which Germany promoted the games and the athletes and the "very good front [Hitler] put up for general visitors" helped convince the international community that perhaps they needed to reconsider their original impression of Hitler and Nazism. As one Jewish writer observed: "It's incessantly drummed into the people and foreigners that you can see the revival, the blossoming, the new spirit, the unity, the steadfastness, the glory, [and] naturally too the peaceful spirit of the Third Reich lovingly embracing the whole world."

Meanwhile, at home, President Franklin D. Roosevelt was reelected overwhelmingly in November of 1936, crushing Kansas Republican Alf Landon in the greatest electoral defeat of modern times up to that point. Roosevelt won forty-six of the forty-eight states—Landon won only Maine and Vermont—and 523 of the 531 electoral votes, and captured 61 percent of the popular vote to just 37 percent for Landon. Though he did not run as strong in the Italian districts of East Boston and the North End as he had in 1932, FDR still captured 85 percent and 86 percent of the vote, respectively.

In his inaugural address of January 20, 1937 (the Twentieth Amendment, ratified in 1933, had set this date for the presidential inauguration), Roosevelt focused on domestic policies, offering a comprehensive review of his preceding term and a blueprint for social reforms to come. It was during this speech that he acknowledged the continued ravages of the Depression. "I see one-third of a nation ill-housed, ill-clad, ill-nourished," he said. "I see millions lacking the means to buy products of farm and factory, and by their poverty, denying work and productiveness to many other millions." The president reassured listeners that it was "not in despair that I paint you that picture, I paint it for you in hope—because the Nation, seeing and understanding the injustice in it, proposes to paint it out." Roosevelt acknowledged the importance of individual ambition and achievement but sounded a clarion call for continued national cohesion to help the poor and end the Depression. And perhaps as important, the country needed to continue its progress "to erect on the old foundations a more enduring structure for the better use of future generations."

The strength of Roosevelt's words comforted Americans, and although the president barely mentioned international affairs in his address, he did mention that the people of the United States expected their country to be "strong among the nations in its example of the will to peace." At the conclusion of his remarks, he asked for "Divine guidance" to help give "light to them that sit in darkness" and to "guide our feet into the way of peace."

Ten days later and thousands of miles away, on the anniversary of his takeover of power, Adolf Hitler delivered a three-hour speech on *his* first four years that would soon threaten the peace Roosevelt prayed for. Hitler roared that he had restored Germany's honor by reintroducing the military draft, creating the Luftwaffe (the air force), and rebuilding the German navy.

Perhaps most significant of all, biographer Ian Kershaw pointed out, Hitler announced that he was "solemnly withdrawing the German signature from the admission of war-guilt in the Versailles Treaty." That admission, the Fuehrer declared scornfully, was "wrung out of a weak government" that was but a distant memory in a glorious new Germany, now led by a Reich that would endure and prosper for a thousand years.

CHAPTER 23

"Nearly 100,000 Massachusetts citizens of Italian extraction . . . supported Governor Saltonstall" in his "great landslide" in November of 1938, editorialized James Donnaruma in the April 15, 1939, issue of *La Gazzetta*. "[Yet] a growing feeling of disillusionment is spreading among them."

Donnaruma's strong editorial argued that a few months into Governor Leverett Saltonstall's administration, he had yet to live up to his promise to appoint more Italian Americans to state positions. "Italian racial groups have anxiously scrutinized the newspapers each time a list of appointments has been issued by the Governor's office [and] we must admit that we fail to understand and are at a loss to explain the apparent lack of recognition of the Italian group up to the present time," Donnaruma wrote in his editorial, entitled "More New Appointments, but No Italian Names."

For Donnaruma, fighting with unresponsive politicians on behalf of Italians for jobs and appointments was certainly nothing new; indeed, he had made a career of it from behind his editor's desk at *La Gazzetta*. But Saltonstall's failure to deliver was an entirely different matter—in more ways than one, this was personal. For, in addition to supporting the Republican candidate on the pages of his newspaper, Donnaruma had stumped for Saltonstall in cities and towns throughout the state. From Fall River to Brockton to Gloucester to Clinton to Pittsfield, Donnaruma spoke to Italian American organizations and virtually anyone else who would listen. At the behest of the Saltonstall campaign, he mailed letters of support to friends and colleagues in Lowell, New Bedford, Bridgewater, Concord, Plymouth, Swampscott, Wellesley, and many other communities. He organized meetings, dinners, and get-out-the-vote rallies. When Saltonstall defeated James Michael Curley by nearly 150,000 votes, Donnaruma took pride in the fact that he likely delivered thousands of Italian votes by himself. He had put his reputation on the line and succeeded; now it was time for Saltonstall to reciprocate. While Italians had been "more calm and patient than other groups" in awaiting the spoils of victory, Donnaruma's editorial now scolded the new administration, asserting that "it is high time that action were taken toward satisfying the just demands of the Italian racial group in Massachusetts."

Yet, in this case, Donnaruma was not only seeking justice for Italians, or merely concerned about his own reputation and credibility in the Italian community; he had other, more personal motives for his editorial stance. First, he had formally requested that the Saltonstall administration find a job for his son Guy Paul, thirty-five, a former officer at the Charles Street Jail who had been discharged by the sheriff after James Donnaruma supported his political opponent. Second, in exchange for *La Gazzetta's* editorial support of Saltonstall, Donnaruma had specifically sought advertising for his newspaper from the state public works department, metropolitan district commission, and insurance commission. Third, and perhaps most flagrantly, Donnaruma had requested advertising "from private concerns with which the Governor is connected." An irritated aide to Governor Saltonstall wrote to Donnaruma in late March: "I have you and your son in mind and at the first opportunity you may be sure we will try to help out. However, there has been very little to give anyone as yet. You may rest assured that we are well aware of what you did during the campaign and it isn't necessary to go over the matter again."

In seeking personal favors from Saltonstall, in addition to largesse for his people, Donnaruma perhaps marred what otherwise was a long, selfless career seeking economic justice for Italians in Boston. Yet, his personal situation provides a window of understanding into his thinking. Saltonstall's aide may have been aware of Donnaruma's contributions to the campaign, but not the high cost that the editor paid for his efforts, a price that perhaps makes it easier to forgive the blatant crassness of his requests. Whereas the Depression had taken its toll on Donnaruma's financial health, the Saltonstall campaign had proven physically debilitating. Donnaruma's grueling pace during the fall of 1938 landed the sixty-five-year-old publisher in the hospital for thirty-seven days in January and February to treat stress and exhaustion. Even then, money worries never disappeared. The resulting $400 hospital bill "placed me in a worse position than I was before," he wrote to a friend.

In a picture that first appeared in the *Boston Traveler* on October 11, 1937, James Donnaruma sits for a portrait by John M. Quinlan (standing), head of a Boston printing firm. The finished Donnaruma portrait was on display at an October 31, 1937, banquet at the Hotel Statler to commemorate the fortieth anniversary of Donnaruma's newspaper, *La Gazzetta del Massachusetts*. *(Courtesy of the Boston Public Library, Print Department)*

Donnaruma returned to work in late February of 1939 ("I am in the office every afternoon and feeling stronger and gaining my lost weight," he wrote to a friend) but perhaps sensed that he would never resume the same robust pace that had made him a leader of Boston's Italians and earned him the respect of city fathers. A few months after his April editorial criticizing Saltonstall, he would be hospitalized again with angina pectoris, severe chest pains associated with emotional stress, an affliction that would hamper his activities for several years. "I have hardly done any work in the last three years," he would write to a friend in January of 1942. To make matters worse, in the midst of a recurrence of angina on Labor Day, 1941, Donnaruma reported that he had "met with a serious automobile accident when a woman smashed into the side of my car and made my illness worse."

James Donnaruma continued speaking out and writing letters on behalf of Italians for appointments, jobs, parole, and other important issues. He continued in the role of esteemed leader emeritus within the Italian community. But, more and more as the 1930s came to a close, Donnaruma was transferring daily control of La Gazzetta over to his son, Caesar, who would turn forty in 1940. The newspaper's circulation still exceeded a healthy ten thousand readers despite a nationwide decline of Italian-language publications as their target audience fully assimilated into American society. (By comparison, Philadelphia's only Italian-language paper, Il Popolo Italiano, which served a community three times as large as that of Boston, sold only sixteen thousand copies in 1940.) Yet, the future health of La Gazzetta would soon become Caesar Donnaruma's primary responsibility.

Meanwhile, as the end of Prohibition slowed and then stopped the millions of dollars organized crime syndicates were reaping from illegal liquor sales, gambling—primarily slot machines and numbers—returned to its number one position as the principal source of underworld income during the 1930s. Millions more poured in from loansharking, prostitution, and racketeering. In Boston's North End, gambling thrived; average residents played the numbers, and a "live and let live" feeling developed between the vast majority of honest Italians and the small gangster element that profited from illegal activities. "The bad reputation of the North End [regarding crime] was based entirely on a very few individuals who were involved in violence and lawlessness," wrote Angelo Ralph Orlandella, one of the subjects of William Foot Whyte's study, years later. "Beyond the small number of people involved in organized crime, the North End was a very peaceable district, with close-knit family ties. We experienced a general high degree of personal safety and security in the North End, both day and night, and robberies and vandalism against home and business were almost non-existent... My mother would not even let us *discuss* anything illegal."

Nonetheless, the rise of the Italian mafia continued in the 1930s. Phil Buccola still ran the Boston underworld, but another gangster, the son of Italian immigrants, was making a name for himself and rising in stature. Raymond S. Patriarca had a lengthy criminal record for hijacking, armed robbery, assault, safecracking, and burglary but was proving a tough, loyal, and resourceful criminal. Buccola elevated Patriarca to the status of right-hand man; eventually, Patriarca would rise to run the entire New England underworld enterprise.

Another North End name from this period is worth mentioning, one of five sons of an Italian grocer. Gennaro "Jerry" Angiulo turned twenty-one years old in 1940 and was just beginning his career in organized crime. Within twenty years, he would be running the Boston Italian mob as an underboss to Patriarca.

Most Boston Italians knew, but did not speak about, Buccola, Patriarca, and Angiulo. Yet they spoke proudly of two other fellow Italians they had never met who were making national headlines as 1940 began, one in sports and the other in entertainment.

Joe DiMaggio was patrolling center field for the New York Yankees, and since his 1936 rookie season, when he hit twenty-nine home runs and led the Yankees to a World Series title, Italians across America had embraced the hitting and fielding sensation. DiMaggio's stature would only grow in 1941, when he hit safely in an astounding fifty-six consecutive games, a record that still stands today.

Another young Italian American, just twenty-five in 1940, had not yet attained "Joltin' Joe's" status. But he soon would equal and surpass it. This skinny kid from Hoboken, New Jersey, named Frank Sinatra, possessed a singing voice that would make women swoon and men envious. His first big break came when he joined the Harry James band in 1939. "The kid's name is Sinatra," the bandleader told a reporter. "He considers himself the greatest vocalist in the business. Get that! Not even one hit record. No one ever heard of him. He looks like a wet rag. But he says he is the greatest." Later that year, the twenty-four-year-old Sinatra cut his first record, on which he sang "From the Bottom of My Heart" and "Melancholy Mood." After six months with Harry James, he was lured away by rival bandleader Tommy Dorsey and would become a sensation in the 1940s and for nearly a half century after that. Sinatra, who would also be known as "The Voice" and the "Chairman of the Board," was an honorary member of virtually every Italian American family in Boston and across America during the second half of the twentieth century.

In the early 1940s, Italians knew DiMaggio and Sinatra were talented, popular, and among the best in their fields. But they could not have imagined that both men would become American icons for decades to come.

For Italians and everyone else in America, organized crime, DiMaggio, Sinatra, and the lingering effects of the Depression were all overshadowed on September 1, 1939, when Adolf Hitler's German forces invaded Poland and conquered it within days, due largely to the efforts of the Luftwaffe, the rebuilt German air force. Norway, Holland, and Belgium all fell soon after to the invading Germans, as World War II began with thunderous successes for the Third Reich.

Italian Americans were chagrined again ten months later, when on June 10, 1940, the Associated Press reported that Benito Mussolini's Italy had joined forces with Germany, "as Nazi legions are pressing down perilously on France and Paris itself." Italian troops invaded France through the Riviera as Mussolini delivered a "wildly cheered, bombastic speech" from the balcony of the Palazzo Venezia to thousands of Fascist Blackshirts gathered below.

After months of teetering on the brink, Italy's declaration of war and its alliance with Germany shocked and angered America's elected officials and its people and, as a result, profoundly affected Italians in Boston and throughout the United States.

CHAPTER 24

A steady rain fell outside as President Franklin D. Roosevelt delivered the commencement address to more than five hundred University of Virginia graduates inside the college's gymnasium on June 10, 1940. Dressed in a crimson robe and hood, Roosevelt delivered a thundering oration whose message carried far beyond the academic halls in Charlottesville and within days would reverberate in Italian neighborhoods in Boston, Chicago, New York, Philadelphia, New Orleans, San Francisco, and enclaves in between. "There could be no missing the depth of his feeling," the *New York Times* wrote, "since he put into his words all the emphasis at his command."

The president's speech came just hours after Benito Mussolini announced his decision to join forces with Hitler and unleash his armies against France and Great Britain. As faculty members stomped their feet and applauded, and graduates wildly cheered and screamed the rebel yell, Roosevelt strongly condemned Italy for its action, calling it "a disregard for the rights and security of other nations," and pledged America's support in materiel and aid to those who were staking their lives in the fight for freedom overseas. "The gods of force and hate would endanger the institutions of democracy in the Western World," the president said. "The whole of our sympathies lie with those nations that are giving their life blood in combat against those forces." While still maintaining America's desire to stay out of war, FDR said the nation would "harness and speed up the use of [its] resources in order that we ... may have equipment and training equal to the task of any emergency and every defense."

Yet, another Roosevelt utterance, one that was a departure from his prepared text, angered Italian Americans, diminished the president's support in Italian American communities, and forced them to again encounter discrimination and disparagement from other Americans. Of Mussolini and Italy, Roosevelt proclaimed: "On this, the 10th day of June, the hand that held the dagger has struck it into the back of his neighbor." The interpolated remark would be highlighted by major newspapers across the country, and Roosevelt's Virginia address became known as the "stab-in-the-back" speech among a dismayed Italian American community that believed the president had gratuitously resorted to the darkest of stereotypes to stigmatize Italy's actions. "Roosevelt's words struck a sensitive nerve among the American population of Italian descent," wrote historian Stefano Luconi years later. "His remarks not only brought shame on Italy. They also drew upon the notorious stereotype of Italians as stiletto-prone people that had haunted the members of this ethnic group since the beginning of mass immigration from Italy to the United States in the 1880s."

American newspapers led with the "stab-in-the-back" speech, some focusing on Roosevelt's seeming vacillation on neutrality, others picking up on the phrase itself. "Mr. Roosevelt understated the case when he asserted that the hand that holds the dagger has struck into the back of its neighbor," asserted the *Chattanooga Times and Democrat*. Of Mussolini's "ambush," the *New York Times* editorialized: "Fascism marches when it thinks that it smells carrion."

Meanwhile, Italian Americans, resentful of Roosevelt's characterization of their ancestral country, also feared that the president's statement would trigger a new wave of anti-Italian bigotry in America. While *La Gazzetta*'s criticism of Roosevelt's remarks was not surprising, considering James Donnaruma's Republican leanings, other Italian-language newspapers also expressed concern. "Since President Roosevelt made his speech . . . many of our people have been fired from their jobs," asserted *Unione,* an Italian-language weekly in Pittsburgh, just three weeks after Roosevelt's speech. "[And] the members of their families, though born in America, have been deprived of all protection." The Philadelphia-based *Il Popolo Italiano* accused the "stab-in-the-back" address of fanning the flames of anti-Italian prejudice. Democratic congressman James A. Shanley of Connecticut wrote to Roosevelt on July 9 that the president's Charlottesville speech had prompted "a wave of sentiment in New England particularly against Italians" and "under the cover of false patriotism certain Italians are being dropped from jobs." An English-language newspaper serving Little

Italy in South Philadelphia noted that "already in the name of patriotism, some of our citizens . . . are leading the attack on aliens, refusing them relief, denying them ordinary rights, taking away their work."

Italians spent the days and weeks after the University of Virginia speech scrambling to prove their loyalty to the United States. In Boston, navy recruiting was booming, with many Italian Americans among the enlistees. The *Boston Globe* published a large photo of Stephen Cammarata enlisting above the caption "Boy of Italian Descent Measured for Navy." The *Globe* reassured its readers that "Italy entering the war against the Allies did not bother Stephen Cammarata of Brighton, who comes from an Italian American family." Cammarata told the *Globe* reporter: "I feel that I am a 100-percent American, and am ready to give my full loyalty to America. What Italy does causes no change in my American ideas. My parents and sister were born in Italy and *they* are also more interested in being loyal to America."

Boston newspapers also reported a rush by local Italians to be naturalized, noting that Italy's entrance into the war generated a wave of patriotic excitement among Italians. In the days following Roosevelt's speech, scores of Italians jammed the corridors of the naturalization bureau in Boston for first and final citizenship applications. "Most of the [Italian] applicants expressed disgust with Mussolini's actions," the *Globe* noted, "declaring they were more anxious than ever to become full citizens of this country and sever all relations with Italy." One Italian awaiting application stated that all the Italians he knew "would shoulder arms for the United States if necessary, even against their own relatives in the home country." Still, clerks in the naturalization offices pointed out that most applicants "spent considerable time pondering the question that read, 'If necessary, are you willing to take arms in defense of this country?'"

Meanwhile, prominent Boston Italians rushed to condemn Italy's actions. Harry Stabile, president of Stabile Bank and Trust, and esteemed Italian lawyer Peter Borre both expressed regret at Mussolini's decision, as did the Women's Italian Club of Boston. The *Boston Herald* reported that in Boston's North End, "there was sadness and tight lips and even a few women weeping in the streets." Boston judge Felix Forte, leader of the national Sons of Italy, denounced Mussolini's declaration of war and pledged the support of his organization's 200,000 members to "stand shoulder to shoulder with other Americans in assuming responsibility and preserving the principles of democracy. We have been hoping and praying for peace. We hoped that this hour might never come to pass." Michael Fredo, a trustee of the Massachusetts General Hospital, deplored Italy's alliance with the Nazis, calling it "sheer madness." While Italians had admired Mussolini's achievements in the past, Fredo said they should strongly condemn *Il Duce*'s latest decision for "[linking] up with one who has trampled underfoot" the principles of "democracy and Christian civilization." And Donnaruma's competitor P. A. Santosuosso, who published the *Italian News,* characterized the reaction in the North End as "a pall of gloom." He chastised members of the press not to "make foreigners out of us because our names end in a vowel. I enlisted once for America and I would again. This is our country and our children's country." Santosuosso compared Italian American affection for Italy with the affection American descendants of the Puritans felt for England or fourth- and fifth-generation Irish Americans felt for Ireland. "But we have loyalty only to this country," he said. "We deeply regret that Mussolini found it necessary to join with Hitler. Go to our churches tonight and you will see them filled with people praying for peace."

One *Herald* account said the most common reaction in the North End was a "gesture of the hand and a shrug of the shoulders" followed by the general comment: "What Italy does is not our business. We are American citizens." In the course of nearly fifty street interviews, the reporter noted, "only two . . . did not say openly they wished Italy had stayed at peace."

Despite these assurances, Italians feared reprisals in the wake of Mussolini's actions and Roosevelt's speech. Even as crowds gathered on Boston Common on June 14 to celebrate Flag Day, even as Mayor Tobin told an audience of more than eight thousand that the nation must be armed so effectively that no other country would dare attack it, the relationship between Italian Americans and other Americans was showing signs of strain. The Italian freighter *Dino,* loading cargo at Charlestown, immediately barred all American visitors upon learning of Mussolini's announcement and officially halted conversations with the crew of the British freighter

Selveston, docked just twenty feet away. At Woburn's June 13 St. Anthony's Day celebration, its Italian American representatives decided it best to withdraw the Italian flag and banners festooned with Italy's national colors of red, white, and green.

At the state level, Governor Saltonstall's choice for a $6,000-per-year post with the state industrial accident board, Nazzareno Toscano, was asked to pledge his loyalty to America before the governor's executive council would confirm him. Toscano, a former officer in the Italian navy, described himself as a "thoroughly loyal American" who stood ready to "defend with his life the American way of living." Councilor Bayard Tuckerman, who urged that Toscano proclaim his allegiance to the United States "considering his past connection," said he was satisfied with Toscano's declaration of loyalty. He denied that his request had "any semblance of intolerance . . . Mr. Toscano's service in the Italian navy is too recent to be brushed off without some interrogation." After Toscano issued his public reassurances, Tuckerman said: "I had hoped he would make such a statement. Of course, I knew myself that he was a loyal citizen." Governor Saltonstall assured residents of Massachusetts that Toscano was "a loyal American citizen who practices the ideals of our American life."

Nationally, there was a similar mix of anti-Italian sentiment and Italian pronouncements of loyalty to the United States. Just four days after Roosevelt's Virginia speech, secretary of state Cordell Hull announced an investigation of Italian consular officials in the United States after a report that Italy's consulate general in New York, under orders of Mussolini, was seeking to promote Fascism in America. Hull's actions prompted a protest by Italian ambassador Don Ascanio del Principi Colonna, who accused the secretary of state of engaging in an "unjustified effort to foment anti-Italian feeling in the United States." As tempers flared in New York, Italian American public officials attempted to cool things down, all the while proclaiming the loyalty of Italian Americans. Lieutenant Governor Charles Poletti declared that Italians in the United States were "wholeheartedly loyal to America, and as loyal Americans we stand ready." New York City mayor Fiorello LaGuardia warned his one million Italian residents that the city would not tolerate any demonstrations "for or against a foreign power," and affirmed that Italian Americans sided with the president. "We recognize no other loyalty [than to America]," he said in an emotion-filled address. "[We appreciate] the privileges and rights of our adopted country." And Luigi Antonini, New York chairman of the American Labor Party and leader of forty-two thousand Italian dressmakers in the city, sent a telegram to President Roosevelt endorsing his attacks on Mussolini and condemning Italy's entry into the war as a "criminal" act against democracy.

Mussolini's decision to join Hitler, coupled with President Roosevelt's "stab-in-the-back" speech, left Italian Americans dispirited and once again on the defensive fighting prejudice and stereotypes. Throughout 1940, many Americans cast a wary eye toward Italians, who were forced once more to defend their integrity—as they had during George Scigliano's battles with the Black Hand, or when they had to distance themselves from the violence of the anarchists, or avoid the stigma attached to them when the public identified organized crime figures.

World War II would become a watershed event for the nation and the world, and a turning point in the history of Italian Americans. In the meantime, as the 1940 presidential elections approached, Roosevelt and his advisors recognized that the stab-in-the-back speech had opened a deep fissure between Italian Americans and their once beloved president.

Sometime during the spring or early summer of 1940, as Britain's fate hung by what Winston Churchill described as "a slender thread," as Americans pondered their own possible involvement in a European war, Franklin D. Roosevelt decided to buck one hundred fifty years of custom and tradition and run for an unprecedented third term. "No man before him had dared breach George Washington's two-term example," noted historian David Kennedy. He was nominated on the first ballot by the Democrats during their July convention in Chicago. Republicans, in what David Kennedy described as "one of the most astonishing surprises in the history of American presidential politics," chose political amateur Wendell Willkie, a corporate attorney and utilities executive who just a few years earlier had been a registered Democrat.

Italian Americans had been a major component in the ethnic coalition that Roosevelt built to amass his overwhelming victories in 1932 and 1936, but his stab-in-the-back speech and denunciation of Italy were liabilities for

Democrats among Italian voters as the 1940 elections drew near. Stefano Luconi wrote that Democratic workers were unable to campaign in New York City's Little Italy without police escorts—such was the extent of the anger toward Roosevelt. Democratic activists in many cities wired the White House, urging Roosevelt to say anything in praise of Italian Americans to make amends for his Charlottesville speech. In New York, party leader Mark Bogart warned that the Italian vote was at risk throughout the state and advised Roosevelt to utter "some statement adequate to offset the whispering campaign actively being conducted within the City of New York to the effect that the President is anti-Italian." The chairperson of the Italian Democratic Committee in Pittsburgh urged Roosevelt to make "some favorable comment about the Italians in America." And from Hartford, Democratic activist Herman Koppleman wrote:

> In a conference with several outstanding and loyal Italian Democrats, it was suggested that the boss [Roosevelt] take advantage of Columbus Day for some kind of laudatory statement concerning the Italians here in America. They are very strongly of the opinion that the Italians here in this country could be turned away from their opposition to the boss on account of the "stab in the back" statement. They feel that everything would be forgiven if in some manner the Italians of America were given some praise."

Inside the White House, Roosevelt's administrative assistant, attorney James Rowe, prepared a memorandum for the president about his forthcoming Columbus Day address that expressed similar concerns: "Would it not be helpful if an indirect reference was made to the fact that Columbus was an Italian?" Rowe wrote. "Reports are that some of the Italian groups in New York are still shakey [sic]."

Roosevelt's support among Boston Italians was also shaky. In *La Gazzetta,* Donnaruma editorialized in October that the president's angry words in Virginia had paved the way for American participation in the war, arguing that a vote for Roosevelt was a vote for war, while a vote for Willkie was a vote for peace. William Foote Whyte acknowledged that any anti-Fascist rhetoric would have alienated some Italian voters, but the impact "could have been minimized had the President not phrased his attack to strike [the North End] in such a sensitive spot." He pointed out that Boston's Italian immigrants "have for years been trying to live down the reputation of being people who are inclined to stick knives in the backs of their enemies. Roosevelt's phrase opened an old wound." Throughout the summer of 1940 and into November, Whyte pointed out that North End Italians were "constantly reminded of the stab in the back [statement], and all my informants agreed that this was the most effective weapon used in the [North End] presidential campaign."

Roosevelt heeded his advisors and the political winds by attempting to reconcile with Italians in his Columbus Day message on October 12, 1940. He celebrated the explorer's brave deeds and used the occasion to extol the contributions of Italian immigrants to America, "and to acknowledge once and for all that they were no longer aliens but a key component of US society," Luconi pointed out. Later, in an address Roosevelt delivered in Dayton, Ohio, he elaborated on this theme:

> Many and numerous have been the groups of Italians who have come in welcome waves of immigration to this hemisphere. They had been an essential element in the civilization and make-up of all the twenty-one Republics. During these centuries, Italian names have been high in the list of statesmen in the United States and in the other Republics—and in addition, those who have helped to create the scientific, commercial, professional, and artistic life of the New World are well known to us.

Would Roosevelt's words be enough to stem his eroding support in Italian communities? Not if Republicans had their way. They continued to hammer home their message that the president was anti-Italian and criticized the Columbus Day speech as a weak and transparent attempt at placating and pandering to Italian Americans. "The insult against the Italians in Virginia, when he uttered those famous words—stab in the back—can never be forgiven by Italian Americans and shall never be excused," wrote Herman Carletti, secretary of the Italo-American Republican League of Pennsylvania. A GOP activist from Buffalo told the state Republican committee that most Italian votes in his city would go for Willkie, "and one of our main arguments which is meeting with enthusiastic response is the reference to the President's speech at Charlottesville, the infamous 'Stab in the Back' speech." A respected former Italian American Republican state senator from Chicago urged Italians there to vote against Roosevelt.

Many Italian-language newspapers and neighborhood leaders echoed the fears of Donnaruma and *La Gazzetta*—that Roosevelt's election in 1940 would propel the United States into war against Germany and Italy. The Italian press argued in many cities that the president's Charlottesville speech not only insulted Italian Americans but also served as a harbinger of Roosevelt's foreign policy intentions; a vote for Willkie, they argued, would keep the United States out of a European war. Even after Roosevelt promised American mothers and fathers that "your boys are not going to be sent into any foreign wars," many Italian Americans, and even his "closest associates and staunchest supporters," remained skeptical about the president's real intentions, Stefano Luconi noted. Ernest Cuneo, Democratic National Committee counsel and a member of the Office of Strategic Services, later recalled: "The only time I winced was when the President . . . assured the electorate 'again and again and again that their sons would fight in no foreign war.'"

Willkie continued attacking Roosevelt as a warmonger in the closing days of the campaign, a perception that the president's Charlottesville speech had fostered well beyond Italian communities. "We do not want to send our boys over there again," Willkie said in a speech in St. Louis. "If you elect the third-term candidate, I believe they will be sent." Roosevelt's clear vulnerability on this issue unsettled his advisors. "This fellow Willkie is about to beat the Boss," fretted presidential advisor Harry Hopkins.

In a crucial speech in Boston on October 30, 1940, Roosevelt focused mostly on economic gains the country had made under his leadership but again reiterated his promise that America's sons would not be sent into any foreign wars. "Conspicuously," David Kennedy noted, "Roosevelt omitted the qualifying phrase that he had used on previous occasions: 'except in case of attack.'"

Listening on the radio, Willkie exploded: "That hypocritical son of a bitch! This is going to beat me."

When an advisor asked Roosevelt about the absence of a qualifier in his Boston speech, the president replied: "If somebody attacks us, then it isn't a foreign war, is it?"

On November 5, 1940, by a comfortable margin, Franklin Roosevelt became the first president in American history elected to a third term, though, as predicted, his popularity in some Italian American communities plummeted. Compared with 1936, Roosevelt's Italian American vote fell from 85 percent to 72 percent in Hartford, 83 percent to 74 percent in Pittsburgh, from more than 70 percent to 54 percent in New Haven, and from 65 percent to 53 percent in Philadelphia. In New York City, the Democratic Party even lost its prewar majority among Italian Americans. Stefano Luconi noted that 79 percent of New York's Italian Americans cast their ballots for Roosevelt in 1936, compared with only a shocking 42 percent four years later.

In Boston, Roosevelt won the majority of the Italian votes in East Boston (63 percent) and the North End, though just barely in the latter neighborhood. Whereas 89 percent of North End Italians voted for Roosevelt in 1936, the president eked out only a 51 percent majority in 1940, a precipitous drop likely aided by *La Gazzetta*'s influence. FDR's North End margin of victory in 1936 exceeded 3,280 votes; in 1940 he won the neighborhood by a mere 117 votes.

Despite the fall in Italian support, it is noteworthy that a majority of Italian Americans did stick with Roosevelt and the Democrats in 1940, largely on the grounds that they, like other ethnic groups, had benefited from New Deal social and labor legislation. Their indignation at the stab-in-the-back speech and their doubts about the president's foreign policy direction notwithstanding, Italians ultimately endorsed him largely on domestic grounds. "The patronage controlled by the Democratic party played a leading role in curbing the defection of voters of Italian descent from Roosevelt's ranks out of retaliation for the President's attitude toward Italy in foreign policy," pointed out Stefano Luconi.

Boston mayor Maurice Tobin was able to secure enough New Deal money to enable Democrats to strengthen their hold on Italian and other ethnic voters. Between 1934 and 1940, Luconi reported, the percentage of

Italian Americans working on government projects rose from 3 to 11 percent in the North End and from 5 to 11 percent in East Boston. While Tobin's predecessor, James Michael Curley, had conflicts with Roosevelt, "Tobin was on good terms with the President and succeeded in having local WPA [Works Progress Administration] rolls increase in 1940," despite a nationwide drop in relief projects after 1938. Thus, while only one-third of North End Italians had a favorable opinion of Roosevelt as late as June of 1941, a narrow majority still voted for him in the 1940 election based on the jobs his administration had provided.

Roosevelt's stab-in-the-back speech was an important moment in the history of Italians in the United States. Sixty years after the first Italians had arrived, three decades after the floodtide of Italians to America's shores, and nearly twenty years after the imposition of stringent immigration restrictions, Italians believed that the president's Virginia speech had turned back the clock on their progress in the United States. With one callous metaphor, accurate though it may have been in describing Mussolini's actions, Roosevelt dredged up dark stereotypes that Italians had struggled to overcome. It forced them to refight battles they thought they had won, and to give ground in the progress they had made against discriminatory attitudes and practices, once again placing them in the position of having to prove their loyalty to America.

The whole question of Italian loyalty and Roosevelt's treatment of Italians was fresh in the minds of Americans, and thus became an even bigger issue when the United States entered World War II.

For Italians, things would get worse before they got better.

CHAPTER 25

My grandmother, Angela Puleo—all five feet and 130 pounds of her—was officially classified as an "enemy alien" by the United States government in mid-February of 1942. Her alien registration card bore a fingerprint of her right index finger, a grim-faced head-shot photo, and a description of her black-and-gray hair and the scar on her left cheek. At the age of fifty-one, after living in the North End for nearly thirty-five years and raising ten children, she still had not obtained her American citizenship. Though the United States Army would eventually draft and ship overseas three of her sons, including my father, to serve in World War II, in the early days of February 1942, she endured the bewilderment and indignity of registering as an enemy alien.

That label was assigned to her after a breathtaking series of events that occurred in early December of 1941. On December 7, the Japanese attacked United States naval and air bases at Pearl Harbor, Hawaii, destroying most of America's planes on Oahu and two-thirds of its total navy and killing more than 2,300 U.S. servicemen. The next day, President Roosevelt declared December 7, 1941 "a date which will live in infamy" when he sought and received a declaration of war against Japan from the United States Congress. On December 11, Hitler and Mussolini, who had alliances with Japan, declared war on the United States, which then recognized a state of war with Germany and Italy. The day after Pearl Harbor—three days before the declaration of war against the United States by Germany and Italy—President Roosevelt signed and issued Proclamation 2527, designating 600,000 unnaturalized Italians as enemy aliens; the alliance between Germany, Italy, and Japan was enough to prompt his action.

Then, in February 1942, Roosevelt signed one of the most controversial documents in American history, Executive Order 9066, authorizing the relocation and detention of enemy aliens from the West Coast to internment camps in the western and mountain states. Japanese Americans (many of whom were U.S. citizens who were also interned) bore the brunt of this decision. However, one of the little-known stories from the early days of World War II was that as many as ten thousand Italian American noncitizens, mostly but not exclusively on the West Coast, were driven from their homes and jobs, restricted from traveling, and interned in camps for a four-month period in 1942—for reasons of "military necessity." Authorities confiscated shortwave radios and flashlights from Italian fishermen up and down the West Coast, from San Diego to San Francisco. The army imposed curfews and travel restrictions against Italians and issued ID cards. It was not until June of 1942 that the government recognized its mistake and permitted Italian (and some German) aliens to return to their homes.

Italian Americans bristled at the enemy-alien designation and the executive order allowing internment. Even citizens of Italian descent, who were not directly affected by either government order, resented the hardship imposed on their unnaturalized relatives and friends of Italian background. They also recognized the suspicion of Italians that both Proclamation 2527 and Executive Order 9066 would engender among other Americans. "[These orders] helped spread distrust in people of Italian descent who were characterized as potential fifth columnists in the eyes of the U.S. society at large," noted Stefano Luconi.

Italians were further outraged that some of their countrymen classified as enemy aliens had sons fighting in the U.S. Army, as was the case with my grandmother. The *Boston Post* picked up an Associated Press story headlined DEAD HERO'S MOTHER ORDERED TO MOVE, which told the story of Rose Trovato, who lost one son at Pearl Harbor and had a second in the navy. Classified as an enemy alien, she was "ordered today to move from her home in a prohibited zone." Another couple, Mr. and Mrs. Louis Nolfo of St. Louis, both natives of Sicily who were forced to register as enemy aliens, "feel they have the right to call themselves 100 per cent Americans," since five of their six sons were serving in the United States Army.

In the midst of their ire, Italians spent the early part of 1942 "proving" their loyalty in a variety of ways. In Milford, Massachusetts, the Sons of Italy banned the Italian flag and language, its 1,200 members agreeing that "hereafter the organization's meetings must be carried on in English" and the Italian flag "must be put away for all time." In the same town, members of the Sons and Daughters of Italy agreed to change the name of their lodge. The Sons of Italy in Woonsocket, Rhode Island, decided to conduct its business in English "as an indication of loyalty to the United States." In Providence, city councilman Angelo Aiello introduced a resolution to change the name of Mussolini Street to Russo Street, in honor of Albert Russo, the first Rhode Islander of Italian extraction who died in action. In St. Louis, members of the Society of the Immaculate Conception, an Italian organization, burned the Italian flag—its emblem heretofore—and substituted the American stars and stripes at a courthouse ceremony. "The match was applied before about 200 spectators by Anthony Trapani, marshal of the society, after a member had crumpled the flag, flung it on the ground, and saturated it with gasoline," the AP reported. "As the last bit of flame flickered out heads were bared and the United States flag was raised. Many of the members are Italian born." The crowd dispersed quietly. Members of the society explained that the burning of the Italian flag "was voluntary," according to the AP.

Watching all of this from Boston was an irritated James Donnaruma. After he received a form letter from the Inter-Racial Press of America, written to government leaders and media outlets, expressing the strong loyalty of foreign-language newspapers to America's cause, Donnaruma fired off a response to the organization's president. "The conduct of the Italian people in the United States and the Italian newspapers [has] proven their loyalty beyond the least doubt," Donnaruma wrote. "Every Italian organization in the United States are [*sic*] buying defense bonds more than they can afford. The military camps will prove by facts and figures that the Italian young men can easily claim first place amongst all the racial groups in America...and the same thing can be said about the number of Italians that have joined the Navy." Donnaruma said the Italian flag-burning incident in St. Louis was "not the way to prove patriotism" and added: "There isn't a single Italian that can be accused of sabotage or any other disloyalty to this country."

Eventually, President Roosevelt and the U.S. government agreed. Once again, in a last-minute attempt to regain the support of Italian Americans before the 1942 midterm elections, the president instructed attorney general Francis Biddle to revoke the enemy alien status of Italians living in the United States who weren't citizens. In Roosevelt's opinion, the country had nothing to fear from Italians—"they are a lot of opera singers," he told Biddle. The official announcement, once again, came on October 12, Columbus Day, to "let the decision have a broader echo in Italian-American communities nationwide and a deeper impact on the vote," according to a Roosevelt campaign strategist. Biddle himself called the repeal of the enemy alien designation "an important weapon of political warfare" and a deed of "good politics." However, the cumulative effects of the stab-in-the-back speech of 1940, the enemy alien classification, and the internment of Italians on the West Coast proved too much for Democrats to overcome; the GOP made major gains in virtually all Italian American communities in 1942. One campaign report from Cambridge, Massachusetts, said Italian Americans there still resented Roosevelt's Virginia speech two years later "because it implied that Italians are cowards."

For all the injustice toward Italians that President Roosevelt's executive orders bespoke, it is certainly a fact that Italians in America felt a tug of love for the Old Country when the United States joined the battle against Italy. Hundreds of thousands of Italian Americans had been born in Italy, and thousands more still had close relatives there; as the most recent large immigrant group to arrive in the United States, Italians were the ethnic group closest to the people and events back home. Italians were loyal to the United States, but they still loved Italy. One American sociologist remarked that after war broke out between Italy and the United States, "most American Italians looked for a mirage: American victory without Italian defeat." Renzo Sereno of the U.S. Office of War Information put it this way: "[Italian] people of rank and file are in an altogether pathetic situation. They are sincerely attached to America and many of them have children and relatives in the United States Army. At the same time, they have a keen and noble attachment to the country that gave them birth." Indeed, Italian American novelist Gay Talese, whose family lived in New York, described his father's outrage when he learned that American bombers had destroyed the 1,400-year-old Abbey of Monte Cassino, located in southern Italy, northwest of Naples. Joseph Talese "smashed to smithereens" his son's collection of model American aircraft, "framed with balsa wood, covered with crisp paper, suspended from [Gay's] bedroom ceiling by almost invisible threads." Joseph did not seem to hear Gay's cries to stop, "but kept swinging wildly with both hands until he had knocked out of the air and crushed with his feet every single plane that his son had for more than a year taken countless evening hours to make . . . and until that moment had been the proudest achievement of Gay's boyhood."

Joseph Talese's emotional response illustrated Italian scholar Sergio Campailla's simple description of the struggle and the dilemma the war posed for Italian Americans: Fighting against Italy was like fighting against themselves.

Indeed, as Stefano Luconi observed, when Italy signed an armistice with the United States in September 1943 after the fall of Mussolini and the collapse of his dictatorship on July 25, most Italian Americans rejoiced primarily because, as one of them said, "Now our boys in the American Army won't have to kill their own kind."

World War II marked a turning point for Italians in Boston and throughout the United States, a period when their experiences and sacrifices bonded them to Americans of all ethnic groups more tightly than ever before. On the home front, Italians heeded President Roosevelt's clarion call for a unified war effort and joined other Americans by participating enthusiastically in paper drives, tin drives, bond drives, blood drives, clothing drives, and scrap-metal drives. With other Americans, they struggled through the rationing of gas, meat, butter, sugar, and rubber. Italian mothers who lost sons in combat hung gold stars in their windows and grieved like Gold Star mothers of every ethnic group. Italian American women joined "Rosie the Riveter"s of all nationalities to help the country's factories manufacture and deliver more ships, tanks, planes, jeeps, rifles, ammunition, artillery pieces, clothing, blankets, helmets, boots, and other materiel than any nation ever had—enough to supply millions of troops in two separate theaters of combat along ocean and land supply lines that stretched thousands of miles. No nation had ever accomplished such a feat, and this remarkable unifying effort drew Americans of all nationalities closer.

Ultimately, though, it was the contributions of Italian American GIs that once and for all buried any notions of Italian disloyalty toward America and instilled pride in their families and countrymen. More than one million Italian Americans were among the sixteen million soldiers, sailors, airmen, and marines of all ethnic and geographic groups who donned American uniforms during World War II. "The sons of [Italian immigrants] flocked to military recruiting offices and induction centers," wrote United States Air Force major Peter Belmonte. Fighting bravely side by side with other Americans from across the country, young Italian American GIs broke down the stereotypes that had plagued their parents and laid to rest questions about their loyalty.

To tell the full story of Italian American contributions in World War II would require an entire volume, but it is important to list some of their noteworthy achievements and sacrifices. World War II unit histories and memoirs are replete with Italian surnames and references to the contributions and deeds of Italian Americans. Thirteen Italian Americans earned the country's highest honor, the Congressional Medal of Honor, during the war, and Peter Belmonte observed that at least three U.S. Navy warships were named for Italian American war heroes. The USS *Carpellotti* was named for Private First Class Louis J. Carpellotti, a member of the First Marine Raider Battalion killed in action in August of 1942 on Tulagi in the South Pacific. The USS *Damato* was named for Marine Corps corporal Anthony P. Damato, who was killed in action in February 1944 in the South Pacific and posthumously awarded the Medal of Honor. And the USS *Basilone,* a destroyer, was named for the most decorated Italian American of all, Marine Gunnery Sergeant John Basilone. Basilone was the first enlisted man to receive the Medal of Honor during World War II, and is the only soldier in United States history to receive both the Medal of Honor and the Navy Cross, the nation's two highest awards for extraordinary heroism. He was killed in action on Iwo Jima in 1945. In addition, Captain Don Gentile became one of America's leading air aces by downing thirty enemy aircraft during the war. Gentile won two Distinguished Service Crosses, eight Distinguished Flying Crosses, and the Silver Star, among other decorations (tragically, he was killed in a military flying accident after the war).

Other Italian Americans who were, or later became, successful in other fields served in the armed forces during the war, thereby raising visibility and credibility of Italians. These included ballplayers Joe DiMaggio, Dom

DiMaggio, Yogi Berra, Phil Rizzuto, and Joe Garagiola, as well as singers Mario Lanza, Lou Monte, and Tony Bennett, composer Henry Mancini, actor Ernest Borgnine, boxer Rocky Marciano, poet John Ciardi, football coach Joe Paterno, and future Massachusetts congressman Silvio Conte.

These were the heroes and the celebrities, but Italian American servicemen were involved in every military operation in all theaters of the war, "from Europe to Japan, from Africa to Iceland, and from Brazil to Canada," Peter Belmonte noted, "wherever American men and women were stationed during the war, Italian Americans were to be found among them." From the beginning of the war to the end, Italian Americans contributed. Forty-five Italian Americans were among the 2,350 members of the U.S. military killed at Pearl Harbor, and an unknown number were wounded; two Italian American paratroopers were among the first eighteen men to parachute into France just past midnight on D-Day, June 6, 1944; and Italian American airman Sergeant Anthony J. Marchione suffered the last combat death of the war when his plane was attacked by Japanese fighters during a photo reconnaissance mission nine days *after* the second atomic bomb was dropped on Nagasaki. The army also created special units, made up largely of Italian American soldiers and assigned to the Office of Strategic Services (OSS), that operated behind enemy lines in Italy.

The contributions of Italian American GIs to the U.S. military effort —though fighting against their parents' beloved Old Country—changed perceptions of Italians among other Americans, and even among themselves. With their loyalty to the United States now above reproach, Italian Americans no longer felt defensive or even embarrassed about their ties with Italy.

During World War II, Belmonte observed, American GIs with Italian surnames were "fighting and bleeding, not for an adopted country, but for a beloved homeland."

"Italian American families throughout the war felt the impact of the war in a personal way," Peter Belmonte wrote. This was certainly the case in Boston's North End and East Boston, where Italian Americans like my father, who had traveled little, entered the service as youngsters and returned home from combat and foreign locales as veterans. Young men of Italian descent whose social gathering spots were specific "corners" or perhaps taverns in the North End either enlisted or were drafted, and then were trained and shipped overseas at a lightning pace after Pearl Harbor. "The war cleared out my corner and just about every corner in the North End," my father recalled. "The place was deserted in a hurry."

Indeed, my father remembers vividly the day his older brother Jack was drafted in early April of 1942, as the United States desperately sought to beef up its woefully inadequate armed forces after Pearl Harbor. "I remember the day he was supposed to report to the draft board," said my father. "He left at six in the morning and it was chilly outside. I was going to get up and wish him well, but I figured, I'll just see him later at supper when he gets home and hear all about it. So I stayed in bed. Well, he didn't come home—not for another three and a half years. The army was so desperate for men that they took him on the spot without even letting him come back home to get his things. I was upset with myself afterwards for not getting up, but who knew they were going to take him so fast?"

Another of my father's brothers, Charlie, left in the summer of 1942, and my own father reported for duty in September of 1943 at the age of eighteen, after an emotional farewell with his family. "My mother was devastated," he said. "Any mother would be. I was the third son to go and I was the baby. We both cried when I left." As she kissed her third son farewell and sent him into war, it is doubtful that my grandmother took any solace from the fact that she was no longer considered an enemy alien by the government that had drafted her boys. My grandfather, stoic as always, hugged my father and wished him well. "He didn't say much," my father remembered, "but he was very emotional. I could see it in his face."

By the time my father departed, it had been more than a year since his two brothers had entered the service. In September of 1943, it would be another two years before the three Puleo brothers would return home. My two uncles spent their entire tour in Europe, and my dad, who would serve in both Europe and the Pacific, was wounded in action and earned a Purple Heart medal.

That they returned home at all made Jack, Charlie, and Tony Puleo three of the lucky ones.

CHAPTER 26

Sacred Heart Church in Boston's North End was mostly deserted in the cold early evening of Monday, December 10, 1945. Inside the large stone structure that occupied a corner of North Square, a few worshippers sat in the hard wooden pews, praying or watching the candles flicker near the altar rail. One of these people, my grandmother, sixty-year-old Angela Puleo, kerchief covering her head and shawl pulled tightly around her, knelt in a pew near the rear of the church, silently mouthing the rosary as she clutched her strand of beads between her fingers. It was a ritual she had performed most days since April of 1942, when the first of her sons had gone to war. She felt comforted in this church, where nine of her children had been baptized—this church, located mere yards from her home, where she had attended Mass for the thirty-eight years she had lived in America and the North End. Her prayers had worked for her son, Jack, who had arrived home safely in November, after more than three years away, to songs of praise and kisses and tears, one of the North End's sons who had made it home when others had not.

Angela Puleo still had two sons who had not returned, despite the fact that V-E Day had been celebrated seven months ago and the Japanese had surrendered in August to bring an end to the bloody Pacific War. One son, Charles, was still in Europe. He had served as a member of the Army Medical Corps and had been one of the first Allied liberators to witness the horrors of the Buchenwald concentration camp. Another son, Anthony, the youngest of her children, was returning home from Japan, where he had been serving as a member of the occupation force in Yokohama.

Tonight my grandmother prayed for both of those sons, but most fervently for the man who would become my father, who was so much closer to home. There would be time to pray for Charlie later; Anthony had called about two weeks earlier from the state of Washington to say he had arrived safely on American soil after twenty months overseas. "In *America!*" Angela Puleo had cried and then whispered countless prayers of thanks when she had received the phone call, a call she was never sure she would receive, but one she would now never forget. Eleven days later, though it had seemed like a lifetime, Anthony had called again—this time from Fort Devens in nearby Ayer, Massachusetts, not sixty miles from the church in which Angela now prayed. The call from Fort Devens had come on December 7, 1945, exactly four years after the Japanese attacked Pearl Harbor, and her whole, long nightmare had begun. Anthony said he was being discharged but that he would not be home for a few days. Angela prayed now that the last leg of his long journey would pass quickly, and that God would see him safely to his home and his parents and his siblings in the North End. She took nothing for granted—no one had since the war began—which was why she was in church tonight.

Once Anthony Puleo arrived on U.S. soil in Tacoma, Washington, he had embarked on a long troop-train ride across the country that dropped off servicemen along the way—men from Montana, the Dakotas, Chicago, Pennsylvania, New York, and places in between. Stepping off the train would complete a transformation for these servicemen. The occupants of the troop train, including my father, had been frightened boys when they shipped out months or years before to do battle against enemies about whom they knew little. Today, they were men who had played a part in saving the world. Private First Class Anthony W. Puleo was one of these men, though to his mother he would always be her youngest boy, taken from her when he was a tender eighteen-year-old and ordered to fight on two continents. He was returning home at the age of twenty, older than his years, perhaps, but alive and healthy, and desperate to see his ma, pa, sisters, and brothers again. Angela had heard the longing in his voice across three thousand miles of telephone line when he called from Washington, and again when he had spoken to her from Fort Devens.

Fort Devens was his final stop, his last official checkpoint. The army's addiction to paperwork had delayed Anthony's homecoming for another few days while he was examined by a doctor, received his mustering-out pay, and signed up for GI benefits. Angela knew all these things were important, but they were still frustrating because they were delaying her son's return to Boston.

All of these thoughts flashed through her mind as she prayed, and she chastised herself for becoming distracted as she worked her way through the decades of the rosary. She began to concentrate again, so hard that she did not look up at first when her daughter Josephine touched her sleeve and quietly called her name.

"Ma," her daughter said. "Tony just called from North Station. He and a couple of other guys grabbed a taxi at Fort Devens. They couldn't wait for the train to leave. Pa and Gaspare went down to pick him up and take him to the house. He's home, ma."

Angela Puleo looked at her daughter, blinked once, as though not comprehending, blinked again as her eyes filled with tears. "Antonio?" she said.

"Yeah," Jo whispered. "Tony's home. Come on, Ma, let's go see him."

My father's return home on December 10 was followed by his brother Charlie's arrival on December 23, which meant that all three Puleo sons made it home for Christmas of 1945. Caught up in the joy and relief of his three sons' safe return, my grandfather, Calogero Puleo, asked one of his daughters to tear into small pieces of confetti the letters his sons had written home from overseas, including the twice-a-week messages my father mailed home (my father's 1944 Christmas card from Belgium survived).

As a historian, that story breaks my heart. My father's letters would have provided precious material for his World War II story; a treasure trove of memories was lost on that day more than sixty years ago when the letters were destroyed. But as a human being, I think I understand my grandfather's decision. When he asked his daughter to tear up the letters from overseas, there is little doubt that his number one reason was the great relief he felt that his sons had returned home whole and intact. But he also must have been thankful that the rest of his family would no longer be required to sacrifice as they had for the past four years. He never told the family his reasons, but my belief is that Calogero Puleo ordered the letters destroyed as a symbolic gesture; they were, after all, reminders of the fear and unrest his family had endured for four long years. The letters were no longer needed now that the Puleo family was reunited and life would return to normal.

My grandmother's joy when my aunt met her in church, my grandfather's relief when he ordered the letters torn into confetti—emotions and scenes like this were repeated in thousands upon thousands of American homes when World War II ended. For Italian American families, though, the end of the war also meant full acceptance as Americans, a meaningful milestone that cannot be overlooked or overestimated. Too many Italian American families had lost sons, too many Italian American boys had suffered wounds or had risked their lives on the battlefield to save comrades, for their loyalty ever to be questioned again. Their stories came back from Europe and the Pacific and were either printed in newspapers or repeated in conversations. Even Hollywood contributed to the image of Italian Americans during and after the war; the "Italian kid from Brooklyn" became a requisite (albeit clichéd) member of virtually all movie platoons or squads portrayed in World War II films.

Learning English helped and obtaining American citizenship helped even more. But more than anything, it was their contributions and sacrifices during the Second World War that enabled Italian Americans, sixty years after they first arrived in the United States, to finally shed their persona and their stigma as strangers in a strange land.

Still, during the war and afterward, even as Italians in the United States solidified their reputation as "loyal Americans," the strong tug of the homeland, the deep affection for its people, persisted. Italians in America felt sympathy and a kinship to their brethren from Europe. For example, more than fifty thousand captured Italian soldiers were interned in twenty-seven POW camps throughout the United States, according to author Louis Keefer, a fact the War Department kept largely shrouded in secrecy. Yet, New England's large Italian population became aware, "through Italian language newspapers and their local Italian parishes," that nearly seven thousand Italian prisoners of war were interned in Massachusetts, writer Sylvia Corrado noted. Prisoners were housed at Columbia Point in Dorchester; Deer Island; and Peddocks Island off Hull, Massachusetts. Young Italian American women from Boston and surrounding communities often brought these prisoners food, flowers, and supplies, which was permitted by authorities once Mussolini fell in 1943. "[They were] generous and caring to the POWs, hoping that their boys were being treated well by the people of Italy," Corrado said. "The arrival of the Italian POWs was their link to the old country, and they embraced them like brothers." In many cases, she noted, young women became acquainted and fell in love with Italian soldiers.

And later, shortly after the war ended, North End Italians showed their affection for the Old Country by establishing American Relief for Italy, whose mission was to solicit donations of blankets, clothing, food, and other supplies to ship to war-torn Italy. Such organizations sprang up in Little Italy communities throughout the United States. "Italy is one of the countries hardest hit [by war] and therefore aid to its citizens is of an impelling nature," noted advisory committee member Gina Langone in her letter to James Donnaruma asking him to become a committee member. Donnaruma replied on October 1, 1945, that while he was "not in a position to accept" a committee membership, he fully supported and would cooperate in its activities.

Most Boston Italians agreed. Perhaps because their World War II contributions and sacrifices equaled those of any ethnic group, perhaps because they no longer feared any significant backlash, Boston Italians responded with overwhelming generosity to assist their brothers and sisters in Italy.

part 6

The GREATER BOSTON ITALIANS

Some things remained the same after World War II ended. James Donnaruma, who turned seventy in 1944, had turned most of the daily editing responsibilities of *La Gazzetta* over to his son, Caesar, but he continued to assist Italian Americans when they needed help. His work on behalf of the little guy against the major institutions of business and government in Boston was now well known across the city. In February of 1946, he extended his help on behalf of Dante Gregorio, who worked as an advertising agent for *La Gazzetta*. Gregorio had spent a short time at Boston City Hospital after collapsing and suffering a minor head wound. When Gregorio returned home from the hospital, he found that approximately $50 of the $120 he had had in his possession was missing. "I do not imagine how you can trace the man that stole this money," Donnaruma wrote to James Manary, the superintendent of the hospital. [But] if you can find [him] I would advise him to give it back." Donnaruma informed Manary that he had dissuaded Gregorio from complaining to the mayor about the theft and was counting on Manary to make things right quietly, and notify him once the situation was resolved. "Kindly let me hear from you," Donnaruma wrote.

Donnaruma's consistent and tireless toil to benefit Boston Italians was familiar to all who resided in the North End, East Boston, and neighborhoods across the city; World War II had not changed Donnaruma's passion or commitment. Yet, the war and its aftermath spawned other upheaval among Boston Italians and other ethnic groups that packed the power of a cultural and demographic earthquake. The end of World War II represented yet another watershed period in the history of Boston Italians that would alter the face of their neighborhoods and the nature of their relationship with other Americans.

At first, when Italian American servicemen returned home from World War II, they mostly went back to the urban neighborhoods from which they hailed, to reconnect with family and friends and girlfriends and wives. For the most part, single Boston Italian servicemen like my father, and unmarried GIs of all ethnic groups, spent the first few months or years reentering civilian life from their parents' homes. For a year after the war, my father and most of his fellow ex-GIs took advantage of the "52–20 Club," in which veterans received $20 a week for one year (fifty-two weeks) to help them adjust to being home. My dad and his buddies called it the "9–20 Club" because they had to go to 9 Beacon Street to pick up their checks. After the year was up, Boston Italian servicemen found their first postwar jobs in or close to the city in an economy that continued its wartime boom (and would, over the next thirty years, with the exception of occasional mild recessions, bring about the most astonishing levels of production and middle-class affluence in history). They socialized in restaurants, taverns, and coffee shops, often finding their way to Scollay Square by subway from East Boston or by streetcar or on foot from the North End, and enjoying burlesque at the Old Howard Theater, an evening out at the Crawford House hotel nightclub, or a nickel hot dog at Joe & Nemo's. On warm summer evenings, they strolled the streets of the North End and East Boston, tipping their hats and exchanging greetings with the old-timers who gathered on front stoops or sat on chairs outside their apartment buildings. Or they waved up to their mothers' friends, who hailed them from upper-story windows, sometimes in Italian, sometimes in broken English, welcoming them home and blessing their safe return. At first, Boston Italian neighborhoods—like the entire city—were crowded, alive, and flush with excitement when their sons returned home from Europe and the Pacific.

Over the next several years the shift happened, slowly at first, and then with inexorable momentum. These World War II veterans, these sons of Italian immigrants, began to marry, have children, and leave the inner city in droves. During the late 1940s, the 1950s, and into the 1960s, the Boston Italians without question became the Greater Boston Italians, moving to nearby communities such as Chelsea, Winthrop, Revere, Medford, Malden, Somerville, Everett, and Quincy and even to a ring of communities beyond, such as Wakefield, Stoneham, and Arlington, and further still to small towns like Woburn, Winchester, and Burlington, where my parents moved in 1956, when I was two years old, much to the chagrin of their parents, who wondered how they would ever survive in "farm country" so far away. "Where is it—how do you get there?" their parents, older siblings and city friends asked.

It was a combination of factors that produced this exodus. Ex-servicemen had fought alongside comrades of so many nationalities, and while thrilled to reacquaint themselves with the old neighborhoods immediately after the war, they now yearned to move beyond the boundaries of the enclaves and fully assimilate with non-Italians. Leaving the North End and East Boston was more than a geographic relocation; it was a symbolic move into the American mainstream. More practical reasons for leaving the city included the stellar postwar economy, which made it possible even for skilled blue-collar workers like my father to start and raise a family and buy a house; the advent of the GI Bill, which made it possible for thousands of Italian Americans to attend college and provided low-interest home loans from the Veterans Administration (VA) or the Federal Housing Administration (FHA). Education provided these veterans with the opportunity for higher-paying jobs, and the loans offered them a chance to buy single-family homes; both enabled them to join the middle class and improve the economic status of their fledgling families. "The GI Bill gave many of our men the economic ladder to go up and the FHA gave them the money to get out," one Italian American recalled. "[These benefits] made it possible to live in a house that had [at least] three cubic inches of grass and assured status. If you moved to suburbia, you would finally find the recognition and acceptance from the larger America that the people in the old neighborhood had always wanted."

Across the country, the population shift in Italian neighborhoods was sweeping. Chicago's Near West Side Italian community held an Italian immigrant population of nearly 13,000 in 1920, according to historian Humbert Nelli. By 1960, the same area contained a combined total of only 5,100 first- and second-generation Italians, and only 1,800 ten years after that. In Boston's North End, the Italian population decreased more than 45 percent between 1950 and 1960, and 40 percent in the following ten years. The decline was attributable "to younger people and couples moving out of the area," historian Spenser DiScala pointed out. It would still be years before forced school busing (which affected other neighborhoods more directly than the North End) exacerbated "white flight" from Boston even further, but the population decline in Boston's Italian neighborhoods began in earnest during the 1950s and continued in the 1960s. For the first time Italians were leaving the safety and comfort of the enclaves in large numbers and settling in mixed ethnic neighborhoods.

"After World War II, Italians were no longer marginalized and their presence was neither resented nor threatened," historian Marie-Christine Michaud observed, calling Italians' assimilation during this period "one of the most significant examples of success" in the United States.

As its population dwindled, as its younger people sought better economic conditions, the North End continued as the center of life for Greater Boston Italians. Young families still visited their grandparents in the North End every Sunday. Italian American men from Medford, Somerville, and elsewhere still gathered at their fraternal societies on a regular basis to socialize or bartered with the pushcart vendors in Haymarket. Women, mostly, returned to the North End to shop for "real" Italian cheese or olive oil or sausages or pastry or pasta (they still called it "macaroni"). For parades and religious feasts, Italian Americans made the pilgrimage from the suburbs to the North End to hear marching bands play or pay homage to saints as their statues were carried in processions through the neighborhood's narrow streets.

And each year they returned, Italian Americans from the suburbs, along with those from the old neighborhood, commented on how things were not quite the same. "The North End has changed," they would say, meaning there were fewer Italians living there and that some of the old customs were slowly dying. That mantra, "the North End has changed," continued for several decades, well into the 1970s and 1980s, when young upper-middle-class non-Italian suburbanites flocked to the neighborhood and the surrounding waterfront because it had become fashionable to live there; old tenements were converted into some of the most expensive condominiums in the city. Still, even as late as 1980, the North End's population was about 60 percent Italian American (the figure is under 40 percent today), and it retained its character, reputation, and heritage as one of the nation's best-known Italian neighborhoods.

Gathering on the corner on a Sunday morning in the North End *(Photo by Jules Aarons. Courtesy of the Boston Public Library, Print Department)*. Looking out the window to the busy street below was a popular pastime among Italians in the North End *(Photo by Jules Aarons. Courtesy of the Boston Public Library, Print Department)*.

In many ways, though, even as early as the 1950s, Boston Italians, young and old alike, were correct: the North End *had* changed. So had East Boston and Italian neighborhoods in Hyde Park, Roslindale, Dorchester, and Roxbury.

Just as important, as they moved out of these neighborhoods and into the American mainstream, Italians changed, too.

World War II enabled Italians to dispel any myths of their disloyalty to the United States, hastened their arrival into the American mainstream, and bolstered their standing as solid citizens. Yet, one stereotype continued to plague them, dragging down their reputations, a cultural ball and chain that hampered both their progress and their acceptance. As the 1950s began, the image of law-abiding Italian Americans was once again broadly tarnished by the common view that, because of their last names, they were either sympathetic to or associated with organized crime and the Mafia. This stereotype—Italians as criminals—would be promulgated in movies, books, television shows, and common cultural references for decades to come, continuing even to the present day.

In the 1950s, it did not help that many of the most celebrated syndicate criminals and Mafia members *were* of Italian heritage. While Jewish mobster Benjamin "Bugsy" Siegel first recognized the tremendous opportunities for profit from casino gambling in Las Vegas, many casino backers and investors were Italian. In addition, two developments during the 1950s underscored Italian involvement in mob activities: the Kefauver hearings and the now-famous Apalachin Meeting of crime bosses in central New York.

First, in 1950, United States senator Estes Kefauver of Tennessee headed a committee investigating organized crime, called the Senate Special Committee to Investigate Crime in Interstate Commerce, more popularly known as the Kefauver Committee. A number of the six hundred witnesses who testified in fourteen cities were high-profile crime bosses, including Italians Willie Moretti and Frank Costello, the latter "making himself famous by refusing to allow his face to be filmed during his questioning and then staging a much publicized walkout," according to one account. Willie Moretti was one of the few witnesses who joked and spoke candidly with the committee—his reputation and the growing violence of the Mafia were confirmed in 1951 when Moretti was gunned down at lunchtime in retribution for his loose tongue. The Kefauver Committee hearings were televised as Americans were beginning to buy televisions in large numbers, making Kefauver nationally famous and introducing Americans to the concept of a widespread criminal organization. "The Kefauver Committee [also] emphasized the role of Italians and publicized the alleged existence of a 'nationwide crime syndicate known as the Mafia,' " noted Humbert Nelli.

The Apalachin Meeting, a 1957 summit of U.S. mafia bosses at the home of mobster Joseph "Joe the Barber" Barbara, was arranged by Vito Genovese, who at the time was competing with Frank Costello for control of a substantial portion of the New York underworld. Genovese had tried to have Costello assassinated, but the attempt failed, and the meeting was an attempt to settle matters diplomatically. The meeting "descended into a farce when those attending fled in panic after their gathering aroused the curiosity of local police," one account noted. Mafia chieftains fled the house, trudged through the woods, "ruining their expensive suits and tossing guns and cash away in case they were caught." Locals reported finding $100 bills scattered about the countryside for months afterwards. About fifty men escaped, but another sixty-three were captured, including Genovese. According to one report, "virtually all of them claimed they had heard Joseph Barbara was feeling unwell and had popped in to see him and wish him well." Because no crime was committed, all the attendees were later released, "but publicized information about Barbara's guests fanned public fears about Italian criminal activities since all the men identified by authorities were of Italian birth or extraction," Nelli pointed out. Most of the guests had arrived from New York, New Jersey, and Pennsylvania, though others had made the trip from Florida, Texas, Colorado, and California. As one account noted years later: "Everyone thought it was very curious that so many men of Italian descent from various cities, the majority with criminal records, should just happen to be all gathering at one place at the same time."

In Boston, postwar Mafia activity was also in full swing by the mid-1950s. Phil Buccola had fled the country to retire in Sicily, clearing the way for Raymond Patriarca to take control of the New England syndicate. Patriarca quickly named Gennaro "Jerry" Angiulo to run the Boston rackets from his North End offices at 98 Prince Street. Angiulo consolidated power and controlled gambling, racketeering, and loansharking in the North End and throughout Boston for the Patriarca family. Gambling and playing the "number" were commonplace in the North End. "It is not uncommon... to see a $10 bill plummet from a fourth-floor window from which a mother instructs her young daughter in the street below, 'Go see C., the bookie, and put it on 'Many Harvests,'" one writer noted in *The Nation* magazine. "Everyone in town knows you don't have to go a third of a block to book a horse, a dog, a number, or to borrow from 'the shylock.' Everyone knows that certain florists sell no flowers, that certain dry-cleaning establishments clean no clothes."

Though the kinds of activities Angiulo and his cronies participated in were limited to a tiny percentage of Italian Americans, the stereotype of Italians as criminals persisted and was strengthened by two watershed events in the next two decades.

First, former syndicate "soldier" Joseph Valachi, who was serving a twenty-year term in federal prison on a narcotics conviction, offered extensive testimony in 1963 on the structure of Mafia families and their methods of operation. "[He] reinforced the prevailing public impression that syndicate crime involved Italians almost to the exclusion of other groups," Humbert Nelli wrote. Valachi's story was later immortalized in a best-selling book, *The Valachi Papers,* by Peter Maas.

Then, in 1972, Francis Ford Coppola's classic, gripping film *The Godfather* (based on Mario Puzo's novel)—widely considered one of the top five movies of all time—indelibly seared the image of the Italian American crime family upon the American consciousness. "[Its] spectacular success made the 'Mafia Family' a permanent part of popular culture," historian Francis Ianni observed. The *Godfather II* sequel, other popular Mafia films that followed in later years (*Goodfellas, A Bronx Tale, Casino*), and HBO's immensely popular cable television series *The Sopranos* continued Hollywood's fascination with the Mafia in general and, in particular, with portraying Italian Americans as gangsters. Subsequent television dramas, sitcoms, and even commercials made those portrayals commonplace, accepted, and even expected. In essence, these televised political hearings, films, and TV shows picked up where newspaper headlines of the 1920s and 1930s left off, conveying in a more widespread and visually powerful way the image of the Italian mobster.

And, as they had done in the 1930s, Italians themselves played a role in perpetuating this image and, sadly, continue to do so. Italian movie directors (like Coppola and Martin Scorsese) and actors (Marlon Brando, Al Pacino, Robert DeNiro, Joe Pesci, Paul Sorvino, and scores of others) built their reputations and their financial success on gangster movies. Italian American citizens, even today, struggle with a dichotomy they have wrestled with for decades. On the one hand, they labor to distance themselves from the aura of organized crime by stressing the hard work and outstanding achievements of the overwhelming majority of their ethnic group; on the other, Italian Americans as much as anyone—perhaps more than most —frequently glorify the Mafia mystique. They often express misplaced pride in the allure of the "wise guys," defending them for participating in "victimless crimes" such as gambling and prostitution, romanticizing them as swashbuckling characters who do little harm to "innocent people," and offering their begrudging admiration for the brazen rogue or outlaw and the code of honor the Mafia "family" demands. Many law-abiding Italians had, and have, a love–hate relationship with gangsters of their own nationality.

In short, as they struggle to battle Mafia stereotypes that fill the electronic media today, a phenomenon that began with the televised Kefauver hearings in the early 1950s, Italian Americans are often their own worst enemies.

CHAPTER 28

A relaxed and smiling seventy-eight-year-old James V. Donnaruma left the offices of *La Gazzetta* at the end of the work day on May 7, 1953, promising his colleagues that he would be in early the next day.

Later that night he was dead of a cerebral hemorrhage.

Ironically, Donnaruma was stricken while on his way to visit a sick friend prior to returning home. He was transported by ambulance to the intensive care unit at Massachusetts General Hospital and died at 11:30 P.M. without regaining consciousness, his wife, children, and other family members at his bedside. After a funeral High Mass at St. Cecilia Church in Boston, "celebrated with much emotion," Donnaruma was buried in the family tomb at St. Michael's Italian Cemetery in Forest Hills, founded fifty years earlier by his old friend George Scigliano. James Donnaruma was survived by his second wife, Margaret, "who was in profound mourning," according to *La Gazzetta,* his sons, Caesar and Guy Paul, his daughter, Florence (Yurko), six grandchildren, and three great-grandchildren. In addition, "he has left an open painful void in the heart and soul of his many friends," the *La Gazzetta* article noted. "With [his] departure, the Italians of America . . . lose one of their most fierce and valued defenders of their rights, culture, and ideals. [With] the irreproachable loyalty of an American citizen, he [also] admired the noble ideologies of his new-found country."

La Gazzetta's long and colorful non-bylined tribute, written in Italian, began on the front page and continued inside, a mix of Donnaruma's personal history and his contributions and dedication to Italian causes. "His life was spent on the existence of the struggling and the difficulties of young immigrants trying to survive in a strange land, the lonely times, [when] every crumb of bread earned was bathed in tears and sweat and bittered by the insufferable injustices of prejudice of race, religion, and nationality," *La Gazzetta*'s paean exulted. "His strength of spirit and his mind guided him on [his] mission." Donnaruma went to his death with some satisfaction, the paper continued, because "he lived to see his dreams and ideals and hopes come to fruition. The Italians in America have in fact already shown in a considerable, remarkable manner, their success in politics, socially, and professionally in this Democracy."

Condolence letters and telegrams poured in to *La Gazzetta,* far too many to print all of them. Judge Vincent Brogna of the Massachusetts Superior Court, Donnaruma's friend of more than forty years, wrote that "his death is a great loss for all Americans of Italian descent in our beloved State of Massachusetts." Brogna said Donnaruma knew the "inner souls" of Italians, and thus could describe their "characteristics and personalities so that people would understand their ways and beliefs." Professor Angelo Papa, who attended Donnaruma's funeral, urged *La Gazzetta* readers to "keep his thoughts and beliefs alive . . . Remember his honorable victories for the good of the people of Italian descent." And to the newspaper itself, Papa implored its staff to "carry on . . . spiritual force and material force will help you continue your triumphant walk as your great founder did."

A fellow newspaperman and Donnaruma's friend for more than fifty years, Agostino de Biasi of New York lauded the late editor for "his work, his time and effort, his joy of family life, his personal ambitions, and his heartbreak. His life was dedicated to the existence of the newspaper." De Biasi called Donnaruma a "gentle man, the ultimate citizen," and "devoted friend." Perhaps de Biasi's most poignant tribute: "He never abandoned or misrepresented the weak."

More than a half century after Donnaruma began publishing and editing *La Gazzetta,* the newspaper concluded its mournful tribute to its founder with words that, in all likelihood, would have pleased him most:

"We, your humble and faithful admirers, gather up the Italian ideals, faithful in the final triumph of your cause . . . Know that your noble spirit will brighten and be heard in the pages of this, 'your' newspaper, a monument to the defense and protection of the rights of the Italian people."

CHAPTER 29

"On March 2," publisher Caesar Donnaruma wrote to President John F. Kennedy in February of 1962, "*La Gazzetta* . . . will become the all-English, all Democratic *Post-Gazette*." Part of the reason for the transition, Donnaruma explained to President Kennedy, was the "urgent need of a newspaper which will be representative of the Democrats of Massachusetts who lack one spokesperson in the newspaper field."

Caesar Donnaruma's letter to Kennedy announced two major changes to Boston's oldest Italian newspaper. First, though its shift to a Democratic-leaning publication would have roiled James Donnaruma's soul, Italian support for Kennedy in the 1960 election convinced Caesar that there was a strong need for a Democratic voice in the community. Kennedy's Catholicism and charisma endeared him to Boston Italians, just as these two attributes—along with his heritage—elevated him to iconic status among Boston's Irish population. (The inconsistency of the "Italian vote" was illustrated when Boston Italians supported Republican John Volpe for Massachusetts governor in the same 1960 election. Volpe was the second consecutive Italian American governor elected in the Commonwealth; Democrat Foster Furcolo, Massachusetts's first Italian American governor, served two two-year terms prior to Volpe.)

Caesar Donnaruma first developed a friendship with Jack Kennedy in the mid-fifties, when the then senator invited him and his wife, Phyllis, to a reception to honor Italian ambassador Manlio Brosio upon his visit to Boston. Like his father, Caesar labored on behalf of Italians awaiting entry into the United States or seeking to avoid deportation, for which he petitioned Kennedy on occasion. Later, in 1957, while he served as state commander of the Disabled American Veterans (he had been injured in the First World War), Caesar Donnaruma and an Italian American citizens' committee organized a testimonial for Jack Kennedy to honor his World War II service. The Kennedy–Donnaruma friendship grew and continued while Kennedy occupied the White House.

But it was the second decision Donnaruma articulated in his 1962 letter to Kennedy, news of *La Gazzetta's* conversion to English as the *Post-Gazette,* that represented an even greater change than the publication's political party affiliation. Boston Italians had moved beyond the city's borders and into the suburbs; among the ones who remained, the number of those who could speak and read Italian had dwindled since the Second World War, and so, too, had the number of *La Gazzetta* readers. In Caesar's first full year as publisher in 1954, *La Gazzetta* had shown an operating loss of more than $100,000 in the first four months and was saddled with liabilities exceeding $600,000. He had since returned the paper to profitability, and still had never missed an issue, but he recognized the need to transform the business to continue its progress.

Caesar Donnaruma's excited words to Senator John F. Kennedy did not prove entirely accurate. *La Gazzetta,* soon to be the *Post-Gazette,* would not become *all* English for another nine years, after Caesar retired and his wife, Phyllis, became publisher. In 1962 most of the paper switched to English, but Caesar decided to publish two pages of Italian in the newly named *Post-Gazette.* Nonetheless, New England's largest Italian newspaper would never be the same.

The North End neighborhood, the city, and Boston Italians were changing. It was incumbent upon *La Gazzetta* to change with them.

Since Caesar Donnaruma took over from his father as editor of the *La Gazzetta* in 1953, much of the change in and around the North End and the Boston Italian community had manifested itself with one big event after another—some positive and others not. One of the first of these events sent waves of jubilation through the North End. In 1955, for the first time ever, the neighborhood celebrated one of its own as world welterweight champion. Boston Italians had taken great pride when an Italian American son of a nearby city, Brockton, became heavyweight champion of the world. Rocky Marciano held the title from 1952 to 1956 and finished his undefeated career with an astounding 49–0 record. But when North End native Tony DeMarco was crowned welterweight champ in 1955, the feeling was different among Boston Italians.

Tony was one of their own, a favorite son, born on Fleet Street during the winter of 1932 to Sicilian immigrant parents. He was christened

Leonardo Liotta, and like all babies born to working-class people during
the Depression, he faced an uphill struggle as his parents scraped to eke out
a living. In this case, Leonardo's father, Vincenzo, worked as a shoemaker
in Copley Square to support his family, including his newborn, whom family members and friends would come to refer to as Nardo.

When North End native Tony DeMarco was crowned welterweight boxing champion
in 1955, the entire neighborhood celebrated. *(Courtesy of Pam Donnaruma and the* Post-
Gazette*)*

At the time of his birth, there was little remarkable about Nardo or his family. Like most Italian families, they likely survived the Depression by doing without: buying inexpensive foods such as pasta and beans (with perhaps a little meat on Sundays), wearing hand-sewn clothing, perhaps relying only on the heat from an open oven door to warm their apartment on the coldest of days. When Nardo was born, the Liottas' *paesani* had no inkling that one day he would become famous and that the mention of his name—he chose Tony DeMarco as his ring moniker—would cause North End Italians and their brethren across the city to swell with pride.

Tony developed into a powerful puncher with quick hands and a rocketing left hook. When he defeated Philadelphia's Johnny Saxton with a fourteenth-round TKO to claim the title, partying in the North End lasted four days and was characterized by the *Boston Globe*'s John Ahern as a Mardi Gras worthy of New Orleans. Tony's reign was brief—just sixty-nine days later, Carmen Basilio knocked him out in Syracuse in the twelfth

Photograph by Jules Aarons

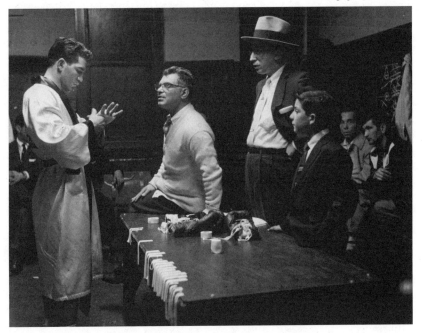

North End native Tony DeMarco tapes up before a fight in the 1950s. *(Photo by Jules Aarons. Courtesy of the Boston Public Library, Print Department)*

round, and later, in July, with the Boston Garden packed to the rafters ("It felt and sounded as though the populace of DeMarco's motherland, the North End, had relocated to the Garden," wrote the *Globe*'s Bud Collins fifty years later), Basilio successfully defended his title in a classic rematch that boxing aficionados labeled the "fight of the year." Years afterward, De-Marco said of his title: "If it had been only one day, I would have been happy. That was my dream—to be a world champion."

Boston Italians may have been overjoyed, but their joy was short-lived. In 1958, Mayor John B. Hynes launched one of the most ambitious and controversial urban renewal projects in the city's history—the redevelopment, and ultimate destruction, of Boston's West End. The neighborhood, which abutted the North End on the west side of the Boston Garden, was one of Boston's oldest communities, and consecutive waves of immigrants —Irish, Italians, Jews, Greeks, Armenians, Poles, Russians—"had turned the neighborhood into a seething and colorful melting pot that at one point was home to as many as twenty-three thousand residents," historian Thomas O'Connor pointed out.

Its residents and its neighbors regarded the West End as a warm, hospitable, close-knit community—a multiethnic version of the North End —in which to live and raise children. "The West End was beautiful and unique," O'Connor quoted one former resident as saying. "One of the city's crimes against itself is that the West End's narrow and mysterious European streets and alleys are not there for the old men to walk, for me to walk, for everyone else to walk."

Yet, Hynes and other liberal urban planners viewed the West End as overcrowded and impoverished, a slum area that would be a perfect spot to take advantage of federal funds that were available to launch a massive urban renewal project. "With a closely packed population that was susceptible to contagious epidemics . . . and those mysterious European streets so narrow that fire engines could not reach a conflagration, social scientists regarded the West End as a disaster waiting to happen," O'Connor noted. The Boston Redevelopment Authority declared that the area was "so clearly substandard" that the only solution was a "sweeping clearance of buildings."

Despite neighborhood and political protests, the wrecking ball and the bulldozer soon destroyed the neighborhood, pulling down homes and tenements, clearing entire city blocks, and displacing more than 3,200 families, for whom the city had made no adequate housing provisions. At the last minute, a few important historic sites such as the Old West Church and the first Harrison Gray Otis House were saved from destruction, but "the rest of the West End was completely obliterated," O'Connor wrote. Years later, city councilor Fred Langone, who at the time was a member of the committee fighting the West End urban renewal plan, called the West End project a "catastrophe.... the irony of the whole shameful episode in the city's history is that the whole purpose of urban renewal was to rebuild cities." Langone noted that the West End and North End people were two close-knit communities "bound by friendships and relations that tied them together." Italian-speaking West Enders worshipped in the North End, mostly at Sacred Heart Church. Many Italian fruit and produce dealers who lived in the West End peddled their wares at Haymarket with their North End brethren. "The tragedy of the West End would not have happened if the elected officials had followed the [urban renewal] guidelines," Langone wrote. "Some politicians serve their own self-interests and forget the public consequences."

O'Connor pointed out the long-term impact of the West End disaster: "The totality of the destruction and the ruthlessness with which it had been carried out engendered such bitter feelings that the future of any further urban renewal projects in Boston was very much in doubt. Residents of other sections of the inner city and the outlying neighborhoods became so terrified at what had happened to the people of the West End that they were determined not to allow the bureaucrats, the technocrats, and the real estate developers to destroy their communities and displace their people."

Perhaps so, but another long-term construction project that had begun with a wrecking ball in 1951 created even more heartbreak in Boston's North End Italian community. A massive elevated highway, known as the Central Artery, under construction throughout the 1950s, resulted in property takings and evictions from the North End, as "a cloud of impending disaster wafted gradually over the city's oldest and most cohesive residential neighborhoods," wrote Yanni Tsipis. The project created "a swath of destruction ... through the commercial heart of the North End." Some merchants and residents held out, refusing to move, but they only delayed the inevitable. Work was delayed for a month near Fulton Street when a young boy was injured, but again, this was only a temporary stoppage.

When it opened on June 25, 1959 (already obsolete for the growing traffic flow), the serpentine three-mile elevated highway wound its way through the spine of the city, a giant steel snake, severing the North End from the downtown area. Hanover, Salem, Blackstone, Cross, and other streets now halted abruptly as they bumped up against the artery, or their traffic flow was disrupted dramatically. The new elevated highway shrouded the western portion of the North End in shadow for almost the entire day, and neighborhood residents were now subjected to the noise and pollution generated from the thousands of vehicles—more than 200,000 daily in the peak years—that traversed the new highway day and night.

Progress, perhaps, but the Central Artery project represented yet another signal to Boston Italians that they retained second-class status in their city. The North End neighborhood, for years a tight-knit, closed enclave, was now literally cut off from the rest of the city, and would remain so for the next forty-five years.

The same year the Central Artery opened, 1959, personal loss struck the Puleo family when my grandfather, Calogero, died from heart failure at the age of seventy-seven, leaving my grandmother and his ten children. I was only five years old when he died, but I still remember the visits my parents and I made to my grandparents' North End home. He was a strong, quiet, and gentle man. I would sit on his lap, my shoulder pressed tight against his broad chest, place my small hand against his cheek, and slide my smooth palm against the sandpaper stubble of his beard. "Grandpa, it's scratchy, you forgot to shave this morning," I said each time I repeated this ritual. He would emit a low, musical chuckle from deep inside and squeeze me tighter with his thick forearms. "Tomorrow," he promised with a wink, his still-heavy Italian accent evident even in that single word. "I shave tomorrow." I still hold in my mind the vivid image of my father, then thirty-four, on the day his father died, sobbing in our living room, holding me close, repeating the words, "He's gone, pal. He's gone." It was my first memory of my father shedding tears.

Like so many other Italian immigrants, my grandfather had spent his entire life doing menial outside work to support his family—first as a pick-and-shovel laborer and then as a pushcart vendor—all the while struggling against poverty, discrimination, illiteracy, and a daunting language barrier. Fifty-three years after he crossed through the gates of Ellis Island and started a new life in the United States, the patriarch of the Puleo family could finally rest.

Boston and Massachusetts politics were changing, too, and Italians, while never achieving the success of the Irish during the 1960s, 1970s, and 1980s, made significant progress.

Following in his father's footsteps, Caesar Donnaruma issued his clarion call for Italian political strength immediately after assuming the reins of *La Gazzetta*. To an Italian American group in 1954 he said: "I can assure you that we have an abundance of men and women among the more than half-million Italo-Americans in Massachusetts whose qualifications for leadership can easily match those of any other racial group." To those who argued that Italians had "done well" because "a handful of Italo-Americans have been placed in positions of responsibility," Caesar Donnaruma suggested otherwise. "There are 240 members of the House [and] we can point to 25 Italo-Americans," he said. "We can't boast or call this an achievement because it is just about 10 percent of membership and we [Italian Americans] number more than 20 percent of the registered voters of the state."

In the decades following Donnaruma's remarks, Italians made their political presence known. Furcolo and Volpe were elected just a few years later as governors, and Volpe, after a heartbreaking loss to Endicott Peabody in 1962, was reelected in 1966 as the first governor in Massachusetts history to serve a four-year term (the result of a change to the state constitution), by the largest margin accorded to a Massachusetts gubernatorial candidate: more than 500,000 votes. Democrat Francis X. Bellotti, who served as lieutenant governor in the mid-sixties, became attorney general in 1974 in a close election against Republican Josiah Spaulding. Bellotti's squeaker came in a year when other Democrats rolled to victory, a fact that the *Post-Gazette* laid at the feet of the *Boston Globe*, accusing it of "trying to smear Bellotti in its news and editorial columns." The Globe, wrote *Post-Gazette* reporter Joe Altano, printed a poll the day before the election showing Spaulding as frontrunner, "and charges were rife that this supposedly impartial poll was rigged" by former supporters of Endicott Peabody, whom Bellotti had defeated in the Democratic primary for governor ten years earlier. "The residue of ill will against him [Bellotti] apparently hasn't diminished with time on the part of [the *Globe*'s] Peabody adherents," Altano wrote.

Several Italian Americans also became state legislators or prominent and influential members of the Boston school committee or city council. (The latter group followed in the footsteps of Gabriel Piemonte, a North End lawyer who became the first Italian American to win a citywide race in 1951, capturing a seat on the newly created nine-member at-large city council. "On his first day in office, he was elected president of that body," wrote William Marchione, "the first Italian-American to hold the post.") Italians reacted with pride when Larry DiCara, a Harvard graduate, was elected to the council in 1971. In 1973, another Harvard graduate, East Boston's Michael LoPresti, following in his father's footsteps, was elected to the state senate, where, for nearly twenty years, he served a district that included his home neighborhood, the North End, and parts of Cambridge. His father had served the same district in the 1940s and 1950s. Chris Ianella ("Chick Morelli" in William Foote Whyte's *Street Corner Society*) served with distinction on the Boston City Council, becoming president in 1980. East Boston's Elvira "Pixie" Palladino was a vocal and controversial opponent of forced busing as a school committee member in the mid-1970s.

Yet the strongest Italian American force for two decades was the irrepressible, colorful, irascible voice of the Boston City Council, Fred Langone, better known as Freddie to his constituents. In the mold of his father, Freddie was regarded as a tireless worker for the "little guy," battling other politicians and downtown developers to preserve neighborhood rights. Langone had his foibles, to be sure, but his blunt speaking style masked a quick wit, a sharp mind, and the keenest of political instincts, and almost always caused his political enemies to underestimate him. His supporters and his opponents often said that Freddie Langone knew where every dollar was buried in the Boston city budget. Freddie Langone's quips and plain speech, which made him one of the most quotable of Boston politicians, endeared him to North End Italians. When Massachusetts passed a property tax restriction law in 1980 known as Proposition 2½, Langone, fearful of its impact on the city, quickly labeled it "Proposition two-and-a-laugh," pronouncing the final word as "laahhhhf" in his classic Boston accent. When Pope John Paul II visited Boston in 1979, Langone, as chairman of the city council's Ways and Means Committee, argued in favor of appropriating $750,000 for security, traffic, and crowd control. "Boston is an international city," he said. "This ain't Toledo."

In the mid-1990s, after he had left the council, Langone wrote glowingly of the North End and its people, dedicating his words to "the early Italian pioneer immigrants... if it weren't for their perseverance and tenacity, there would be no North End as we know it." It was that spirit, Langone said, that would inspire future generations to preserve the neighborhood, so that "no matter how many highways and tunnels they build in and around the North End, it will live on forever because the people are proud of it and won't let it die."

Most people who observe that "the North End has changed" are not referring to the nature of organized crime, but the phrase certainly *could* apply to mob activities in Boston.

In the early 1980s, the FBI—with the help of Irish mobster James "Whitey" Bulger—bugged Gennaro Angiulo's 98 Prince Street headquarters and gathered enough evidence to bring his mob empire crashing down. Angiulo and his brothers were convicted of illegal gambling, racketeering, and extortion; Gerry Angiulo was sentenced to forty-five years in prison. Later, court testimony and published accounts revealed that Whitey Bulger, in one of the most intriguing and shocking alliances between organized crime and law enforcement, had worked as an FBI informant for years, and that most of his criminal activities—even murder—were carried on with the knowledge, and often the protection, of the FBI, particularly his boyhood friend, agent John Connolly. The subsequent scandal rocked the Boston office of the FBI. The demise of Angiulo and the Italian mob bolstered Bulger's illegal activities, at least until the South Boston mobster became a fugitive in 1995.

With the destruction of Angiulo's organization and the Patriarca crime family in the late 1980s, the Italian mafia in Boston fell into disarray. Italian criminals were now mostly small-time hoods rather than big-time gangsters. There would still be crime, of course, some of it organized, but other ethnic groups began to control illegal activities in Boston and surrounding areas.

The true heyday of the Italian Mafia "family" in Boston, glorified by many and resented by others, was, like much in the North End, a thing of the past.

Caesar Donnaruma retired in 1971, turning the title of publisher and editor of the *Post-Gazette* over to his wife, Phyllis, who became a leading figure in Boston in her own right, counseling immigrants, doing charity work, and maintaining an open-door policy at the paper's 5 Prince Street offices for Boston's Italian community. One of the nation's first Italian American woman publishers, Phyllis had enormous influence in Massachusetts and national political circles. State politicians and candidates made her office an early stop on their campaign trail, and she even made the short list for the ambassadorship to Italy during the Carter administration. While honored, she asked that her name be withdrawn from consideration; remaining close to home and family was more important to her.

In 1974, Caesar and Phyllis offered the papers of James Donnaruma to Professor Rudolph Vecoli, director of the Immigration History Research Center (IHRC) at the University of Minnesota. "We are anxious to have the . . . materials you mentioned," Vecoli said. "[They] would be a welcome addition to our Italian-American Collection . . . so please save everything for us." In addition, the IHRC microfilmed virtually every issue of *La Gazzetta*. To this day, the James V. Donnaruma papers make up one of the most comprehensive and important collections for any Italian American in the IHRC's holdings.

Caesar Donnaruma died in June of 1989, at the age of eighty-nine. The *Post-Gazette* published its tribute under the headline HAIL CAESAR AND FAREWELL. Seventeen months later, after her own nineteen-year stint as publisher (she changed the *Post-Gazette* to all English in 1971), Phyllis Donnaruma died at the age of seventy-four. "I know that Auntie is proud of us for never missing an issue," wrote Phyllis's niece, Diane Greene, in her *Post-Gazette* tribute in the November 9, 1990, issue. "This one is dedicated to her memory. I pray that she gives us the courage to continue her mission."

PART 7

Boston Italians *as* Leaders: Emergence *and* Accomplishment

CHAPTER 30

The way Sal Balsamo figures it, his old boss did him a favor in the mid-1960s when he told Sal flat out that there was no room for Italian Americans in his company's senior management ranks.

Though Sal was among the temporary staffing company's top salesmen year in and year out, helping the company grow from $880,000 to $13 million in four years, his boss made it clear that he would never gain admittance to the company's upper echelon. Sal had an inkling that something was amiss when his CEO started hiring layers of management above and around him, blocking his entrance to the executive suite. "Finally," Sal recalled in a 2005 interview, "I asked him, 'why are you putting these people around me? They don't have the talent I have.' He said, 'Sal, to tell you the truth, I'm not going to have any Italians in the top echelon of my company.' God's truth. He just said matter-of-factly that Italians were not welcomed on the senior management team. I knew what I had to do. At that moment, I made up my mind to start my own business and compete with him. I waited until the right time and then said good-bye." Four years later, Sal Balsamo and a partner started TAC Worldwide. With immense confidence in his own ability to become successful, Sal did not view the venture as a gamble. His wife, though, was fearful. "I was married with three children," he said. "My wife said I needed to have my head examined. I had a good job with the old company, I had a company car. We had just bought a new house. But I couldn't see myself working for a company that didn't want me around. That was okay—they actually did me a favor."

From there, Balsamo's story assumed Horatio Alger status. He founded and became CEO of TAC Worldwide, headquartered in Dedham, Massachusetts, which went on to become a billion-dollar enterprise, one of the largest and most prestigious temporary staffing companies in the world. As he built his company and wielded more influence as a business force, Balsamo used his status to advance Italian American causes in Boston and across the United States. While he is no longer a young man, he does represent one of the new breed of Italian American professionals, entrepreneurs, and elected officials who are attempting to shed light on the achievements of Italian Americans, leading by example, fighting continued discrimination, and more important, passing along to their children, grandchildren, and society at large an awareness of the contributions and essence of Italian culture. They are the twenty-first-century versions of George Scigliano, James Donnaruma, and the dozens of other leaders who have shared the Boston Italian experience.

Among the general public and even the media, many of these individuals continue to fly under the radar when Boston's most influential leaders are mentioned; despite his company's success, Sal Balsamo is far from a household name in the city.

Yet, through their words and deeds, they are spreading their message.

If there was a secret to Sal Balsamo's success, it lay in his ability to create a workplace atmosphere that exemplified the best virtues and values of the Italian family, and then apply the business precepts that his father taught him. These were lessons about the bottom line, for sure, but mostly, Anthony Balsamo shared with his son a lifetime of lessons about people.

Born in 1933 in a three-decker in Boston's Dorchester section to Anthony and Rosalia Balsamo, Sal learned quickly the value of hard work and the pride his parents felt about living in America. His father emigrated from Carini, Sicily, in 1907 at the age of sixteen, the oldest of five brothers, and believed the best chance he had of contributing to his family was to earn money in the United States. He struggled for the first several years, but then during World War I he became a cook in the army, where he learned enough to launch an extraordinarily successful culinary career. From opening what Sal described as "the first Italian restaurant in Boston" —where he served a plate of spaghetti, a meatball, bread, and a glass of wine for a nickel—Anthony Balsamo became a skilled and highly sought-after chef who worked in major restaurants and hotels. He was head chef at the first major hotel in Miami Beach and became the first chef for the Sheraton Corporation.

Every week throughout the course of his career, Anthony Balsamo sent money back to his family in Italy, Sal remembers, until he had sent enough to bring all of them to the United States. "My father loved this country for the opportunity it gave him," Sal said. "He loved being an American. He made the best of the opportunities this country gave him, and he wanted the same for his family."

Finally, in 1955, Anthony Balsamo bought his own restaurant, and for the next six years Sal worked for his dad, during what he called the best years of his life. "He taught me something every day, simple commonsense lessons that stayed with me." Sal recalled one example: At his father's restaurant, workers had to walk through a storeroom to the changing area to don their uniforms for the meal period. Soon, the Balsamos noticed items missing—tuna cans, coffee, other canned goods, and Anthony told his sons that he would build a cage around the storage area. "I'll buy the materials and you guys build the cage," Sal's father said. Sal and his brother scoffed when his father brought back flimsy wood strips, "chicken wire you could break with your hands," and a thin-hasped lock that a strong child could break. " 'Dad,' we said, 'who do you think this will keep out?' " Sal recalled. "My father said, 'Boys, it will keep the honest people out because it will remove the temptation. All they need is this simple cage to get the message.' And he was right. We built this cage that you could probably knock down with one hand, and the pilferage problem went away. That's the kind of thing I learned from him. He was not an educated man—only went to school through the sixth grade—but he was the smartest man I knew."

Anthony Balsamo's smarts rubbed off on his son. Under Sal's leadership, TAC Worldwide, which opened as Technical Aid Corporation in 1969, experienced enormous growth. By the end of the twentieth century, the company hit the $1 billion revenue mark, making it the largest privately held company of its kind. TAC's corporate headquarters were in Dedham, Massachusetts, and its far-flung reach included 150 offices in fifty states and twenty-three countries in North America, Europe, and Southeast Asia. Beginning in 1995, TAC was included on the Forbes 500 list of top private companies. Balsamo finally sold the company in September of 2005 to a large Japanese staffing company and established his own diversified investment company.

Balsamo's success is rooted in simple values. "If you asked every employee in our company, and that's eight hundred to nine hundred employees, what it was like to work at TAC, they would tell you it's like being in a big family. That's the number one value we tried to instill here—a sense of family. Family is number one, and I think that's true in the workplace, too." Indeed, this is far from an empty corporate platitude; TAC had the usual president's club and corporate recognition programs, but the family commitment went far beyond that. From TAC's inception, Balsamo and his wife would visit every single office in the company once a year and have dinner with every one of its employees (1,500 at the company's peak), in small groups, large groups, or even one on one. Up until a few years ago, his wife, Yvonne, "knew every single person, every single child, every graduation, every wedding our employees had. That's what I mean about family."

Balsamo's instincts on the importance of creating a family culture were borne out by the fact that TAC had the lowest employee attrition rate in the industry. "Headhunters come up to me, shaking their heads, and saying, 'We don't even call your people anymore because we know they won't leave,'" Balsamo said. "I've tried to stress the importance of people my whole career." Such an approach has benefited Balsamo, too. "I haven't stayed in business all this time just to make money," he said. "Money is fine, but you can only drive one car at a time or wear one suit at a time. Where I get my thrill, my kick, is from watching other people grow. That's where the real joy is for me."

For more than a decade now, Sal Balsamo has directed his passion and energy toward sharing and promoting his Italian heritage. He serves as vice president of the National Italian American Foundation's (NIAF) New England region and as a member of the board of directors for the Massachusetts Chapter of the National Italian-American Sports Hall of Fame, and he has established a charitable foundation that conducts fundraising activities on behalf of charities serving children and the elderly.

Perhaps his greatest honor as an Italian American occurred in 2003, when he received the Ellis Island Medal of Honor from the National Ethnic Coalition of Organizations Foundation (NECO) for his work on behalf of Italian Americans. The award is given to citizens of various ethnic backgrounds for promoting cultural awareness; other winners have included Martin Scorsese, Danny Aiello, Mike Wallace, Lee Iacocca, Coretta Scott King, Ronald Reagan, Colin Powell, and Madeleine Albright. In 2003, 130 recipients were chosen from ten thousand nominees.

For Balsamo, who dedicated the award to his immigrant parents, the real joy was renting a bus and taking thirty-five family members with him to New York for the ceremony, including his ninety-seven-year-old mother (who died the next year). "To get the award was one thing, but to have her there was so special," he recalled. "The whole thing was an extraordinary experience—it gives you such a feeling of heritage. It's so important to retain that."

Balsamo believes that the current resurgence, in the Boston area and nationally, in preserving the Italian American culture derives from Italians' fear that the old ethnic values are eroding. "You had a generation where Italian families would spend every Sunday dinner together, and that's gone away," he laments. "The Italian language is not taught as much in schools, something the NIAF is trying to change. If we don't preserve it, there will be no Italian heritage in one hundred or two hundred years. We have to at least put our finger in the dike and slow down the erosion. It's why I insist that my children, my grandchildren, all know about their Italian heritage."

His love of and commitment to his heritage is one other thing Balsamo attributes to his late father's influence. "His approach seemed like a contradiction," Balsamo said. "He loved this country. Unlike most Italians, he became a citizen as fast as he was able. He wouldn't allow Italian to be spoken by us—he would only speak it to my mother. In all ways, he wanted to be an American. But yet, despite all of that, he was fiercely proud of his heritage. He would never let us forget where he came from. He knew you could be a great American and still love your Italian heritage."

It is a creed that Sal Balsamo has adopted as his own.

CHAPTER 31

"Let me tell you a secret," said Barbara Summa, owner of the La Summa restaurant on Fleet Street (aka Tony DeMarco Way) in the North End. "Most of the people who own restaurants in the North End today are not from the North End. They're here to make money. So when they bring down the grate at night, they go home. They aren't concerned about what happens to the *people* here. That was never the case. Business owners used to live here and take a personal interest in the neighborhood. That's just one way the North End has changed."

There are others, of course, and Summa, a North End resident for her entire life, symbolizes another piece of the change; when Summa opened her popular restaurant in February of 1983 as a way to support herself and her children after a divorce, she was (and still is) one of the few women who owned eating establishments in the neighborhood. Today, her restaurant, a cozy place with family photos on a bookcase near the front door, a wine rack against one wall, and white linen–covered tables, provides an intimacy that is a metaphor for Barbara's North End of old. La Summa is frequented by Boston mayor Tom Menino and other elected officials and local notables, but this is not a spot that caters to celebrity. "Regular people love it here, because it's clean, the food is good, and there is warmth here," Barbara said. Couples, friends, old-timers—all of them frequent La Summa for a taste of good Italian food and a slice of North End nostalgia. It is Barbara's way of keeping alive a way of life that she believes is long past, and one she misses with wistful sadness.

"My son is right—he says to me, 'Ma, unless you experienced it, you can't explain it,'" she said, and then proceeds to explain it very well. "This was a neighborhood where everyone looked out for everyone else. Sunday mornings, all the church bells would ring at St. Leonard's and St. Mary's and Sacred Heart. Windows would be open—no one had air conditioning —and you could smell the sauce simmering and the coffee perking. Maybe you'd buy coffee and a paper and visit someone. I'd visit my grandmother and help her roll meatballs in the breadcrumbs before they were fried. My other job was to cut the fresh parsley. I still smell the smells, I still hear my grandmother. And I miss it, because I think so much of it is going away."

Soft-spoken yet intense, Summa laments the rise in property values that has driven so many "original North Enders" from their homes (she bought an apartment house in 1969, before prices spiked, that has allowed her to stay in her beloved neighborhood), and the gentrification that has brought about a collision of values and cultures. "I feel that if you move into my neighborhood, you should respect my ways," she said. "We have people here today who don't do that. They complain about the feasts, they complain about the procession of the saints, they complain about the church bells. These are small things—the Italian people here, the minority that are left, don't ask for much. Neither did the old-timers. That should be respected, just as every nationality should be respected. People should not try to change us."

Born in 1940 (her grandfather emigrated from Italy, went back to marry and have children, and then returned), Barbara suffered through both scarlet fever and diphtheria as a child, spending three months at City Hospital, including a long stretch in quarantine. "My parents couldn't come in the room—they had to wave to me through a glass enclosure." Even that ordeal, however, taught her something about her parents' capacity for hard work and sacrifice. "I remember how hard they worked later to pay that stupid hospital bill," she said. "My father worked so hard his whole life. He had so much pride in his family and work was the way to take care of us."

The day Barbara opened her restaurant, her father sat in one of the chairs for much of the day, greeting well-wishers and patrons. "He'd say, 'This is my daughter's restaurant, you know,' and shake their hand," Barbara recalled. "And you could just see the pride—it started at his feet and just went up his entire body until he was ready to explode. I'll always remember that."

From her parents and grandparents and other old-timers, Barbara said, she learned that most obstacles could be overcome and that experience is the best teacher, values she has tried to pass on to her two children. "Think

Photograph by Jules Aarons

An Italian woman watches from her doorway in the North End. *(Photo by Jules Aarons. Courtesy of the Boston Public Library, Print Department)*

about how tough they [immigrants] had it," she said. "I always do. They couldn't speak the language. They didn't have skills. Non-Italian people despised them. Yet, again, they asked for so little. And they saved money and they bought homes and they built lives. And without any education, they handed out so much wisdom, so much common sense. I wish everyone could have experienced it."

Her son, a Boston police officer, recalled an image of his grandmother that seemed to capture for Barbara the example of quiet grit and resolve that Italian immigrants set for their families. "He remembered seeing his *nonna* sitting on a chair, hand-sewing something," Barbara said. "There she was, her hands all gnarled and her fingers bent, and she was sewing so fast and with such ease and without complaint. He still pictures that in his mind. He says, 'Ma, you never heard a peep out of her. She must have been in pain, but she just did it because it had to be done.' That's the way the old-timers were. Today, it's different. We have so much more than our parents and grandparents in terms of money and *things*—but I feel, in many ways, that we have so much less."

Barbara Summa tries to rekindle some of those memories at La Summa, fostering an atmosphere where family and friends can gather and talk and laugh. One of her traditions is an open house on Christmas Eve when patrons can savor the "seven fishes" Italian feast that she and so many Italians grew up enjoying, and in which many still partake.

"It's my way of trying to recapture some of that nostalgia," she said, "some of that good feeling that was always such an important part of my life. Of our lives."

CHAPTER 32

Never in his wildest dreams did Boston attorney Al DeNapoli imagine taking on actor Robert DeNiro.

Not in the courtroom, but in the court of public opinion.

As national president of the Sons of Italy (OSIA) Committee on Social Justice, DeNapoli, together with OSIA president Joseph Sciame, coauthored a letter in August of 2004 to Italian prime minister Silvio Berlusconi urging him to cancel his government's plans to confer honorary Italian citizenship on DeNiro (whose paternal grandfather was born in Italy). The letter said DeNiro "has made a career of playing gangsters of Italian descent," and as a case in point, the American actor was planning to be in Italy to promote his latest film, *Shark Tale,* "a children's gangster movie [animated, and featuring DeNiro as the voice of a "gangster boss shark"], produced by Steven Spielberg's company, DreamWorks, SKG.... [which] will perpetuate the image of Italian Americans as gangsters... we are especially concerned since this movie is directed at children who are particularly susceptible to absorbing negative stereotyping." In short, the OSIA letter stated bluntly, DeNiro did not deserve the Italian citizenship honor, since "he has done nothing to promote Italian culture in the United States. Instead, the OSIA and its members hold him and his movies responsible for considerably damaging the collective reputations of both Italians and Italian Americans."

The OSIA letter started a firestorm around the world, as newspapers all over the globe picked up the story. DeNiro, who played Mafia boss Vito Corleone in *The Godfather II,* Al Capone in *The Untouchables,* a crime boss in the "Mafia comedy" *Analyze This,* and other mob roles, dismissed OSIA's criticism, saying: "The characters I played are real. They have as much right to be portrayed as any others." The Columbus Citizens Foundation joined OSIA by blasting *Shark Tale* for stereotyping Italian Americans as "thugs and mobsters" and singled out DeNiro, calling him "the Italian-American equivalent of Uncle Tom" who has "profited from negative stereotypes of Italian-Americans for years." In the midst of the uproar, DeNiro declined the honor from the Italian government.

For DeNapoli, the victory was small but symbolic, one step along an uphill road of reducing the prevalent Italian American stereotyping in the media (he thinks "eradication" is probably impossible) and reeducating both Italians and non-Italians alike on the "positive Italian experience" in the United States. "The Italian as a gangster is such an easy depiction for a creative person to fall back on," he said. "Either that, or you see popular media portray Italians as buffoons or brutes—*cafoni*—and it's so pervasive that people just take it for granted." Since the early 1990s, DeNapoli, a founding member of the Boston law firm of Tarlow, Breed, Hart & Rodgers, has involved himself in promoting Italian American culture. The grandson of Italian immigrants, DeNapoli was raised in a close, loving family environment in Roslindale and now lives in Walpole, a Boston suburb, where he is a member of the board of selectmen. His father was a World War II veteran who earned a Bronze Star and returned home and supported his family as a crane operator; his mother worked as a hairdresser. Al attended parochial schools, then graduated with an English degree from Boston College and a master's in American Studies from the University of Maryland. He taught junior high English for a time before he decided to attend New England School of Law at night. He "crossed the Rubicon" in the early 1980s, when he went to work for a downtown Boston law firm, "an amazing step for my family... here I was the son of a construction worker, certainly the first person in my family with an advanced professional degree. I felt honored by the privilege."

He was slow to embrace his own heritage, struggling with identity issues that Italian Americans have battled for years because of discrimination and stereotypes. "I didn't want to embrace it at first," he said. "I didn't want to be perceived as a dago, as *too* Italian. I was so slow to be proud of who I was. It wasn't until after I graduated from high school that I realized I didn't have to be ashamed of being Italian. Then I embraced the whole culture—the food, the wine, the music, the hard work. I realize I'm a product of all of it and how great that is. That's what I'm fighting for now, so my kids and other young people of Italian descent realize what a great culture they're a part of—something they'd never know from watching TV or going to the movies."

It was in high school at Catholic Memorial on the outskirts of Boston that DeNapoli encountered his first taste of discrimination from an authority figure. One of the Brothers during freshman year would strike him for no reason during Latin class, and called him "Al Capone." DeNapoli's father visited the school and asked him to stop. "My father wouldn't have minded if this Brother picked on everyone in the class, not at all," DeNapoli said. "But he sensed, from my stories, maybe before I did, that I was singled out because I was Italian."

DeNapoli believes that Italians themselves are in large part responsible for ethnic stereotyping, that their lack of protest—even their complicity—stems from fear they will be labeled as "bad sports" or "unable to take a joke," or otherwise viewed as overly sensitive. "Let me generalize myself," he said. "Italians tend to be relatively easygoing and they pride themselves on having a good sense of humor. We don't want to be portrayed as sticks-in-the-mud. We want to be able to take a joke, to poke fun at ourselves, to prove we can 'lighten up.' The problem is, the constant negative stereotyping does long-term damage, especially to our kids. One, it makes them ashamed of being Italian. Two, it conveys to them that the mob life, the Mafia life, is the glamorous life. That's the long-term downside." Such a message is especially crippling to teenage boys, DeNapoli said. "It says to them, 'This [becoming a gangster] is how you earn respect, this is the way it is.' Well that isn't the way it is—so it's bad for everyone."

In addition to the DeNiro episode, the Sons of Italy protested strongly against the HBO hit series *The Sopranos* for its portrayal of Italians as violent mobsters, and also protested vigorously the American Red Cross's nationwide sponsorship of *Joey and Maria's Wedding* (and its various spinoffs, such as *Tony and Tina's Wedding*), a dinner theater production that exaggerates the vilest Italian American stereotypes, portraying the family as loud, boorish, vulgar, and disrespectful to women. "During the 'wedding reception,'" noted the OSIA press release on the interactive dinner theater production, "the groom gets drunk, the bride goes to the Ladies Room to sniff coke; the in-laws have a food fight while a nun does splits; and the groom's father arrives with his girl-friend, a stripper." This all takes place with the actors sporting strong Italian accents and exaggerated gestures.

"We informed the Red Cross that the 600,000 Italian-American members of the Sons of Italy would not donate to their charity in light of their support," DeNapoli said. "To their credit, they pulled their support."

DeNapoli's concerns are borne out by statistics and observation, and in many ways, his is the modern-day fight that George Scigliano waged a century earlier and James Donnaruma fought his entire life. In the summer of 2003, the Sons of Italy published a white paper entitled *Italian American Stereotypes in U.S. Advertising,* which included the results of a Zogby poll of American teenagers (thirteen to eighteen years old) revealing that 78 percent of them associate Italian Americans with criminal activities. It also cited a Princeton-based Response Analysis Corporation (RAC) poll revealing that an astonishing 74 percent of adult Americans believe most Italian Americans have some connection to organized crime, when Department of Justice statistics suggested that the percentage of Italian Americans involved in organized crime was infinitesimal, perhaps twenty-five hundredths of 1 percent of the 26 million Americans of Italian descent.

In its white paper, OSIA cites the following examples of anti-Italian print and television advertising:

• **Ragu "Rich and Meaty" meat sauce print ad**—Graphics show three butchers with olive complexions scowling into the camera. Behind them hang sausages and a salami. "We asked these butchers what they thought of our new meat sauce," the ad reads. "They beat us up."

• **Uncle Ben's Pasta Bowl print ad**—"If you eat an Uncle Ben's pasta bowl," the copy reads, "don't be surprised ifa youa starta talking likea this afterwards."

• **The International Dairy Food TV commercial**—"Vinny" and a friend try to break the bones of a man who owes them money, but since the intended victim drinks milk, they can't hurt him.

• **AT&T broadband TV commercial**—A teacher warns a student that he will fail her class because his assignment is late. Two characters from

The Sopranos appear and threaten the teacher if the student doesn't receive an A.

• **Lycos Internet search engine TV commercial**—As a mandolin plays Italian music in the background, an older man (clearly Italian) carries furniture up the steps of a brownstone apartment, while his dark-haired daughter and grandchild look on. He tells his daughter that the furniture "fell off a truck." In the next scene, more furniture is moved in, but the daughter holds up a bill of sale so that FBI agents in a parked car nearby can see that she bought it on the Internet, using Lycos.

The OSIA list goes on and on with examples, far too many to reprint here. If taken separately, the stereotypes are bad enough; cumulatively, the mass media's linkage between anything Italian and the implicit or explicit visage of organized crime is astonishingly pervasive. *Hartford Courant* business columnist Matthew Kauffman wrote in 2003: "Madison Avenue tolerates a dwindling number of stereotypes. Gays are still fair game. Blondes rarely stand a chance. And then there are Italians, and the seemingly irresistible desire to paint them as silk-suit-wearing, pinky-ring-waving, New Joisey-talking galoots with a penchant for violence." In the column, Kauffman issued the caution that Italian Americans themselves struggle with: "This is not a plea for runaway political correctness and the blandness it engenders . . . that's silly. But . . . that's a far cry from routinely endorsing the image of Italian Americans as violent gangsters. What is it that makes the stereotype of the violent Italian so embraceable?"

Again, part of the answer aligns with DeNapoli's thesis: the reluctance of Italian Americans to complain, and their willingness to accept, if not embrace, the stereotype. "Those of us who are sensitive to the narrow stereotyping of Italian Americans are chastised for not getting 'with the program,'" wrote Daniela Gioseffi in an essay entitled "What Would Your Dead Immigrant Father Say About: 'The World According to Tony Soprano'?" "But we are chagrined because this stereotype has occurred and succeeded more than *any* other ethnic stereotype in the Hollywood and television industry" [Gioseffi's emphasis]. These endless portrayals, Gioseffi says, have led "even Italian-Americans to buy and consume as the main image of their own people [these stereotypes]. So brainwashed are they!" Another writer pointed out that the film *Moonstruck* was so popular among Italian Americans not only because it portrayed the warmth of an Italian American family—"even still, in the most stereotypical way, with all the hysteria and pathos"—but because Italians were "relieved" that Hollywood had finally released a movie about Italians that did not include mobsters.

It's not just advertising and movies, but news, politics, the literati and glitterati, liberals and conservatives alike. An Americans for the Arts advertisement in the *New York Times* promoting a cultural event was headlined: "No Wonder People Think Caravaggio Is a Guy on the Sopranos," and incorporated the phrase "Fuggedaboudit." The organization contended that the ad was not intended to offend Italian Americans, and that some Italian American organizations even applauded its cleverness. "We are still waiting to hear which Italian-American organization applauded such an advertisement," the National Italian American Foundation (NIAF) wrote. "Linking mobsters with the great Italian Baroque artist . . . was perceived as insensitive by many in the Italian-American community. We can't imagine this kind of stereotyping with any other ethnic group."

Moving to politics, there is a famous exchange in the Watergate tapes during which President Richard Nixon and high-ranking aide John Ehrlichman are conversing about Italians in the early 1970s. "We must do something for them," Nixon says. "They're not like us . . . they smell different, they look different, act different . . . you can't blame them, oh, no . . . They've never had the things we've had." After Ehrlichman agrees with Nixon's last statement, the president replies: "Of course, the trouble is . . . the trouble is, you can't find one that's honest."

Nor are such examples restricted to one political party thirty years ago. In late 2005, after President George W. Bush had nominated Judge Samuel Alito for the Supreme Court, political commentator Chris Matthews (host of *Hardball* on MSNBC) blasted Democrats for placing at the top of their list of opposition "talking points" a claim that Alito had not come down hard on sentencing members of the Gambino crime family in New Jersey fifteen years earlier. "Wait a minute," Matthews said to Democratic Party chairman Howard Dean, "this man has been an appeals court judge for fifteen years and issued hundreds and hundreds of opinions and you have to go back to when he was a trial judge for this talking point?" Matthews said the decision was either "incredibly naive" or "a blatant case of ethnic discrimination." Dean denied both labels, calling the Gambino–Alito link a "coincidence." Ironically, a few nights later, Matthews's own network ran a feature package on Alito's background and philosophy and entitled it "Alito's Way," a clear reference to *Carlito's Way,* a mob movie. As Daniela Gioseffi says, "They just can't help themselves."

The NIAF also protested attempts by some Democrats to "marginalize [Judge] Alito's outstanding record by frequent references to his Italian heritage and by the use of the nickname, 'Scalito'" in an attempt to link him philosophically with Justice Antonin Scalia, another Italian American. The organization argued that the combined name was intended to be more than an ideological link—noting that Alito also shared many views of justice Clarence Thomas and newly confirmed chief justice John Roberts—and was designed to focus on the ethnicity of the two men. "Appropriately, no one mentioned that Justice Breyer was Jewish or suggested that he was in lock-step ideologically with the other Jewish Supreme Court Justice, Ruth Bader Ginsburg," the NIAF statement read. "It would have been outrageous to do so."

Al DeNapoli is far from naive. He recognizes that Italians played a major role in organized crime, that the Mafia has its origins in Southern Italy, and that such history should not be quashed or whitewashed. "You can't deny reality," he said. "But when that's the *only* thing you see or hear—that's what we have to fight." He also recognizes that Italian Americans, like other Americans, are attracted to the rituals and secrecy of the Mafia mystique and Mafia television programs and movies. (I agree. For example, I think *The Godfather* is one of the top five movies of all time; it would be virtually impossible to cut a single scene from the film, and its lure is nearly irresistible to me when it pops up on cable television channels, as it does frequently.) As one Italian American, active in the NIAF, said to me: "I hate the 'goombah assumption' we put up with, the automatic conclusion people reach that if a guy has an ethnic-Italian first name, like Sal or Vinnie or Domenic, or a last name that's hard to pronounce, he must be 'connected' or a Mafioso. That infuriates me, even when it's said in jest." But then he acknowledged to me, sotto voce, "On the other hand, I'm a closet *Sopranos* lover. It's a can't-miss show for me."

DeNapoli fully understands the apparent contradiction. "I don't want to be overly sensitive, either," he said. "I recognize that some of these [movies] are great works of art by great artists. We can and should enjoy them, but we have to understand that they're not the whole story."

Does anyone ever accuse him of overreacting in his vigilance? "Yeah, my kids, sometimes," he said. "They'll say, 'Dad . . .' and roll their eyes, and say I'm being too much of a watchdog. But we need to tell them the real story, *our* story. The Mafia is colorful and carries a sense of romance and mystery, but it's on the periphery of the story. But, how Italians left their homes to get here with virtually nothing, how they struggled and worked hard once they arrived, and how they've succeeded and become great Americans—that's the heart of the story. I want to make sure *that* isn't lost. That's why I do what I do."

CHAPTER 33

"I am deeply proud of my heritage," Salvatore F. DiMasi told his legislative colleagues on September 29, 2004, the day he was elected the first Italian American Speaker of the House of Representatives in Massachusetts history. "Growing up in the North End shaped my values. I grew up during a time when the North End had tenements, not condominiums...We were poor, but we were rich in our family and in our friends and neighbors...I learned a lot about the importance of community—the moral obligation that we share to look out for each other...If a neighbor was sick, you took care of him. If a neighbor was out of work, you brought food to his family. These are the values I learned in the narrow streets of the North End."

With those words during his inaugural address, Sal DiMasi joined two fellow Italian Americans who held political leadership positions in Boston, a triumvirate whose collective achievement is unprecedented in the history of the city and the state. Less than two years earlier, East Boston's Robert Travaglini had become the first Italian American president of the state senate. Both DiMasi and Travaglini followed Boston mayor Thomas M. Menino on this list of firsts; Menino became Boston's first Italian American mayor in 1993, when he won 64 percent of the vote and eighteen of the city's twenty-two wards. He won reelection in 1997, without opposition, and landslides in 2001 and 2005. All three men held their prestigious offices as this book went to press, and while DiMasi and Travaglini govern at the state level and Menino's responsibility stops at the city line, they wield their power within two blocks of each other in Boston.

The close geographic proximity of three of the city's, and the state's, most powerful elected officials—men who ply their trades in the Commonwealth's largest city and media market, men who were born and grew up in different Boston neighborhoods— provides a visible and frequent reminder of just how far Italian Americans have come in Boston.

———

An enormous mural in Mayor Tom Menino's outer office virtually covers one wall and beckons visitors to study its details. Painted by Menino's cousin, the scene depicts the mayor's grandfather sitting in his Italian village, awaiting passage to America. Across a wide body of water that dominates the painting is the skyline of an American city, its shores a two-week voyage away in real life but just a few inches away on the canvas. The mayor describes the painting with pride; it is, he says, the beginning of the Menino story in the United States. Without Thomas Menino's monumental decision to leave Grottaminarda, Avellino, and travel to a strange country, his grandson would never have had an opportunity to make his own special history in Boston. Thomas Menino settled in Boston's Hyde Park section, at the far western corner of the city, a neighborhood his grandson still cherishes and lives in today, and from which he built the political base that has enabled him to lead the city for more than a dozen years.

When we met on a summer Friday at Boston City Hall, the then sixty-three-year-old Tom Menino was dressed in an open-collared, short-sleeved blue shirt and khaki slacks, and looked tan and fit. For nearly two hours he was articulate, expansive, and relaxed, qualities not often evident in the mayor's public persona. There were none of the uncomfortable grimaces that frequently accompany his interactions with media members, none of the guarded hesitancy to share his personal life, none of the syntax struggles that punctuate his public speaking. Perhaps it was the familiar nature of the subject matter and the mayor's comfort with it, or the fact that elected officials, in the rush of daily media pressures and the desire to avoid verbal missteps, are not often afforded the opportunity to step back and reflect on their own families and backgrounds. Whatever the reasons, Menino's language brimmed with confidence and color as he described the depth of his pride in his Italian heritage and the manner in which it has shaped his life and his politics. "Every day, it affects me," he said. "My Italian heritage taught me the importance of family, the importance of hard work, the obligation we have to help others, the strength to never give up. Every single one of those lessons affects the way I go about my job."

Still, the mayor acknowledged that he is reserved about proclaiming his Italian heritage on the public stage. Why is this? In March of 2003 (be-

Boston's first Italian American mayor, Thomas M. Menino, addresses a crowd at Faneuil Hall. *(Courtesy of Pam Donnaruma and the* Post-Gazette*)*

fore DiMasi was chosen as Speaker), political columnist and commentator Jon Keller wrote a piece for *Boston* magazine noting that "Italians are now as much in charge of this town as the Irish. Why are they so shy about it?" (In light of the discussion in the previous chapter, it is worthwhile to note that *Boston* entitled Keller's piece "The Godfathers.") Keller ran through a list of noted Boston Italian American luminaries in business, media, and public service, yet pointed out that Italians themselves had understated their political achievements. "Even successful Italian-Americans often find themselves deferring to the omnipresent Irish culture," Keller wrote. "It's sometimes said of Menino, a proud Italian-American who vacations in Ireland and leans on a predominately Irish-American inner circle, that he 'thinks he's Irish.' " Keller then suggested that "Tony Soprano may have something to do with it [Italians' reticence to celebrate their heritage too publicly]." "Don't laugh," Keller said to readers, and then he quoted Rina Crugnale, regional vice president of the Italian American cultural and education organization Fieri: "As soon as you put the word 'Italian' out there, you're immediately stereotyped as a Mafia person." Boston city councilor

Paul Scapicchio, of the North End, echoed Crugnale's position in Keller's article: "I am very guarded about whom I associate with and who I'm seen with in public. In one fell swoop someone can totally cast your career in a negative light."

Menino, though, discounts Keller's "shyness" label and the "goombah assumption" put forth by Crugnale and Scapicchio, insisting that his reluctance to inject his "Italian-ness" into his public life is simply an instance of the political practicality he has had to exercise since he first ran for office. "When I was a city councilor representing Hyde Park-Roslindale-Jamaica Plain, I represented a district that was 50 percent Irish, 20 percent Italian, 10 percent black, and a variety of other ethnic groups," he said, rattling off the section's demographic breakdown with the encyclopedic knowledge of all good Boston politicians. "Now I'm mayor of a city with a wide diversity of ethnic and racial groups. So, yes, I'm extremely proud of being Italian, but I don't make it a big part of my politics because I represent people of so many different backgrounds. I feel I have to speak for them, too." Menino said he never "dodged" his Italian background, but his "quiet pride" stems from the values he grew up with that emphasized "humility and hard work, not boastfulness."

Was Menino so immersed in becoming mayor of "all the people" that he was unaware during the 1993 campaign that, if elected, he would become the first Italian American mayor in Boston history? "Oh, no," he said, and winked. "I knew it all the time. I was very proud of it and my family was, too. I just never broadcast it." Menino acknowledged that he has "known anti-Italian prejudice" but never on any sort of widespread basis, and never in a way that has made him feel different from anyone else. "In the old days, it was more prevalent," he said. "I had people tell me when I ran for mayor, 'an Italian will never be elected mayor of this city.' Things are different today. It [prejudice] still exists, but not nearly the way it was. Everyone has experienced it in some manner, and that's a shame," he said. "But we don't live in a perfect society."

Menino took an unlikely route to the mayor's office, an acknowledged "shy kid" who became hooked on politics at age thirteen while distributing campaign flyers for a Hyde Park candidate. When Boston redistricted and went to a thirteen-member city council (nine district councilors and four at large) in 1983, Menino ran for the district seat from Hyde Park, despite skepticism from his father. "My dad said, 'You have two kids and a wife. What happens if you lose?' I told him: 'Dad, don't worry. I'm not going to lose.'" Menino won easily and was reelected four more times to the city council, eventually becoming president of the body. Initially, his plan was to serve for ten years and then leave politics. But while he was city council president, at the nine-and-a-half-year mark of his council career, then mayor Ray Flynn was appointed ambassador to the Vatican, and Menino became acting mayor. He won in his own right in the 1993 city election and, assuming he serves out his entire current term, will become the longest-serving mayor in Boston history when it concludes in 2009. "I'm proud of that," he said. "I never had the ambition to become mayor and I didn't think I'd ever be in politics because I'm not handsome and I'm not articulate. I've always had confidence, though, and I've always had a desire to help people."

Menino believes his Italian heritage, his family-oriented background, and the closeness of the Italian enclave in which he grew up have made him a better mayor by enabling him to understand the importance of bridging the gap between Boston's neighborhoods and the downtown business community. "You have to balance interests for the benefit of the entire city," he said. "Any city that is going to be great has to have strong neighborhoods, so you have to emphasize them, make them viable, strong, make sure people want to live there. I think I have great credibility in the neighborhoods because of who I am and where I came from. But you also have to have jobs in a city. You need to work with the business community to create them, and work on the issues they're concerned about. Without jobs, you have neglect and abandonment of downtown areas and you have a phantom city. So you have to focus on both [neighborhoods and downtown] to make a great city. That's what I've tried to do in my administration."

Menino said the influence of his working-class Italian parents helps him better understand the struggles faced by Boston residents, including new immigrants, every day. He remembers the role his mother—who was born in America but spoke fluent Italian—played in his Hyde Park neighborhood, helping Italian immigrants fill out job applications, get their children into schools, or translate the bills they received in the mail. "She always taught me to work hard and do whatever you could to ease the struggles of others," he said. "She was probably my strongest influence." Menino's father, who worked at Westinghouse in Hyde Park, instilled in him a "set of high standards and a respect for others, no matter where they fell on the pecking order" that Menino said he tries to remember every day. "Little things, like he told me to always be on time, because if you're late, that shows disrespect for other people's time," Menino recalled. The mayor's greatest political hero is President Harry Truman. "Tell the truth, be a plain talker, get the job done, and don't whine," Menino said. "It's why I like and respect Truman. I try to conduct myself the same way he did."

Menino has battled and overcome cancer and other health issues but retains a palpable vigor for life and for his work as mayor. He cherishes his family, and his old friends are still his best friends. On Christmas Eve morning, he and "the guys from the old neighborhood" still go out at 5 A.M. and buy the shrimp, smelts, and *baccala* that will form the heart of the "seven fishes" feast that evening. He enjoys visits to North End restaurants with friends, including La Summa, his "favorite," and frequents Parziale's Bakery to buy his scala bread and chat with patrons. Hyde Park is his home, but there is a soft spot in his heart for the North End, where his uncle and other relatives lived many years ago, a neighborhood in which Menino has always felt welcomed and one he has supported personally and politically. (When he was a city councilor, Menino convinced his colleagues to pass a fifty-five-foot maximum height restriction in the North End so the neighborhood "wouldn't become Manhattan-ized.")

Now in his sixties, Menino said he reflects on his heritage frequently, and admires and appreciates deeply the accomplishments of his parents and grandparents. "You don't even think about your heritage, or I didn't, until you hit age thirty-five or forty, and then you say, 'Wow, those people had it tough and look at what they did.' That feeling grows as you get older." The mayor continues to use those ancestral accomplishments as inspiration. "I'm never happy professionally," he said. "You can't be happy because then you'll get too satisfied. I don't want that. I want to continue to bring this city to new heights and provide more opportunity for her citizens. If you're satisfied, then why are you here?"

"When I'm finally satisfied, then I'll leave," he said. "Otherwise, I'd be bored. Like the old Italians, I try to challenge myself every day to make Boston a better place."

———

Bob Travaglini was seventeen years old when his father died suddenly of a heart attack at age forty, and the second-oldest son knew his life had changed forever. "My dad's death had a profound effect on our family," he said. "My brothers and I got closer and rallied around my mother. There was no more room for error. My mother was so devastated by the loss that my brothers and I knew that if any one of us stepped out of line and deepened her pain in any way, the other four would be very upset." The loss of his father, Travaglini asserted, meant "there was no more time for games . . . it forced us to focus on what was important in life."

Travaglini was a senior at East Boston's Dom Savio High School when his father died. With one brother already a freshman at college and three others in grammar school, he needed to become a leader in the family and chart a course that would serve as an example for his young brothers. "The foundation had been set by both my parents," Travaglini said. "My father and mother set very strict rules in our household, but in return, we were surrounded by love, affection, stability, high expectations, and an understanding of what was right and what was wrong. We didn't have much, but we had everything. When my father left, he left that as his legacy."

Indeed, when Travaglini first asked his mother for her blessing to run for public office in the early 1980s, she replied with an admonition that the senate president says guides him each day: "She said make sure you pass on your name to your son or daughter in the same condition that you received it from your mother and father . . . that's a very profound message. Obviously I agreed and she gave me her blessing. I've tried to live by that creed in this office."

Like Menino, Travaglini—officially Robert E. Travaglini, but better known as Trav or Bobby Trav—got his start in politics when he won a district city council seat representing East Boston, the North End, and Charlestown. While he was a senior in high school, he had managed a summer recreation program for 1,800 kids in East Boston, many of whom, ten years later, were more than happy to serve as the core of Travaglini's organization. "Your first campaign generates a level of excitement that is never repeated," he recalled. "Mine was stacked with friends who were eager to lend a hand for all that had been done for them."

From those modest political beginnings, Travaglini now holds the distinction of being the first Italian American senate president in the 225-year history of the Commonwealth. It is a title, a charge, he treats with great reverence. "The sacrifices my parents and grandparents made play heavily in the way I execute the duties of my office," he said. "I take seriously the image and reputation I bring to this business. I want to get it right because I am the first [Italo-American]. It took me—us—this long to get here. I want to make it easier for the next person who comes along."

Travaglini said some on Beacon Hill were skeptical of an Italian American's ability to lead. "They set the bar so low for me I thought I was in a limbo contest," he said. "We had a $3 billion deficit [on his inauguration day in January of 2003], and tremendous uncertainty and political instability. There were people saying, 'Let's give it to Trav, we'll let him fail, then throw him under the bus and give it to someone else.' Instead, we've changed the entire atmosphere up here. We've challenged everyone to bring forth their ideas and talents to get things done, and I now have the trust and confidence of every one of my colleagues and everyone who does business in this building. I'm very proud of that."

Still a resident of East Boston, Travaglini remembered his inauguration as senate president as a "very emotional day." Prior to his speech, his mother came into his office and began crying, overwhelmed by the impact of the occasion. "Here I was, reading over my speech, thinking about my dad, but still in control," Travaglini remembered. "Then my mother starts crying, so I had to say to a few of my best friends, 'Please get her out of here.' I was in control and stable and if she had stayed any longer I would have lost it. It's the first and only time I threw my mother out of my office." Later, during the speech, Travaglini looked out into the audience, saw his mother and his wife and three children, and "realized again how blessed I am . . . the essence of my speech, the message I conveyed was that I was going to use my power to help those who could not do it themselves, that the poor and undereducated were not going to be neglected or underserved. Seeing my family reminded me again how important that message was. I have everything a man could want and I'm grateful for it."

An optimist by nature, Travaglini dealt with cold reality in 2001 when he had brushes with both cancer and heart disease—"back to back, first cancer and then quadruple bypass three months later"—yet he remains energetic and enthusiastic about his family, his work, his life. "Make no mistake, you're never quite the same once they do that to you [heart surgery]," he said. "I'm not seventeen any longer and I do have to take care of myself. But I have a beautiful wife, three beautiful children, and I love my job, so I'm hoping to stay around as long as possible."

He says he tries to pass along to his children the essence of their Italian heritage—including visits to their grandmother's house on Sundays, the feasts, the "magic" of Christmas Eve celebrations at his brother's Winchester home—as well as reinforce how fortunate they are by bringing them to soup kitchens, homeless shelters, and Boys' and Girls' Club events. "I want to expose them to different conditions of society, so they realize the blessings they have in comparison to others who are struggling every day," he said. He engages in his own special reflection every Christmas Eve, his "favorite night of the year," late at night when it's quiet, when he "thanks God for the blessings he has given me, for my family, for my heritage. It all comes home to me on that night. It brings tears to my eyes."

Much of Travaglini's ethnic pride is private. Jon Keller spent several paragraphs in his 2003 column focusing on Trav, saying "the persistent cultural stereotyping may be the single biggest reason why Travaglini didn't wave the ethnic flag at his inauguration." Keller added: "Friends say he's so sensitive about it he eschews white ties and other gaudy attire associated with Italian stereotypes, and conspicuously stocks his office with a diverse —but non-Italian—staff." Keller pointed out that Travaglini's sensitivity was not hard to understand, considering that once he had garnered enough votes to assure him the senate presidency, newspaper columnist Howie Carr "unleashed a torrent of Mafia jokes," including the opinion that Trav's victory "was like handing the keys to the State House to Tony Soprano." Carr's remark prompted an outraged response from Italian American superior court judge Peter Agnes, who termed it "far outside the ken of political discourse. It is a slur that should be offensive to every right-thinking person."

Travaglini is reluctant to discuss the entire issue of stereotyping, except to acknowledge that "the undercurrent of discrimination is there . . . I've lived it, I've witnessed it, I'm offended as hell by it, we are deluged with it from Hollywood and television, but I can't fight this fight as one person. It comes with too much baggage that we [Italian Americans] have not been able to overcome for decades. So I don't talk about it. I don't have to talk about it or focus on my ethnicity every day. It's enough that people know who I am, that I am comfortable with who I am, and that there are many people out there taking great pride that an Italo-American is serving in this position after more than two centuries. It's why I feel so strongly that I have to maintain the highest possible standards for this office."

It is an office that Travaglini loves, so much so that he says the one decision he has made for the future is not to seek higher office. He believes he can get more done for more people exactly where he is today. "This is like playing third base," he said. "Nothing gets home unless it gets by me. Everything, no matter who initiates it, comes across my desk and awaits my endorsement or my rejection. That's pretty powerful—and as long as I don't abuse that power, and use that power for the right things, I feel like I'm accomplishing something that benefits society. Being senate president has exceeded my wildest dreams—I have no aspirations for higher office."

He plans to run for senate president again (in 2007), but said after that he would let his health and his professional desires dictate his actions. "I'm not frightened about the day I have to exit this building or this business, because of what I've achieved," he said. "I have had a great run, and I hope it continues for a while. But I'll take whatever comes my way. I told you— I'm very comfortable with who I am."

It is a testament to how far Italian Americans have come in Boston that the most powerful man in the Massachusetts House of Representatives had to walk two blocks to use a shower every day until he was twenty-one years old. Salvatore F. DiMasi was born in the same house as his father, at 181 Salem Street in Boston's North End, adjacent to the Old North Church— a three-floored tenement that his grandfather had purchased when he arrived in America from Southern Italy. DiMasi lived with his brothers and his parents on the third floor, DiMasi's grandparents lived on the second, and "there was no heat or hot water, no shower or bathtub, and a toilet out in the hall," DiMasi recalled. "I had to walk to the bathhouse to take a shower."

Despite the humble beginnings, perhaps because of them, DiMasi has built a long career in elected politics and developed a reputation as a tough, fair, hardnosed politician, a Democrat and social liberal but not an ideologue, a self-effacing leader who is able to work with people of different political persuasions and philosophies to get things done. "When he knows something is the right thing to do or the right way to do it, he doesn't hesitate," Representative Lida Harkins told a newspaper reporter as DiMasi was preparing to assume the Speaker's role. "He stands firm."

Even more than Tom Menino and Bob Travaglini, Sal DiMasi is happy to publicly celebrate his ethnic heritage. "Those values I talked about in my inauguration speech, I learned them from growing up in an Italian family in the North End community," DiMasi said. "It's because of those values that I entered public life—to continue the tradition and to help people." Indeed, just a few days after becoming Speaker, DiMasi presided over ceremonies to kick off Italian-American Heritage Month (October) at the State House. "It's very important for me to attain this position," DiMasi said during an interview at the event. "It's very significant for Italian Americans in this state, as well as this country." Italian-American Heritage Month was first celebrated in Massachusetts in 1998 under then governor Paul Cellucci, the Commonwealth's third Italian American governor, to celebrate the contributions of Italians in the United States. At the 2004 event, state auditor Joe DeNucci, himself an Italian American, praised DiMasi, Travaglini, and Menino but reminded those in attendance that "we're still stereotyped as Italians. We're the goodfellas, the gangsters. It is so nice to finally see Italian Americans on top here in state government, but we have a long way to go."

DiMasi's brand of politics mixes personality and policy, or as the *Boston Globe* once described it: "There is little boundary between the personal and the political. He intertwines the two seamlessly." He cajoles allies and adversaries alike, and his experiences in the North End define who he is and what he believes is important. "For DiMasi, the North End was a rich tapestry of friends and lessons learned," one reporter wrote, "one he weaves liberally into political speeches." A longtime friend, Representative Angelo Scaccia, said of DiMasi: "Sal has the wit of an Irishman and the squeezability of an Italian." If there is a teddy-bear side to his political persona, it coexists with a grizzly-like toughness. DiMasi is also a fighter and, when necessary, an arm twister. He would take each characterization—fighter and peacemaker—as a compliment, relying on whatever approach works to advance his goals. "In the end, all of our work must be tested against one principle: that the decisions we make will make life better for those we represent and those who follow in the future," he said in his inauguration speech. Acknowledging the family that had shaped his values, DiMasi also told the colleagues who had elected him Speaker: "I only wish that my mother and father could be here today to witness this."

The middle child of Celia and Joseph DiMasi, Sal attended Boston College presuming he would graduate and enter the business world. But during his senior year, a constitutional law class convinced him that he wanted to become a lawyer. Upon his graduation from BC, he enrolled in Suffolk University Law School and graduated in 1971. He served as a prosecutor, and later entered private practice and focused on criminal cases, where his storytelling gifts helped him with juries, and eventually led him to consider a political career. He lost his first race in 1976 by 145 votes to the incumbent state representative of the North End ("I do not like to lose," DiMasi said) but formed the North End Neighborhood Task Force, a citizens' watchdog group, to deal with neighborhood issues. The Task Force and his strong family name recognition provided him with the political support he needed when the seat came up two years later; he won it, and his constituents have returned him to Beacon Hill ever since. It is a diverse multiracial and multiethnic constituency, in a district that not only includes the North End but stretches through Chinatown and Bay Village, whose varied demographics illustrate DiMasi's ability to represent many points of view.

While DiMasi commands the respect of his colleagues, he has heard the whispers of stereotyping and discrimination in the corridors of the State House. "It still exists, in my opinion, no question about it," he said. "And yes, it's offensive to me. People still feel they can get away with stereotyping. They're fascinated with the mob and mob stories, and it persists and affects all of us in public life with Italian last names." DiMasi recalled when he was chairman of the House Judiciary Committee and the House was contemplating passing a state RICO (racketeering) statute. DiMasi held hearings and solicited testimony and input from representatives of the Justice Department, the FBI, attorneys, and legal scholars. In his view, the proposed statute went too far and could have violated certain civil liberties and due process laws, so he recommended that the state RICO statute be killed. "People were whispering and writing at the time that Sal DiMasi is a mob attorney and that's why we didn't pass it," DiMasi said. "I said to them, 'If my name was Alan Dershowitz [a prominent Jewish American Boston attorney], you'd be calling me a civil libertarian, but because it's DiMasi and I live in the North End, you're calling me mob-connected. Why would you say that about me?'"

Though perhaps it's not as blatant today, DiMasi and his chief of staff, Maryann Calia, both acknowledge continued stereotyping. "I'm sensitive to it, that you almost have to prove you *aren't* connected," DiMasi said. "This doesn't happen to other ethnic groups." And Calia pointed out that stereotyping doesn't stop at "Italians as criminals," but also ridicules their intelligence. "I remember one person in this building saying they had spoken to the Speaker, 'and the Speaker said. . . .' And the person proceeded to mimic the Speaker in a Rocky Balboa voice. I said to him, 'Why are you talking like that? That isn't how Sal DiMasi speaks.' Many people up here, they are very surprised to find that [an Italian] is bright, educated, has a brain in his head. As annoying as it is, it's really quite interesting to observe." The political bright spot in such assumptions, DiMasi says, is "they're always underestimating us."

DiMasi acknowledges that as a youth, he could have been tempted by unsavory characters and criminal elements in the North End but for the strong influence of his family. "You make choices when you grow up and your choices are based on your family," he said. "My parents valued honesty and a good education, so that's the direction my life took."

Stereotyping aside, DiMasi loves and celebrates his Italian heritage and thoroughly enjoys his job. "Politics have changed, the business has changed, but I still enjoy it," he said. "The media focuses on the sensational instead of the substantive and that sometimes makes it hard. But as long as you can make a difference in people's lives, this is a great job to have."

He, too, was fully aware that his ascendancy to the Speaker's chair made him the first Italian American in Massachusetts history to hold the seat, and he speaks of the accomplishment to groups and organizations as evidence of how far Italians have progressed in politics. "I used to say that an Italian thought he was politically astute when he backed the right Irishman," DiMasi quipped. "It took a long time for Italians to mobilize politically. My accomplishment is a tribute to all the Italian American politicians who came before me. I'm proud to be the first Italian American Speaker and I will *not* be quiet about it."

As Sal DiMasi was poised to become Speaker, a *Boston Globe* reporter walked the streets of the North End to assess the pride in the neighborhood now that Italian Americans would occupy two of the most powerful elected positions in state government and the Boston mayor's office. Pointing out that both DiMasi's and Travaglini's districts included the North End, the *Globe* noted that their elections to lead their respective bodies are "uncorking a wealth of ethnic pride" in Boston's first and most enduring Italian neighborhood. "Across the North End yesterday, from tailors to fruit vendors to retirees relaxing in lawn chairs, the neighborhood brimmed with pride at the rise of a familiar face, known almost universally as Sal, to the pinnacle of political power," the *Globe* observed.

Or, more simply, as now-deceased North End native Jimmy "Nini" Limone, then eighty-six years old, told the *Globe:* "Travaglini and DiMasi. Where'd you ever see that in your life?"

By every statistical measure, we are the Greater Boston Italians now.

Latest census figures place the number of Italian Americans in the metropolitan Boston area at approximately 800,000, second only to the Irish as an ethnic bloc. Massachusetts ranks sixth in total Italian American population (behind New York, New Jersey, California, Pennsylvania, and Florida) with 860,000 people claiming Italian heritage, about 13.5 percent of the state population (Italian Americans make up only 6 percent of the U.S. population). Yet, fewer than fifty thousand Italian Americans now reside in Boston proper, less than 10 percent of the city's population (though the city still ranks seventh in overall Italian American population behind New York, Philadelphia, Chicago, Los Angeles, Phoenix, and San Diego).

Second-, third-, and fourth-generation Italian Americans, like so many other middle- and upper-middle-class ethnic groups, have left the core city seeking better schools, better jobs, larger homes, more open space, and safer neighborhoods.

In so many ways, assimilation is complete. Italian Americans now compare favorably with, or exceed, national averages in many demographic categories. The Sons of Italy, using raw data from the census, reports that as of 2000, Italian Americans had a median income of $61,000 (compared with $50,000 nationally) and a college graduation rate of 18.5 percent (15.5 percent nationally). Italian Americans now attend graduate schools and medical schools at rates comparable to the U.S. population at large. More than 66 percent of Italian Americans work at white-collar occupations, compared with a national average of about 64 percent. A full 96 percent of Italian Americans are U.S.-born, with only 4 percent born overseas.

Within the Boston city limits, gentrification is complete, too.

The North End and East Boston *have* changed; this is no longer an anecdotal refrain, but a demographic reality. Once overwhelmingly Italian, East Boston is now nearly 40 percent Latino; the rest of the neighborhood is an ethnic mix of Italians, Irish, Southeast Asians, Eastern Europeans, and African Americans. The North End population is half of what it was in 1950, tenement buildings that once housed thirty people may now have a handful of residents in condominiums. The Italian population, still significant, is estimated at under 40 percent, though some of the old-timers insist it is lower. "Many non-Italians live in the neighborhood today," the *Boston Globe* pointed out, "often in old buildings that have been renovated into upscale condominiums." A 2004 Prince Street condominium project was the first major housing development in the North End in a hundred years, with the developer offering one- and two-bedroom units at prices of $400,000 to $1.2 million, a figure that sounds incomprehensible to natives who know the neighborhood's history. Also in 2004, North End neighbors battled over whether a Dunkin' Donuts shop should be allowed to open on Hanover Street; opponents feared the Old World feel of the North End was being whittled away by big-name franchises. In 2005, longtime North End Italian residents blamed nighttime rowdiness in the neighborhood on newcomers, many of them college students. "This neighborhood was never like this," one woman told a newspaper reporter. "Everybody used to watch everybody's back. Not anymore."

And yet, particularly in the North End, the Italian character of the city still thrives. Some of the finest Italian restaurants in the country are among the one hundred or so eateries contained within the neighborhood's borders. Italian old-timers are still amused that a bowl of *pasta e fagioli* (pasta and beans) soup sells for $5 or a plate of *pasta aglia olio* (pasta with garlic and oil) will cost $17.95; years ago these were considered the dishes of the dirt-poor, not trendy delicacies that would delight tourists. Italians find it ironic, also, that garlic is so popular with mainstream Americans as a health food; the term "garlic eaters" was once an ethnic slur directed to Italians. North End pastry shops are nationally famous, too, attracting patrons for fresh scala bread or cannoli. Suburban Italian Americans and members of other ethnic groups flock to the North End by the thousands to celebrate religious feasts. And in 2004, Italian Americans appealed to the Archdiocese of Boston not to close Sacred Heart Church—the place where my grandmother prayed awaiting my father's return from World War II—as part of a reconfiguration of parishes. "This is probably the last of the real

Italian bastions, the heart and soul of the North End, and the North End will be little more than a group of Italian restaurants without this church," said a lifelong parishioner.

This latest celebration of North End Italian pride coincided with the reuniting of the neighborhood with the rest of the city in 2005 and 2006 as the overhead Central Artery highway that had caused so much heartache nearly fifty years earlier was torn down, replaced by an underground thoroughfare Bostonians refer to as "the Big Dig." One lifelong resident said the reopening of Hanover Street all the way to City Hall "opened up my heart . . . I never thought I'd live to see this day."

From one century to the next, the North End continues to endure as the symbol of Boston's Italian American heritage and history.

The *Post-Gazette* endures, too. As her grandfather did for more than fifty years, and her parents for nearly forty years after that, publisher Pam Donnaruma plans each issue and directs coverage from a cubbyhole office with the unabashed goal of advancing Italian American ideals and, especially, benefiting young Italian Americans. "I'm a goody-two-shoes editor," she said. "We don't cover crime stories because people get that in the regular [Boston] papers. I want kids to learn about the Italian heritage, to keep in touch with who they are. We do a lot of nostalgia about the struggles Italian immigrants faced, about life in the North End. And we try to promote positive stories. Our kids are doing so many good things—they receive scholarships, they help the elderly, they do charity—and nobody else writes about them. Nobody. What they do is part of the Italian experience, and I see that as part of my mission."

Like so many others, Pam bristles at the Mafia stereotypes and has refused several requests from advertisers to "feature the mob" in her pages as a way to boost circulation. She has even declined to sell the *Post-Gazette* to prospective owners who might transform it into a publication that "glorifies *The Sopranos*." " 'No, no, no' is what I keep telling them. I could never live with myself if this newspaper became a vehicle for that kind of stereotyping."

Pam, who has continued the *Post-Gazette* tradition of never missing a weekly issue, is fiercely protective of the newspaper's reputation. "I tell any-

Photograph by Jules Aarons

A *festa* or "feast" parade in the North End. The Italian feasts are still among the most popular summer events in the neighborhood. *(Photo by Jules Aarons. Courtesy of the Boston Public Library, Print Department)*

one who might speak negatively about me personally, 'Okay, but don't touch this newspaper,' " she said. "I'm very aware and protective of its history, its contributions, of what it represents. It has an impeccable reputation and my number one mission is to keep it that way."

We are members of the American mainstream, perhaps, but there is a resurgence of interest and pride among Italian Americans, in Boston and elsewhere, in our heritage. Organizations such as the Sons of Italy and the National Italian American Foundation have become more active in political and social issues affecting Italian Americans. The Justinian Law Society, an organization composed of judges, attorneys, and law students of Italian American descent, is influential in virtually every major American city, including Boston. So, too, is Fieri, an organization of young Italian American professionals, ages eighteen to thirty-nine, who are interested in celebrating and learning more about their Italian background and culture. A burgeoning interest in genealogy, coupled with the computerization of Ellis Island records, has led thousands of Italian Americans to seek and study the details of their ancestry. The Italian Genealogical Society of America (IGSA) has its headquarters in the Boston area and describes its mission as bringing together the Old World and the New World. Countless other organizations, book clubs, and societies across Boston and the United States focus on Italian American culture and history.

This thirst for knowledge about our ancestors and our past, of course, is our effort to learn more about ourselves and our future.

True, we are the children of Columbus, and for that matter of Vespucci, Verdi, Dante, da Vinci, Machiavelli, Michelangelo, Boccaccio, Puccini, Galileo, Garibaldi, Montessori, and yes, of Caruso, Capra, Coppola, Fermi, Sinatra, and DiMaggio, and of hundreds of others whose genius and talent have shaped the world. The Italian word for achievements such as theirs is *sprezzatura,* defined as "the art of effortless mastery."

Yet, the vast majority of us who live in the United States also hold a different lineage. We are the children and grandchildren of James Donnaruma, Calogero and Angela Puleo, and David Minichiello, Italian immigrants who arrived in America as impoverished and frightened strangers, unskilled and unwanted, illiterate and ill prepared, lost in a language they could neither speak nor understand. In the face of these most daunting odds, they found work, built lives, purchased homes, started businesses, raised families, and came to love their new country for the opportunities it provided them and their children. Where did they find such strength? How did they muster such courage? To what extent did their discouragement approach the unbearable? We seek not just their documents but their stories, not just the skeletal outlines but the flesh and blood and heartbeat of their lives.

They are all gone now, the wave of Italian immigrants who flooded America's shores in the late nineteenth and early twentieth centuries (I was blessed to have my remaining three grandparents into my twenties). Thus, Italian Americans must gather today to share and compare and preserve the stories, and find the collective comfort that a common history brings. One Italian American journalist said that our appetite to know our ancestors is fueled by our desire to build "a spiritual bridge between [our] Italian past and [our] American future."

Only with the presence of such a bridge, spanning generations, can we summon their wisdom and example to guide and inspire our own journey.

ACKNOWLEDGMENTS

Like a lively conversation during an Italian Sunday dinner, many people contributed their voices, opinions, and wisdom to this book to enhance its tone and richness.

It's best to begin at the beginning. Bob Gormley, former editor in chief at Northeastern University Press, first proposed to me (in 2003) the idea of a one-volume history of the Boston Italians. NU Press had published esteemed Boston historian Thomas O'Connor's *The Boston Irish* in 1995, and Gormley felt strongly that a companion book about the Italian experience was long overdue (as did O'Connor, who honored me with his endorsement to write this book). Bob could not see this project through, but it's unlikely you would be reading *The Boston Italians* without his initial inspiration.

I was not surprised at all when Amy Caldwell, senior editor at Beacon Press, enthusiastically concurred on the need for a book that chronicled the history of Boston's second-largest ethnic group. Amy and I worked together on *Dark Tide,* and her sound judgment and wise guidance, evident from the beginning, were largely responsible for that book's success. I am thrilled to be working again with Amy and the entire professional team at Beacon.

Speaking of pros, I owe a debt of gratitude to the terrific team at the University of Minnesota's Immigration History Research Center (IHRC). Curator and assistant director Joel Wurl, assistant curator Daniel Necas, and researcher Jon Openshaw helped me navigate through the Donnaruma and Scigliano papers, and many issues of *La Gazzetta del Massachusetts,* to breathe life into two of Boston's most important Italian American figures.

Most of the IHRC material was in English, but several key documents were written in Italian and needed expert translation. Left to my own devices, who knows how long this task would have taken me! Thus, I'm thankful for the swift and precise translation work of Concetta Antonella DeRosa Snow, whose efforts have made this a better book.

I made so many contacts among Boston-area Italian Americans during my research, many of whom shared their family stories. Two people also shared their impressive research. Jane Pisciottoli Papa provided me with a complete summary of the South Cove (South End) Italian settlement to which I refer in this book. Sylvia Corrado offered her research on the internment of Italian POWs in the United States during World War II. Both of their contributions added important pieces to this story and both are cited formally in the bibliographic essay.

In that same essay, I've also cited the names of those who were kind enough to agree to personal interviews for this book, but my gratitude compels me to list them here as well. Sal Balsamo, Al DeNapoli, Sal DiMasi, Pam Donnaruma, Tom Menino, Barbara Summa, and Bob Travaglini shared their personal and family stories with me, and did so openly and without reservation. I hope I did justice to their accomplishments and accurately conveyed the influence of their Italian heritage on their lives.

I am thankful to Janet Buda, librarian at the Boston Public Library's North End branch, for opening up her photo files, and to Aaron Schmidt of the BPL's Print Department/Photo Division for making available the library's rich collection of photos and images related to Italian Americans and the North End and East Boston neighborhoods.

The photos and images in this book, other than those I provided myself, are courtesy of the following people and organizations: Jules Aarons, Leslie Jones, and the Boston Public Library Print Department; Pam Donnaruma and the *Post-Gazette*; and Paul Yovino.

I am humbled by the personal support of dozens of friends and family members whose interest and enthusiasm infuses me with the energy to work hard and the desire to get it right. These people attend my book signings and presentations, write letters and e-mails of encouragement, and purchase (and urge others to purchase) my books. I can't list all of them here, but they know who they are, and I am appreciative of their efforts.

I would like to single out a few people for their noteworthy contributions.

My friend Paula Hoyt employed her careful and considerable editing skills in her advance reading of the manuscript and, as usual, missed virtually nothing. Further, she is responsible for the overall structure, navigation, content, and ongoing management of my website, a responsibility she embraces with care, creativity, and constancy. Paula lets me share ideas with her on a regular basis, and always responds with patience, honesty, and thoughtfulness. I'm immensely grateful for her talent and friendship.

The photograph on this dust jacket (as well as the photo on my most recent book, *Due to Enemy Action*) was taken by my sister-in-law and friend, Patricia Doyle, who is also responsible for most of the photos on my website and for photography work at my book signings and presentations. Pat's exemplary photo skills are but one aspect of her contributions; I am even more thankful for her continuous encouragement, unwavering support, and steadfast company on my book-writing journey.

As she has with my previous work, my longtime friend Ellen Keefe has contributed in numerous ways to this book. A fellow history lover, she offered her thoughts on my approach at the outset, served as a sounding board along the way, assisted with the research, and edited the final manuscript. Her support is rock steady throughout a project; she offers sage advice and a keen ear during the unglamorous writing phase, and then, once a book is published, promotes it vigorously among her family, friends, and colleagues. The breadth of Ellen's enthusiasm is exceeded only by the depth of her friendship.

My agent, Joy Tutela (once a "Boston Italian" herself), of the David Black Literary Agency, continues to be there for me in every way possible. Joy offers her guidance and support with grace, humor, skill, and honesty. She is, at once, an optimist and a realist, a coach and a critic, tenderhearted and tough-minded—the difficult balance the best agents must strike (she is and she does). This is our third book together, and I will always be indebted to Joy for her confidence and belief in me from the beginning. *Mille grazie,* Joy!

My parents, Rose and Tony Puleo, to whom this book is dedicated, have always warmed my heart with their expressions of pride and the generosity of their love. They have also blessed me with a respect for my heritage—teaching me that understanding my Italian background is part of understanding what it means to be an American. For all the lessons they have taught me and the example they have set, my parents are my heroes. I can only hope they are as proud of me as I am of them.

My final and most profound thanks are reserved for my "First Lady," Kate, my wife and best friend—and yes, though of proud Irish lineage, an "honorary Italian" since joining the Puleo family more than a quarter century ago. During the writing of this book, Kate and I celebrated our twenty-fifth wedding anniversary, and the only thing that astonishes me more than the speed with which the years have passed is the strength with which our love has grown during their passage. We are a great team, standing side by side and sharing and believing in each other's dreams. Throughout this project, as with all projects, Kate has shared the daily ups and downs, offered her wisdom and counsel, and served as confidante and talented editor. More than anything, it is Kate's enduring strength, friendship, and love that have made this book—and everything else—possible. She is, and always will be, my greatest blessing.

STEPHEN PULEO

I am honored to have written the first full-length, 130-year history of the Italians in Boston, and equally grateful to have found and used a wide variety of primary and secondary sources to bring their story alive for readers. The collection of primary sources was particularly rewarding, considering that most Italians did not leave long documentary trails of diaries, letters, or journals. As I have recounted in this book, many immigrants were illiterate even in their own language, and generally, second-generation Italians did not write extensively, either. James Donnaruma and George Scigliano were notable exceptions; their writings provide the richest primary sources for *The Boston Italians* and add immeasurable texture and depth to the story of a people. Immigration and naturalization records (including my own grandparents'), the Dillingham Commission report, church documents, and presidential speeches and other government records (including the Depression reports written for Harry Hopkins), as well as personal interviews, provide the remainder of the most important primary source material.

In my previous books, I provided a list of primary sources and a brief description of how I used them, and grouped secondary sources according to topical categories. I continue this approach here, based upon the many favorable comments readers have shared with me.

In this book, I have built the narrative and drawn conclusions based on a combination of these primary and secondary sources, many of which are listed in the text (the Donnaruma and Scigliano quotes are drawn word for word either from their own writings or, in a few cases, from quotes attributed to them in newspaper accounts). I have taken no "poetic license." In places that call for speculation, I have done so based upon the best available source material and my knowledge of the characters' background and related events. I limited any speculation or conjecture to those matters for which no documentation exists, but where my knowledge of the character or the event places me on solid footing (for instance, James Donnaruma's feelings upon the death of Henry Cabot Lodge); in any case, I have tried to make these few instances clear to the readers.

Otherwise, everything in *The Boston Italians* is drawn from primary documents and personal interviews and an extensive array of secondary sources.

Primary Sources

The James V. Donnaruma Collection
Immigration History Research Center (IHRC)
University of Minnesota

Box 1: Folders 5, 6, 7, 8, 9
Box 2: Folders 11, 12, 13, 14, 15, 16
Box 3: Folders 18, 20, 22, 24,
Box 5: Folders 39, 40, 41, 45
Box 6: Folders 49, 50, 54, 55
Box 7: Folders 56, 61
Various other folders

This fascinating collection of hundreds of James Donnaruma's letters, financial records, pamphlets, flyers, copies of *La Gazzetta del Massachusetts,* and other documents helped me understand and develop the book's main real-life character and, for the first time, present to readers this important, yet largely unknown, figure in Boston history.

Donnaruma was a strong writer with strong opinions, and his words come alive on the page, whether he was crafting an argument to help a countryman avoid deportation, attempting to convince an elected official to vote against a bill that would be detrimental to Italians, or fighting to rename North Square to honor his good friend George Scigliano. The bonus, from my point of view, is that the vast majority of his correspondence is in English; the few exceptions I either translated myself from Italian (slowly and painstakingly) or had translated. Donnaruma was a mover and shaker, a power broker who was well aware that his ability to get things done depended on his persuasiveness in English; otherwise, his character, his story, and the story of the Boston Italians would have been much tougher to build.

His half-century tenure as publisher and editor of *La Gazzetta del Massachusetts* coincided with the most vital years of Italian immigration and settlement in Boston, and thus his writings accomplish the two most critical tasks of the best primary sources: they provide insight about him and offer a window through which to view the overall history of Boston Italians.

The George Scigliano Collection
Immigration History Research Center (IHRC)
University of Minnesota

Though significantly smaller than the Donnaruma Collection, the George Scigliano Collection provides invaluable insight into Boston's first powerful politician of Italian descent. This collection contains many newspaper clippings about Scigliano, as well as columns he wrote, pamphlets, political flyers, his identification card for the Lewis and Clark Centennial in 1905, and other items. These documents enabled me to piece together the previously untold story of "The Battle for North Square" and—as was the case with Donnaruma—provide readers with the first public look of this heretofore unknown Italian American leader.

The Caesar Donnaruma Collection
Immigration History Research Center (IHRC)
University of Minnesota

Like the Scigliano papers, this collection is significantly smaller than the one for James Donnaruma; it contains letters and other documents written by Donnaruma's son Caesar. Included is a detailed accounting (balance sheet and income statement) of *La Gazzetta*'s 1954 financial deficit, to which I make reference in the book, as well as Caesar's numerous letters to and from John F. Kennedy.

Report of the Immigration Commission
United States Immigration Commission ("The Dillingham
Commission"; 1907–1910)
42 volumes; Washington, D.C.: Government Printing Office, 1911

This massive work, still the most exhaustive study of immigration to the United States ever undertaken, assesses the impact of mass immigration on

American society. I concentrated specifically on Volumes 26 and 27, entitled "Immigration in Cities." These two volumes present an analysis of immigrant populations of seven cities: New York, Chicago, Philadelphia, Boston, Cleveland, Buffalo, and Milwaukee, and also selected neighborhoods or "districts" in each city. Two of Boston's "districts" were in the North End.

The Dillingham Commission studied an enormous "sample group" in Boston and the North End, much larger, for example, than modern-day focus groups or even "sample sizes" used in political polling. The commission's total Boston sample consisted of 326 Southern Italian households and 15 Northern Italian households, representing nearly 1,800 people. The two North End districts included 278 Southern Italian households, 12 Northern Italian households, and just under 1,500 individuals; the North End thus represented nearly 86 percent of all Boston Italians in the commission's survey.

Through the years, much of the analysis and many conclusions of the Dillingham Commission report have been criticized for their lack of objectivity and their anti-immigration bias, due mainly to the excess influence of immigration restrictionists on the panel. However, the report's statistical data are generally presumed accurate, and as such, they provide the most important quantitative look at immigrant life in America in the first decade of the twentieth century.

Immigration and Naturalization Records

Records of Naturalization, September 1906–June 1929 (421 vols.)
United States District Court for the District of Massachusetts

Petitions and Records of Naturalization, October 1906–December 1911
   (22 vols.)
United States Circuit Court for the District of Massachusetts

Passenger lists: Ellis Island arrivals, 1900–1921
United States Immigration Service

I used these records as the primary source for my master's thesis (*From Italy to Boston's North End: Italian Immigration and Settlement, 1890–1910.* University of Massachusetts/Boston: 1994) and dug into them again for this book.

The naturalization petitions, especially, are rich in information, particularly after 1906, when the increase in immigration prompted the United States government to require detailed personal and family information from people who applied for citizenship (including the date and place of birth of the applicant and his wife and children; hometown and province or region in Europe; place and date of marriage; date and port of embarkation; name of the vessel upon which the immigrant arrived; port of entry; information on the period between arrival and naturalization, including occupations; and length of time spent continuously in the United States and in the state in which they sought citizenship). Only naturalization petitions after 1906 provide this volume of information, yet they still allow the study of Italians who arrived well before 1900. An immigrant had to be living in the United States at least five years to petition for citizenship, and Italians generally waited far longer to petition.

Included in these records were my grandfathers' and Aunt Angela's passenger manifests, naturalization petitions, and citizenship certificates, and my paternal grandmother's passenger manifest.

"Dear Mr. Hopkins" (Depression-era reports to Federal Emergency Relief Administration director Harry Hopkins)
Martha Gellhorn (November 1934); Robert Washburn (November 1934)
New Deal Network (http://newdeal.feri.org/)
Franklin and Eleanor Roosevelt Institute
These well-written and detailed accounts from Hopkins's team of "reporters" were invaluable in sketching Depression-era life in Boston and Massachusetts.

Correspondence to and from St. Leonard of Port Maurice Church and Sacred Heart Church, North End, Boston
Parish files, Archdiocese of Boston Archives
Details about the families affected by the influenza pandemic are drawn from these records, which encompass correspondence to and from Cardinal O'Connell and his administrators.

Papers Relating to the Foreign Relations of the United States with the Annual Message of the President Transmitted to Congress (1906–1908)
United States Department of State
These documents detail the story of the mistreatment of Italian workers by the Spruce Pine Carolina Company as well as provide information about the earthquake in Messina, Sicily.

"Enemy Alien" registration card and right index fingerprint of Angela Puleo
February 1942
United States Department of Justice

U.S. Army records of Anthony W. Puleo, World War II service
National Military Records Center
St. Louis, Missouri

Statistical Abstract, 2000 Census
United States Bureau of the Census
www.census.gov/prod/www/STATISTICAL-ABSTRACT-1995-2000.html

Parish baptism and marriage records, 1890–1910
St. Leonard of Port Maurice Church
Boston, Massachusetts

Parish baptism and marriage records, 1890–1910
Sacred Heart Church
Boston, Massachusetts

Presidential speeches and remarks (Woodrow Wilson, Warren G. Harding, Calvin Coolidge, Herbert Hoover, and Franklin D. Roosevelt):
DeGregorio, William. **The Complete Book of U.S. Presidents.** *New York: Wing Books, 1993.*

Lott, David Newton. **The Presidents Speak: The Inaugural Addresses of the American Presidents, from Washington to Clinton.** *New York: Henry Holt, 1994.*

Personal interviews (April–October 2005)

Salvatore A. Balsamo
Albert A. DeNapoli
Salvatore F. DiMasi
Pamela Donnaruma
Thomas M. Menino
Anthony W. Puleo
Barbara Summa
Robert E. Travaglini

THESES, DISSERTATIONS, AND UNPUBLISHED RESEARCH

Johnson, Amy. "The Ethnic Shift of Catholicism in Boston During the Second Wave of Immigration." Boston College honors thesis, April 2004.

I found Amy Johnson's chapter entitled "The Italians vs. the Irish: How the Attitudes of One Hindered the Assimilation of Another" particularly helpful for this book.

Papa, Jane Pisciottoli. Research on the Italians who settled in Boston's South Cove (South End) area, 2005–2006.

Jane Pisciottoli Papa has done first-rate research, including the examination of numerous primary sources, on this group of Italian immigrants (mostly *Calabresi*) and was generous enough to share it with me for this book. The discussion of these immigrants in Chapter 8 is drawn from her research.

Parenti, Michael John. "Ethnic and Political Attitudes: An In-depth Study of Italian-Americans." Yale University Ph.D. dissertation, 1975.

This work included information about settlement in cities, discrimination, the *padrone* system, and Italians' slow progress in politics.

Puleo, Stephen C. "From Italy to Boston's North End: Italian Immigration and Settlement, 1890–1910." University of Massachusetts/Boston master's thesis, May 1994.

Much of the material from my own thesis made its way into *The Boston Italians*. Readers can also find a complete bibliography in my thesis that covers a wide range of topics about the Italian experience in America.

Salimbeni, Stefano. "Family Matters: The Post-Gazette, an Example of Longevity in Boston's Ethnic Press." Boston University journalism graduate paper, 1997.

This paper contained helpful information about *La Gazzetta*'s history and mission.

Speranza, Gloria. "When Cultures Collide: A Study of the Relationship Between Education and the Assimilation of Southern Italians." Harvard University master's thesis, June 2001.

Much of the material about Italian American schoolchildren in Boston was drawn from this thesis.

SONS OF ITALY (OSIA) REPORTS AND STUDIES

(Online at http://www.osia.org/public/culture/reports_studies.asp)
Columbus: Fact or Fiction (2002; updated 2003)
Italian American Stereotypes in U.S. Advertising (including results of Zogby poll; 2003)
A Profile of Today's Italian-Americans Based on the Year 2000 Census (2003)

These white papers provided original research on demographics and discrimination as they pertain to Italian Americans.

CONFERENCE PROCEEDINGS

Candeloro, Dominic, Fred Gardaphe, and Paolo Giordano, eds. *Italian Ethnics: Their Languages, Literature and Lives.* Chicago: American Italian Historical Association, 1987.

Egelman, William, and Jerome Krase, eds. *The Melting Pot and Beyond: Italian Americans in the Year 2000.* (Proceedings of the seventeenth annual conference of the American Italian Historical Association). Providence: 1985.

Femminella, Francis X., ed. *Italians and Irish in America.* (Proceedings of the sixteenth annual conference of the American Italian Historical Association). New York: American Italian Historical Association, 1985.

Juliani, Richard N., and Philip V. Cannistraro, eds. *Italian Americans: The Search for a Usable Past.* (Proceedings of the nineteenth annual conference of the American Italian Historical Association, Philadelphia, November 14–15, 1986). New York: American Italian Historical Association, 1989.

Tomasi, S. M., ed. *The Religious Experience of Italian Americans.* (Proceedings of the sixth annual conference of the American Italian Historical Association, November 17, 1973). Staten Island: American Italian Historical Society, 1975.

Tomasi, S. M., ed. *Perspectives in Italian Immigration and Ethnicity.* (Proceedings of a symposium held at Casa Italiana, Columbia University, New York, May 21–23, 1976). New York: Center for Migration Studies, 1977.

These conference proceedings contain original papers on a wide variety of Italian American topics, including settlement, assimilation, work and family life, service in both world wars, religion, Little Italies, business ownership, and social mobility.

SECONDARY SOURCES

Throughout this book, on virtually every subject, I consulted dozens upon dozens of newspaper pages, primarily in the *Boston Globe,* the *Boston Herald,* the *Boston Post,* the *Boston American,* and the *New York Times.* Most of these are referenced directly in the text. In addition, I consulted a vast collection of worldwide newspaper accounts, provided to me by Al De-Napoli, concerning the controversy over the offer of honorary Italian citizenship to Robert DeNiro. As mentioned earlier, other secondary sources that I consulted, and from which I quoted, are cited and grouped according to category.

I think it is important to note that the literature on Italian Americans and their history is vast but little known. Much of it is scholarly and most of it has not worked its way into the mainstream. The works that are most popular, sadly, focus mainly on organized crime. I hope this book helps to change that direction, and that the list that follows encourages readers to explore the full range of Italian American sources, as well as the more general works to which I refer on other topics.

Italian Immigration, Assimilation, and Settlement (General)

I noted in a previous book, *Dark Tide,* that the historiography within this category is lengthy, though largely unknown. Indeed, this category deserves to be divided into subgroupings for easier reference.

For good general studies of Italian immigration, settlement, and assimilation in the United States, see Richard Alba's *Italian-Americans: Into the Twilight of Ethnicity* (Englewood, NJ: Prentice Hall, 1985); Erik Amfitheatrof's *The Children of Columbus: An Informal History of Italians in the New World* (Boston: Little, Brown, 1973); *Studies in Italian-American Social History: Essays in Honor of Leonard Covello* (ed. Francesco Cordasco; Totowa, NJ: Rowman and Littlefield, 1974) and Cardasco's *Italian Mass Emigration: The Exodus of a Latin People—A Bibliographical Guide to the Bollettino Dell'Emigrazione, 1902–1927* (Totowa, NJ: Rowman and Littlefield, 1980); James A. Crispino's *The Assimilation of Ethnic Groups: The Italian Case* (New York: Center for Migration Studies, 1980); Alexander DeConde's *Half Bitter, Half Sweet: An Excursion into Italian-American History* (New York: Scribner, 1971); *The Italian Experience in the United States* (ed. Madeline H. Engle and Silvano M. Tomasi; New York: Center for Migration Studies, 1977); and Francis X. Femminella and Jill S. Quadagno's "The Italian-American Family," in *Ethnic Families in America: Patterns and Variations* (ed. Charles Mindel and Robert W. Habenstein; New York: Elsevier Scientific Publishing Company, 1976).

In this subgroup, I also consulted Patrick J. Gallo's *Old Bread, New Wine: A Portrait of Italian Americans* (Chicago: Nelson Hall, 1981); Richard Gambino's *Blood of My Blood: The Dilemma of Italian-Americans* (New

York: Doubleday, 1974); Dorothy and Thomas Hoobler's *The Italian-American Family Album* (Oxford: Oxford University Press, 1994); Luciano Iorizzo and Salvatore Mondello's *The Italian Americans* (Boston: Twayne Publishers, 1980); Salvatore J. LaGumina's *The Immigrants Speak: Italian-Americans Tell Their Story* (New York: Center for Migration Studies, 1979); Jerry Mangione and Ben Morreale's *La Storia: Five Centuries of the Italian-American Experience* (New York: Harper Collins, 1992); *A Documentary History of the Italian-Americans* (ed. Wayne Moquin, Charles Van Doren, and Francis Ianni; New York: Praeger, 1974).

Other works consulted include Humbert Nelli's *From Immigrants to Ethnics: The Italian Americans* (Oxford: Oxford University Press, 1970); Andrew Rolle's *The Italian-Americans: Troubled Roots* (New York: The Free Press, 1980); *Italian-Americans: A Retrospective on the Twentieth Century* (ed. Paola Alessandra Sensi-Isolani and Anthony Julian Tamburri; Chicago: American Italian Historical Association, 2001); Allon Schoener's *The Italian Americans* (New York: Macmillan, 1987); Lydio F. Tomaso, ed., *The Italians in America: The Progressive View, 1891–1914* (New York: Center for Migration Studies, 1972); and Phyllis H. Williams's *South Italian Folkways in Europe and America* (New York: Russell & Russell, 1938). Also in this subgrouping, the *Summer 1967 International Migration Review* (Vol. 1, No. 3) contains a collection of articles devoted to the Italian American experience.

For the best discussion of Italian birds of passage and repatriation, see Betty Boyd Caroli's *Italian Repatriation from the United States, 1900–1914* (New York: Center for Migration Studies, 1973). Michael J. Piore also deals with this topic in *Birds of Passage: Migrant Labor and Industrial Societies* (New York: Cambridge University Press, 1979).

Religion, particularly Catholicism, was a central component of the Italian experience in America. I found the following works helpful for this book: Lucille Papin Borden's *Sister Francesca Cabrini: Without Staff or Scrip* (New York: Macmillan, 1945); Stephen DiGiovanni's "Michael Corrigan and the Italian Immigrants: The Relationship Between the Church and the Italians in the Archdiocese of New York, 1885–1902," in *Italian Americans: New Perspectives in Italian Immigration and Ethnicity* (ed. Sylvio Tomasi; New York: Center for Migration Studies, 1983); Robert H. Lord, John E.

Sexton, and Edward T. Harrington's *History of the Archdiocese of Boston in the Various Stages of its Development, 1603–1943* (Vol. 3; Boston: The Pilot Publishing House, 1945); Robert Orsi's *The Madonna of 115th Street: Faith and Community in Italian Harlem, 1880–1950* (New Haven, CT: Yale University Press, 1985); James O'Toole's *Militant and Triumphant: William Henry O'Connell and the Catholic Church in Boston, 1859–1944* (Notre Dame, IN: University of Notre Dame Press, 1992); *Catholic Boston: Studies in Religion and Community, 1870–1970* (ed. James O'Toole and Robert E. Sullivan; Boston: Roman Catholic Archbishop of Boston, 1985); O'Toole's own "In the Court of Conscience: American Catholics and Confession, 1900–1975" in *Habits of Devotion: Catholic Religious Practice in Twentieth-Century America* (ed. James O'Toole; Ithaca, NY: Cornell University Press, 2004); Kristen A. Petersen's "Contested Bodies and Souls: Immigrant Converts in Boston, 1890–1940" in *Boston Histories: Essays in Honor of Thomas H. O'Connor* (ed. James O'Toole and David Quigley; Boston: Northeastern University Press, 2004); and Silvano Tomasi's *The Religious Experience of Italian Americans* (New York: American Italian Historical Association, 1975).

For cities and neighborhoods outside of Boston, I consulted many fine regional, local, and neighborhood studies that helped me obtain a good overall view of Italian communities in the United States (works on Boston follow in a separate section). These included Adria Bernardi's *Houses With Names: The Italian Immigrants of Highwood, Illinois* (Urbana: University of Illinois Press, 1990); John Briggs's *An Italian Passage: Immigrants to Three American Cities, 1890–1930* (New Haven, CT: Yale University Press, 1978); Charles Churchill's *The Italians of Newark: A Community Study* (New York: New York University, 1942); Dino Cinel's *From Italy to San Francisco: The Immigrant Experience* (Stanford, CA: Stanford University Press, 1982); Micaela diLeonardo's *The Varieties of Ethnic Experience: Kinship, Class, and Gender Among California Italian-Americans* (Ithaca, NY: Cornell University Press, 1984); Donna R. Gabbaccia's *From Sicily to Elizabeth Street: Housing and Social Change Among Italian-Americans, 1880–1930* (Albany: State University of New York, 1984); Donna Paoli Gumina's *The Italians of San Francisco* (New York: Center for Migration Studies, 1978); Gary Mormino's *Immigrants on the Hill: Italian-Americans in St. Louis, 1882–1982* (Urbana:

University of Illinois Press, 1986); Humbert Nelli's *Italians in Chicago, 1880–1930: A Study in Ethnic Mobility* (Oxford: Oxford University Press, 1970); Judith E. Smith's *Family Connections: A History of Italian and Jewish Immigrant Lives in Providence, Rhode Island, 1900–1940* (Albany: State University of New York Press, 1985); and Virginia Yans-McLaughlin's *Family and Community: Italian Immigrants in Buffalo, 1880–1930* (Ithaca, NY: Cornell University Press, 1971).

To close out this "general" category, I also consulted the following that do not readily fall into handy subgroups: *Italian-Americans in the '80s: A Sociodemographic Profile* (ed. Graziano Battistella; New York: Center for Migration Studies, 1989); Richard Ben Cramer's *Joe DiMaggio: The Hero's Life* (New York: Simon & Schuster, 2000); Peter D'Epiro and Mary Desmond Pinkowish's *Sprezzatura: 50 Ways Italian Genius Shaped the World* (New York: Anchor Books, 2001); *Reaching for the Stars: A Celebration of Italian-Americans in Major League Baseball* (ed. Larry Freundlich; New York: Ballantine Books, 2003); Pete Hamill's *Why Sinatra Matters* (New York: Little Brown, 1998); and Gay Talese's fine novel *Unto the Sons* (New York: Alfred A. Knopf, 1992).

Contemporary Sources (The Immigration Years)

I believe it is important to list separately accounts written "in the day" because they provide a much different perspective than more recent sources. With that in mind, the most compelling sources I consulted that were written during the immigration years were John Foster Carr's *Guide for the Immigrant Italian in the United States of America* (New York: Doubleday, Page & Company, 1911); Robert F. Foerster's *The Italian Emigration of Our Times* (Cambridge: Harvard University Press, 1919); Jeremiah Jenks and W. Jett Lauck's *The Immigration Problem: A Study of American Immigration Conditions and Needs* (New York: Funk & Wagnalls Company, 1917); John Horace Mariano's *The Italian Contributions to American Democracy* (Boston: Christopher Publishing House, 1921) and Mariano's *The Italian Immigrant and Our Courts* (Boston: Christopher Publishing House, 1925); Sarah Gertrude Pomeroy's *The Italians: A Study of the Countrymen of Columbus, Dante, and Michelangelo* (New York: Fleming H. Revell Company, 1914); Frank Julien Warne's *The Immigrant Invasion* (New York:

Dodd, Mead & Company, 1913); and *Americans in Process: A Settlement Study by Residents and Associates of the South End House: North and West Ends of Boston* (ed. Robert A. Woods; Boston: Houghton Mifflin, 1903).

Also of interest in this category was a fictional pamphlet published by the Boston Legal Aid Society in 1923 entitled *Luigi and the Law's Delay,* a story highlighting the difficulties Italian immigrants faced in obtaining good legal help.

Boston and the North End

In addition to the many references to Boston and the North End in sources I've already mentioned, and to my own master's thesis and *Dark Tide,* I also quoted from or consulted the following: Jack Beatty's *The Rascal King: The Life and Times of James Michael Curley, 1874–1958* (Reading, MA: Addison-Wesley, 1992); William DeMarco's classic study of Italian enclaves, *Ethnics and Enclaves: Boston's Italian North End* (Ann Arbor: UMI Research Press, 1981); Benedict Deschamps's "Publisher of the Foreign-Language Press as an Ethnic Leader? The Case of James V. Donnaruma and Boston's Italian-American Community in the Interwar Years," in the *Historical Journal of Massachusetts* (Summer, 2002); Kathleen Kilgore's *John Volpe: The Life of an Immigrant's Son* (Dublin, NH: Yankee Books, 1987); Fred Langone's *The North End: Where It All Began* (published by the *Post-Gazette,* undated); William P. Marchione's photo essay book *The Italians of Greater Boston: A Proud Tradition* (Dover, NH: Arcadia Publishing, 1999); and Anna Maria Martellone's North End neighborhood study (in Italian) *Una Little Italy Nell'Atene D'America: La comunita Italiana di Boston dal 1880 at 1920* (Naples, Italy: Guida Editori, 1973).

Also, the work of Boston College university historian Thomas O'Connor, who likely has written more about Boston than anyone else, provided me with invaluable source material, particularly *The Boston Irish: A Political History* (Boston: Northeastern University Press, 1995) and *The Hub: Boston Past and Present* (Boston: Northeastern University Press, 2001). I also found helpful Anthony Mitchell Sammarco's photo essay books as part of the "Images of America" series, including *East Boston* (Portsmouth, NH: Arcadia Publishing, 1997); *Boston's North End* (Dover, NH: Arcadia Publishing, 1997); and Sammarco and Michael Price's *Boston's Immigrants:*

1840–1925 (Charleston, SC: Arcadia Publishing, 2000), as well as Christopher Small's photo essay book from the same series, entitled *The Italian Home for Children* (Charleston, SC: Arcadia Publishing, 2005).

In addition, I consulted Paula Todisco's *Boston's First Neighborhood: The North End* (Boston: Trustees of the Boston Public Library, 1976); Yanni Tsipis's photo essay book ("Image of America" series) entitled *Boston's Central Artery* (Charleston, SC: Arcadia Publishing, 2004); William Foote Whyte's classic sociological study *Street Corner Society: The Social Structure of an Italian Slum* (Chicago: University of Chicago Press, 1993; first published in 1943); Whyte's "Race Conflicts in the North End of Boston," in *The New England Quarterly* (No. 12, December 1939); and Mitchell Zuckoff's *Ponzi's Scheme: The True Story of a Financial Legend* (New York: Random House, 2005).

Anarchists and Organized Crime

I group these two categories together because the activities of both anarchists and mobsters tarnished the reputations of honest Italians and Italian Americans.

In the anarchist subgroup, I am most grateful to Paul Avrich for his fine book *Sacco and Vanzetti: The Anarchist Background* (Princeton, NJ: Princeton University Press, 1991), the most comprehensive work on both the anarchist underpinnings of the Sacco and Vanzetti case and the anarchist movement in Boston and the United States. I also consulted Avrich's paper "Sacco and Vanzetti—Innocent or Guilty?" which he presented at the nineteenth annual conference of the American Italian Historical Association in 1986 (see full citation under Conference Proceedings, above). In addition, I examined Louis Adamic's *Dynamite: The Story of Class Violence in America* (New York: Chelsea House, 1982); Eric Rauchway's *Murdering McKinley: The Making of Theodore Roosevelt's America* (New York: Hill and Wang, 2003); Francis Russell's *A City in Terror: The 1919 Boston Police Strike* (New York: Viking Press, 1975); and *Italian American Radicalism: Old World Origins and New World Developments* (ed. Rudolph J. Vecoli; New York: American Italian Historical Association, 1973).

In the area of organized crime and the Mafia, the literature is vast, some of it well done and some sensational and loosely documented. For the purposes of this book, I looked at Francis A. J. Ianni's "Organized Crime and the Italo-American Family" in *Ethnic Families in America: Patterns and Variations* (ed. Charles H. Mindel and Robert W. Habenstein New York: Elsevier, 1976); Francis Ianni and Elizabeth Reuss-Ianni's *The Crime Society* (New York: New American Library, 1976); *An Inquiry into Organized Crime* (ed. Luciano Iorizzo; New York: American Italian Historical Association, 1970); Dick Lehr and Gerard O'Neill's *Black Mass: The True Story of an Unholy Alliance Between the FBI and the Irish Mob* (New York: Public Affairs, 2000); Peter Maas's *The Valachi Papers* (New York: G. P. Putnam and Sons, 1968); Humbert S. Nelli's *The Business of Crime: Italians and Syndicate Crime in the United States* (New York: Oxford University Press, 1976); and, of course, Mario Puzo's groundbreaking and culture-changing novel *The Godfather* (New York: G. P. Putnam and Sons, 1969).

Discrimination and Stereotyping

Information about these topics finds its way into most recounts of the Italian American experience, but there are important works devoted to this category that I consulted for this book.

Chief among these is Richard Gambino's meticulously researched and disturbing look at the 1891 New Orleans lynching of eleven Sicilian immigrants, *Vendetta: A True Story of the Worst Lynching in America, the Mass Murder of Italian-Americans in New Orleans in 1891, the Vicious Motivations Behind It and the Tragic Repercussions That Linger to This Day* (New York: Doubleday, 1977). The most thorough treatment of this sordid event, which began the pattern of discrimination against Italians in the United States, it shows how a brutal but localized incident can have far-reaching and long-lasting implications. Readers interested in the origins and ongoing nature of widespread discrimination against Italian Americans—and in the first major event that stereotyped the Italian American culture as inherently criminal—must read Gambino's book.

For a series of essays that touch on, but move past, the issues of stereotyping, see A. Kenneth Ciongoli and Jay Parini's *Beyond the Godfather: Italian-American Writers on the Real Italian-American Experience* (Hanover, NH: University Press of New England, 1997). For accounts of the internment of Italian Americans during World War II, see *Una Storia Segreta: The*

Secret History of Italian-American Evacuation and Internment During World War II (ed. Lawrence DiStasi; Berkeley, CA: Heydey Books, 2001) and Stephen Fox's *The Unknown Internment: An Oral History of the Relocation of Italian-Americans During World War II* (Boston: Twayne Publishers, 1990).

In addition, Salvatore J. LaGumina's *Wop! A Documentary History of Anti-Italian Discrimination* (New York: Straight Arrow Books, 1973, updated 1999) provides a wide collection of anti-Italian writing, much of it virulent and from so-called respectable sources. Finally, for a thorough examination of the entire phenomenon of Southern Italian immigrants being perceived as a different "race" in America, see David R. Roediger's *Working Toward Whiteness: How America's Immigrants Became White* (New York: Basic Books, 2005).

The Great Depression and World War II

I group these two monumental events in the same category due to their profound effect on Italian Americans and Americans in general. Some sources listed here deal with both of these events. It is important to note that the literature on the Depression and the Second World War is enormous and far-reaching; the list here only scratches the surface and represents the sources I consulted most frequently.

For solid accounts of the Great Depression, see David F. Burg's *The Great Depression: An Eyewitness History* (New York: Facts on File, 1996); *Dear Mrs. Roosevelt: Letters from the Children of the Great Depression* (ed. Robert Cohen; Chapel Hill: University of North Carolina Press, 2002); James D. Horan's *The Desperate Years: A Pictorial History of the Thirties* (New York: Bonanza Books, 1962); Robert S. McElvaine's *The Depression and New Deal: A History in Documents* (New York: Oxford University Press, 2000); and T. H. Watkins's *The Great Depression: America in the 1930s* (Boston: Little, Brown, 1993) and *The Hungry Years: A Narrative History of the Great Depression in America* (New York: Henry Holt, 1999).

The World War II historiography could consume several volumes; however, as a start, I would suggest (without false modesty) that readers look at the bibliography in my own *Due to Enemy Action: The True World War II Story of the USS Eagle 56* (Guilford, CT: Lyons Press, 2005) for an overview. For the book now in your hands, I am grateful for Peter Belmonte's "Italian Americans in World War One and World War Two" and Stefano Luconi's "World War II and Italian-American Voters," both in the already cited *Italian-Americans: A Retrospective on the Twentieth Century* [see full citation in the section headed "Italian Immigration, Assimilation, and Settlement (General)"]. For information about Italian POWs imprisoned in Massachusetts, I must acknowledge Sylvia Corrado's extensive research and her article entitled "Love and War: Italian POWs in Smalltown USA" in *Ambassador Magazine* (Spring, 2001). Ian Kershaw's magnificent two-volume biography *Hitler* (*1889–1936: Hubris* and *1936–1945: Nemesis*; New York: Norton, 1998; 2000) provided me with fascinating material on both the man and the Third Reich he brought to power.

Last in this category are three books upon which I relied that covered both the Great Depression and World War II eras. These were Paul Johnson's *A History of the American People* (New York: HarperCollins, 1997); David M. Kennedy's outstanding *Freedom From Fear: The American People in Depression and War, 1929–1945* (New York: Oxford University Press, 1999); and Lawrence W. Levine and Cornelia R. Levine's *The People and the President: America's Conversation With FDR* (Boston: Beacon Press, 2002).

Immigration to the United States (General)

To understand Italian immigration, it is important to explore the entire immigration experience during the late nineteenth and early twentieth centuries. The following are works I consulted for this book: *One America: The History, Contributions, and Present Problems of Our Racial and National Minorities* (ed. Francis J. Brown and Joseph S. Roucek; Englewood, NJ: Prentice Hall, 1952); David M. Brownstone's *Island of Hope, Island of Tears: In Their Own Words, The Story of Those Alive Today Who Made the Great Migration Through Ellis Island from the Old World to the New* (New York: Rawson, Wade Publishers, 1979); Peter Morton Coan's *Ellis Island Interviews: In Their Own Words* (New York: Facts on File, 1997); and Roger Daniels's *Coming to America: A History of Immigration and Ethnicity in American Life* (New York: Perennial, 1991).

Other works I found useful included *Emigration from Europe, 1815–1914: Select Documents* (ed. Charlotte Erikson; London: Adam and Charles

Black, 1976); Herbert J. Gans's *The Urban Villagers* (New York: The Free Press, 1962); Oscar Handlin's *Boston's Immigrants: A Study in Acculturation* (Cambridge: Harvard University Press, 1941) and Handlin's *The Uprooted: The Epic Story of the Great Migrations That Made the American People* (Boston: Little, Brown, 1951); John F. Kennedy's posthumously published *A Nation of Immigrants* (New York: Harper & Row, 1964); "Immigration and American Public Policy" in *The Annals of the American Academy of Political and Social Science* (ed. Richard D. Lambert and Alan W. Heston; Beverly Hills, CA: Sage Publications, September 1986); and Stanley Lieberson's *Ethnic Patterns in American Cities* (New York: The Free Press of Glencoe, 1963).

Additional sources I consulted were John M. Lund's "Boundaries of Restriction: The Dillingham Commission" in the *University of Vermont History Review* (Vol. 6, December 1994); John Namias's *First Generation: In the Words of Twentieth-Century American Immigrants* (Boston: Beacon Press, 1978); Philip Taylor's *The Distant Magnet: European Emigration to the U.S.A.* (New York: Harper & Row, 1971); Stephen Thernstrom's *The Other Bostonians: Poverty and Progress in the American Metropolis, 1800–1970* (Cambridge: Harvard University Press, 1973); and Richard Vedder, Lowell Gallaway, and Stephen Moore's "The Immigration Problem: Then and Now" in *The Independent Review* (Vol. 4, No. 3; Winter, 2000).

Walter Wilcox's two-volume statistical analysis and interpretation in *International Migrations* (2 vols.; New York: Gordon and Breach Science Publishers, 1969) proved immensely helpful.

And finally, readers interested in learning about the history and origins of the Italian character should read the classic, scholarly essay *The Italians* by Luigi Barzini (New York: Simon & Schuster, 1964). Subtitled "A Full-Length Portrait Featuring Their Manners and Morals," this book is considered, still, the definitive portrait of the Italian people. Barzini examines the North–South tensions and the two Italies: one that created and nurtured such luminaries as Dante Alighieri, St. Thomas of Aquino, and Leonardo da Vinci; the other, backward in political thought, "invaded, ravaged, sacked, and humiliated in every century." The book focuses on Italians in Italy but in so doing provides insights on the settlement patterns, social customs, and political behavior of Italians once they arrived in the United States.

INDEX

AAFLN (American Association of Foreign Language Newspapers), 88, 131, 132–33
Abruzzesi, 70
Adamo, Martin, 91
Adams, Charles Francis, 34
Adams, James Tuslow, 167
African Americans, 81–82, 124
Agnes, Peter, 274
agricultural disasters in Italy, 48, 49, 50
Ahern, John, 239
Aiello, Angelo, 211
airport construction, 156
Alito, Samuel, 263–64
Altano, Joe, 244
American Association of Foreign Language Newspapers (AAFLN), 88, 131, 132–33
American Relief for Italy, 221
American Woolen Company, 126
anarchists: and anti-Italian prejudice, 108–9, 118–19, 127–29, 134; anti-WWI activity, 106–7, 116–19; Boston violence by, 108–10; deportation of, 132; ideology of, 106–8, 109, 138; North End as center of operations, 105, 107; post-WWI escalation of activity, 126–29
Angiulo, Gennaro "Jerry," 196, 232, 245
Antonini, Luigi, 203
Apalachin Meeting, 230–31
assimilation: acceptance as dependent upon, 76, 148; and ethnic enclave, xii–xiii, 71–72; and foreign-language newspapers, 195, 236–37; and home ownership, 96; and Italian-American celebrity heroes, 196–97, 214–15; post-WWII completion of, 281; pre-WWI

progress, 90–98; and second generation immigrants, 144–48, 214–20; and suburban migration, 226–28; WWI-era progress, 101–5, 113–16; and WWII loyalty issue, 200–203, 209–20. *See also* language
Avellinese, 57, 69–70, 70, 136
Avrich, Paul, 108, 117, 127, 128, 139

Badaracco, Alessandro, 9
Balsamo, Anthony, 250–51
Balsamo, Rosalia, 250–51
Balsamo, Sal, 249–53
Balsamo, Yvonne, 252
banks, 20–21, 166, 167, 172
Barbara, Joseph "Joe the Barber," 231
barbershop businesses, 183
Basilio, Carmen, 239–40
Battle for North Square, 29–39
Beatty, Jack, 172
Bellotti, Francis X., 243
Belmonte, Peter, 214, 215
belonging, sense of, 30–31, 38–39. *See also* ethnic enclaves; neighborhoods
Berkman, Alexander, 106, 117, 132
Berlusconi, Silvio, 258
Biasi, Agostino, 235
Biddle, Francis, 212
Big Dig, 283
birds of passage, immigrants as, 43, 53–58, 59–60
Black Hand organization, 157
blacks, 81–82, 124
boarders, Italian income from, 94–95
Board of Aldermen, 32, 37, 38
Bogart, Mark, 204